Praise for IF LOOKS COULD KILL

"M. William Phelps, one of America's finest true-crime writers, has written a compelling and gripping book about an intriguing Ohio murder mystery ultimately resolved by circumstantial evidence. Readers of this genre will thoroughly enjoy this book."

—**Vincent Bugliosi,** author of *Helter Skelter* and *Reclaiming History*

"*If Looks Could Kill* starts quickly and doesn't slow down. The author's thorough research and interviews give the book a sense of growing complexity, richness of character, and urgency."

—**Stephen Singular,** author of *Unholy Messenger: The Life and Crimes of the BTK Serial Killer*

"Phelps' sharp attention to detail culminates in this meticulous recreation of a tragic crime. This gripping true story reads like a well-plotted crime novel and proves that truth is not only stranger, but more shocking, than fiction. Riveting."

—**Allison Brennan,** *New York Times* bestselling author of *Fear No Evil*

Praise for MURDER IN THE HEARTLAND

"Drawing on interviews with law officers and relatives, *Murder in the Heartland* will interest anyone who has followed the Stinnett case. The author has done significant research and—demonstrating how modern forensics and the Internet played critical, even unexpected roles in the investigation—his facile writing pulls the reader along."

—*St. Louis Post-Dispatch*

"Phelps uses a unique combination of investigative skills and narrative insight to give readers an exclusive, insider's look into the events surrounding this incredible, high-profile American tragedy. . . . He has written a compassionate, riveting true crime masterpiece."

—**Anne Bremner,** op-ed columnist and TV legal analyst

"M. Williams Phelps expertly reminds us that when the darkest form of evil invades the quiet and safe outposts of rural America, the tragedy is greatly magnified. Get ready for some sleepless nights."

—**Carlton Stowers,** Edgar Award-winning author of *Careless Whispers*

"This is the most disturbing and moving look at murder in rural America since Capote's *In Cold Blood.*"

—**Gregg Olsen,** *New York Times* bestselling author of *Abandoned Prayers*

"A crisp, no-nonsense account . . . masterful."

—*Bucks County Courier Times*

"An unflinching investigation . . . Phelps explores this tragedy with courage, insight, and compassion."

—*Lima News* (Lima, OH)

Praise for SLEEP IN HEAVENLY PEACE

"An exceptional book by an exceptional true crime writer. Page by page, Phelps skillfully probes the disturbed mind of a mother guilty of the ultimate betrayal."

—**Kathryn Casey,** author of *She Wanted It All*

Other books by M. William Phelps

IF LOOKS COULD KILL

M. WILLIAM PHELPS

PINNACLE BOOKS
Kensington Publishing Corp.
http://www.kensingtonbooks.com

Some names have been changed to protect the privacy of individuals connected to this story.

PINNACLE BOOKS are published by

Kensington Publishing Corp.
850 Third Avenue
New York, NY 10022

All Kensington Titles, Imprints, and Distributed Lines are available at special quantity discounts for bulk purchases for sales promotions, premiums, fund-raising, and educational or institutional use. Special book excerpts or customized printings can also be created to fit specific needs. For details, write or phone the office of the Kensington special sales manager: Kensington Publishing Corp., 850 Third Avenue, New York, NY 10022, attn: Special Sales Department, Phone: 1-800-221-2647.

Pinnacle and the P logo Reg. U.S. Pat. & TM Off.

ISBN-13: 978-0-7860-1784-3
ISBN-10: 0-7860-1784-8

First Printing: March 2008

10 9 8 7 6 5 4 3 2 1

Printed in the United States of America

For April,
my wonderful little helper:

You are an inspiration to me,
how fortunate I am to be blessed
with your love & grace.

ACKNOWLEDGMENTS

In lieu of thanking everyone I have in all of my previous books, I wanted to take this opportunity to share the appreciation I have for all of my readers throughout the years. I am grateful for each and every one of you. I understand how overcrowded bookstore shelves are today, with far too many books being published every year, and realize the choices you have are endless. For you to choose my book(s) and spend a few days with my words is an honor for me. I understand the responsibility I have as an author. You are the reason why I write these books.

I need to thank Melissa White, who kindly handed over hundreds of pages of documents and was instrumental in introducing me to several major players involved in this case. Without Melissa's help, or her trusting me with a story she had intended to one day write herself, I would not have been able to give this subject the in-depth reporting I feel it deserved. Additionally, if Akron-area attorney Cindy Mason hadn't introduced me to Melissa, I'm convinced this incredible story would have never been told.

All of the detectives I interviewed while I was in Akron

were kind, courteous and extremely helpful. Dave Whiddon, Russ McFarland, Mike Shaeffer and, especially, Ed Moriarty helped me in more ways than I could ever explain here. Without the time they gave me while I was in Akron and the numerous telephone calls later on, along with the countless e-mails back and forth, I surely would not have been able to get to the core of this incredible crime story. In addition, I'd like to thank Ed Moriarty's wife for the hospitality she showed me while I was in town.

Likewise, Carrie Stoll, who is, I'm told, the heartbeat of the crimes against persons unit inside the Akron Police Department, was always willing to look things up, check details and help me gather some excellent photos.

I am indebted to everyone in law enforcement for their help. They are all true professionals.

What can I say about Christine Todaro? She is a courageous woman in every aspect of the word; someone who was willing to put others before herself, in spite of what might happen to her and what people said about her. She is a person of great moral integrity. Without her, I was told by almost every detective working the case, a murderer would have gotten away with the ultimate crime.

Jeff Zack's mother Elayne Zack—a wonderful, gracious lady, open and honest—allowed me into a part of her life many wouldn't have had the guts to do. I commend Mrs. Zack for her candor and sincerity. I worry that she will have a hard time with some of what's in this book. But I could not ignore the truth.

To the dozens of other sources I used for this book: thank you for your time, honesty and willingness to see that the truth about this case was finally exposed. Without you, I would have been lost.

Lastly, my manager, Peter Miller, president of PMA Literary & Film Management Corp., has been one of my biggest supporters and guides through the landscape of film, books and television. Peter is so much more than my literary agent: friend, business manager, first reader, counselor (at times) and compass. He has been a true blessing in my life. I could never thank him enough for the work he has done for me.

Once again, Stephanie Finnegan did a wonderful job copyediting this book and saved this author some embarrassment.

AUTHOR'S NOTE

In the spring of 2006, I was busy doing media interviews for my book *Murder in the Heartland,* which had just been published. While I was on a Cleveland, Ohio, radio station discussing that book, the host of the show asked me a question: "How do you find the stories you turn into books?" I answered by saying that I relied on readers, for the most part, along with tips from people who write in to my author Web site.

You *must* keep your eyes on the news, the host suggested.

Yes, in fact, I do. It's a combination of all those things, I said, concluding, "Right now, I'm looking for a story in Ohio."

Wasn't sure why I said it. Only that I had looked at several Ohio stories over the years and, for one reason or another, had passed on all of them. My editor, Michaela Hamilton, had also mentioned that Ohio was a great place for a true crime story to be set.

Later that same week, I was on another radio show, in a different part of Ohio. Near the end of the interview, I gave the same answer to basically the same question.

One of the hosts, a female, mentioned a murder case that had been recently adjudicated. After our interview, she e-mailed me several links to the case. "You *have* to do this one," she said. "It's incredible."

After both shows, I checked my Web site e-mail and found several e-mails suggesting I look into the death of Jeff Zack (the case the second host had mentioned), a rather complicated man who had lived in the Akron region of Ohio most of his adult life. One letter was from someone closely connected to the case. From that letter and further encouragement from my new radio friend, I began looking more closely at the case. I was intrigued immediately by the dynamics of it and how long it took law enforcement to solve.

As I made some calls and began interviewing people, I realized there was a great story to tell, not to mention it was set in a location I had never covered in a book. The murder of Jeff Zack and the subsequent arrest of the triggerman and an alleged accomplice are only one small aspect of this story. The city of Akron, for example, a wonderful place I was fortunate enough to spend about a week in during my travels researching this book, became a character in and of itself. The aesthetics of the city, its growth over the years, certainly the world-renowned Tangier restaurant downtown, the Akron Police Department, and all of the people who keep the city living and breathing on a daily basis, make it the perfect location to tell a story. Most locations in crime books are ephemeral, they become an afterthought, a background for the action in the book to take place. Not Akron. It was a setting—at least I saw it that way from the day I decided to take on the project—all of the players had wandered in and out of at various times of their lives. Jeff Zack was murdered in broad daylight on a Saturday afternoon in front of dozens of people at a very popular chain store. Yet no one could identify the shooter. From that perspective alone, what an interesting place, I thought, to tell this story. And as I met people in town and began to investigate this case on a deeper level, I realized that Akron is no different from any other city in America: murder is a part of the dynamic, a crime that, when a high-profileness is attached to it and a city's elite become involved, can put a pockmark on a city that simply doesn't deserve one. The murder of Jeff Zack never defined Akron. Rather, the people of Akron—especially those who came forward and helped crack this seemingly unsolvable crime—defined the true character of community.

The triggerman in this case answered a letter I had written to him at the start of the project. I had explained that I wanted his help. I would offer him all the space he needed to tell "his side of the story." He had gone on A&E's *American Justice* and, through tears, proclaimed his innocence. He said he'd had "nothing" whatsoever to do with this murder—that it was a setup from day one. Organized crime was one theory. Police corruption at the highest level another. Knowing that, I wanted his version of the events so I could go out and investigate his claims and prove them true or false.

In response, he said he wasn't about to help me "if your intention is to portray me as a cold-blooded killer. . . ."

I sent him back a second letter, in which I offered this excerpt:

> *I cannot depict you as anything you are not. I am trying to find out the truth in this case. . . . I am offering you a voice in my book; a chance to tell your side of the story. . . .*

You make some pretty intrepid allegations against the prosecution in your letter. I'd like to look further into that end of your story. But I need to study the documentation first. . . .

You asked me in your letter "what direction" I am going and "what" I "need from you." Simple, actually. I follow the evidence and [dig] below the surface of the cases I write about. Murder cases are inherently predisposed to fault. I conduct my own investigation. If what you claim is true, well, I'll uncover it and expose it. . . . [F]eel free to write to me and tell me whatever you wish; and also send me copies of any documents you feel will help me better understand your plight. . . . If you want to set a time/day every week to chat by phone, let me know. Be glad to.

I never heard back from this man. He stopped communicating with me after I sent my response, which is not at all surprising. You see, I have yet to meet a convicted murderer who admits he or she is guilty. I guess it's part of having to do so much time behind bars: telling yourself— even convincing yourself—that you had nothing to do with the crime in which you are being punished is maybe the only way to deal with your surroundings.

This mentality makes me that much more empathetic to those innocent men and women serving time. Can you imagine, for a moment, what it must be like to be behind bars knowing that you have been wrongly convicted? Some religions teach us to accept heaven and hell. Living your life in prison as an innocent person must be part of that hell, or at least a purgatory that keeps your spirit restrained. Your life, in a sense, has been stolen.

Was my new pen pal one of these men? Had he been wrongly convicted, serving the sentence of another man? I had to take him seriously.

As I headed into the first months of the writing and researching process, learning all I could about the case, I received an anonymous e-mail from a woman who claimed to have information that this convicted murderer was, in fact, innocent. She said he had been set up by powerful people in powerful positions. Akron was full of people like this, she claimed. It is a town, she insinuated, under a cloud of corruption and payoffs at the highest level.

We went back and forth a few times. I figured out she was a relative. And then, when I asked her to come forward and explain, providing me with evidence and proof of her allegations, I never heard from her again.

I have never worked on a book with better documentation. The hundreds of police reports I had access to were written in a way I had never seen. The detail was exceptional. The reason you will see so much dialogue in this book is because those reports, coupled with the hundreds of hours of interviews I conducted with many of the people involved, along with the hours and hours of recorded conversations members of the Akron Police Department made with some of the major players, offered me such a rich overview of every conversation detectives involved in the case had with witnesses and suspects, that I was able to re-create, almost verbatim, many of the conversations that took place over the course of the investigation. Add to that the hundreds of letters, e-mails, the thousands of pages of testimony from two trials, witness statements and transcripts from witness interviews, and the entire story emerged, right there in black and white.

M. William Phelps
Vernon, CT, July 2007

Is history possible? Is anyone serious?
Who do we take seriously? Only the lethal believer,
the person who kills and dies for faith.

—Don DeLillo, *Mao II*

PART ONE

1

It was a typical afternoon in Northeastern Ohio. The type of day when blackbirds, grazing together by the thousands in fields off to the side of the road, are spooked by the slightest sound—a beep of a horn, a shout, a kid speeding by on his skateboard, an impatient motorcyclist whining his engine at a stoplight— and, in an instant, flutter away like a school of minnows, darting from one grassy knoll to the next.

On this day, June 16, 2001, a busy spring Saturday, Carolyn Ann Hyson was sitting inside the employee kiosk of the Akron, Ohio, BJ's Wholesale Club fuel station, going through the motions of her day. At a few minutes past noon, that otherwise ordinary day took a remarkable turn. Carolyn looked up from what she was doing and saw a motorcycle—"black with lime green trim"—speed past the front of her booth and stop sharply with a little chirp of its tire by the pump closest to her workstation.

At first, none of this seemed to be unusual. Carolyn had seen scores of customers throughout the morn-

ing. Some punk on a motorcycle acting unruly was a
daily event.

The door to Carolyn's booth was slightly ajar. It was
pleasantly cool outside, about 71 degrees. Clouds had
moved in and made the day a bit overcast, yet, at the
same time, a cheery manner hung in the air. On balance, what did the weather matter? It was the weekend.
Summer was upon Akron. Unlike Carolyn, who worked
full-time during the week as a teacher's aide, most had
the day off. As she could see, many had decided to go
shopping. BJ's parking lot behind her was brimming
with vehicles, same as the Chapel Hill Mall to her right.
For most, it was just another weekend afternoon of er-
rands and domestic chores, shopping with friends and
enjoying time off. "It was nice," Carolyn remarked later.
"It was not too hot, not too cold. I was sitting there . . .
just sitting in the booth with the door open."

But then, in an instant, everything changed.

While Carolyn went about her work, preparing for
her next customer, the motorcycle captured her attention. "Because," she said, "it was making some loud
noise."

The driver, dressed from head to toe in black, wearing a full-face shield, was rocking the throttle back and
forth, making the engine whine loudly. The black-clad
driver had pulled up almost parallel to a dark-colored
SUV, which was sitting at the same pump on the opposite side of the fuel island, about twenty feet from Carolyn's booth. The SUV had just pulled in. The guy
hadn't even gotten out of his vehicle yet.

After Carolyn shook her head in disgust at the rude motorcyclist, she heard a loud crack—and it startled her. For
Carolyn, who "grew up around guns," and knew the difference between a backfiring car and the steel hammer of

a handgun slapping the seat of a bullet, that loud crack meant only one thing.

Several people stood at the other pumps, oblivious to what was going on. Some were fumbling around, squeegeeing their windows clean, while others pumped fuel, staring blankly at the digits as they clicked away their money. All of them, undoubtedly, thinking about the gorgeous day it was turning out to be.

As Carolyn stopped working, that earsplitting explosion—a quick pop—shocked her to attention. It was rapid. A snap, like a firecracker, or the sound of a brittle piece of wood cracking in half.

Realizing it could possibly be a gunshot, Carolyn jumped out of her seat and followed the noise.

At the same time Carolyn heard the loud pop and saw the person on the motorcycle, *Mark Christianson* (pseudonyms are italicized at first use) was wandering around the "tirebox" area of BJ's, a few hundred yards in back of the fuel station area. A few minutes before, Mark had seen someone on a motorcycle inside the parking lot. "He was riding his bike back and forth," Mark said later. Mark had used the pronoun "he" more as an expression than a literal term, because he had no idea, really, which gender the person on the bike was.

Not thinking anything of it, Mark went back to his business, but was soon startled by the same loud noise Carolyn had heard. "I thought it was the kids up the hill to my left setting off M-80s."

So when Mark heard the loud crack, he took off up the steep embankment, hoping to bag the kids and give them a good tongue-lashing. But when he made it around the corner of the building, near the foot of the hill, he noticed there wasn't anyone around.

Son of a gun. What was that noise?

When Mark got back to the tirebox, he heard Carolyn, who had assessed the situation at the pumps and ran back into her kiosk, "panicking over the PA system." Then Mark looked toward the fuel pumps and noticed two BJ's managers running toward Carolyn and the pumps.

Something had happened. Somebody was hurt.

So Mark took off toward them.

Coming out of the booth a moment later, Carolyn saw the motorcyclist standing near the driver's side door of the SUV. So she stopped by a pillar and stared. Standing, stunned, Carolyn saw "a fully clothed . . . [person]. Let's put it that way because I could not tell you what he was. I see a person standing there. . . ."

The person she saw, Carolyn explained, had his or her hands stretched out, pointed at the SUV, much like a cop holding a weapon on someone and saying *"Freeze!"* But at that moment, the motorcyclist turned to look at Carolyn. The rider, underneath his or her face shield, looked directly at Carolyn for a brief moment, perhaps sizing her up. Then hopped back on the bike and sped off toward Home Avenue, just to the west of the fuel pumps, and down a short inlet road. Carolyn later described the look the motorcyclist gave her as a "chill that went through" her. The person had a steely gaze about him or her. One of those rigid, "forget what you just saw" looks. It seemed threatening to Carolyn. She was terrified.

Within a few seconds—or so it seemed—the person on the motorcycle drove past a small grassy area near the fuel station entrance, stopped momentarily to avoid hitting a car, floored the gas throttle and, leaving a patch of rubber behind, sped off through a red light, took a sharp left near Success Avenue, jumped over the railroad tracks and disappeared out of sight.

The entire sequence of circumstances took about ninety seconds.

Carolyn had already approached the man in the SUV. A big man, she remembered. Tall. Handsome. White hair. "I went over to him," she remembered later in court, "and he was sitting there . . . and his head was rolling back and forth, back and forth. I could see the life going out of him because he was turning completely white."

Then Mark approached. He saw a "white male with his head down," slumped over, inside the same black SUV. "I thought he passed out . . . that there was a fire or something. But when I got in front of the truck, I noticed both windows were busted."

Carolyn was shaking so bad after seeing the color flush out of the man's face that, when she returned to her kiosk, she had trouble dialing 911.

Located about three miles north of BJ's Wholesale Club, Akron City Hospital, on East Market Street, employs dozens of doctors and nurses who stop at BJ's to gas up and grab a few gas-and-snack items—chips, soda pop, gum, candy, whatever—on their way to work. Many even live in the Chapel Hill Mall area and, on weekends, frequent the different shops. After Mark took another look at the guy in the SUV and realized he was hurt pretty bad, he heard one of his bosses call out over the PA system for any doctors and/or nurses in the immediate area. No sooner had the plea gone out when "five women," Mark recalled, "[ran] over, who were nurses and doctors, and proceed to pull the gentleman out of the truck."

One of them, who claimed to be a doctor, asked

Carolyn if she had any alcohol around. Quick-thinking Carolyn grabbed the eyewash solution, which she knew was loaded with alcohol, and poured it over the doctor's hands.

Standing there, watching everything going on, with a crowd of people now swelling around, Mark knew immediately—after the nurses and doctors dragged the man out of his SUV onto the ground and began working on him—that the guy was in serious trouble.

"There was blood all over his shirt," Mark recalled.

Beyond that, there was even more blood draining down the back of his head and a starfish-shaped hole about the size of a dime on the opposite side of his cheek.

2

Ed Moriarty grew up in Akron. He was just a kid when, after leaving high school in 1964 and subsequently spending three years in the military, 1½ of which included a tour with the Third Marine Amphibious Force in Vietnam, he found himself back in the thicket of Akron wondering what to do with his life. In his absence, many of Moriarty's friends had gone on to college to become educators. Moriarty had gone to Catholic schools most of his life. He even understood a bit of Latin. He surely had the skills, definitely the patience, and no doubt the will, to become a teacher himself. It was a noble profession.

So what was stopping him?

As Moriarty settled in back home after returning from Vietnam, the thought of teaching was far from his mind. The first thing he did was get a job with the East Ohio Gas Company. Then he went to a local university to pursue a degree in education—but the prospect soon vanished. Not because he didn't want to sit in class for four more years, or go through the rigmarole of the school system, but all those friends of his who had gone into teaching were leaving the field. The pay was horrible, Moriarty heard. Students were taking control of the classrooms. Teachers had little say anymore in what went on with the curriculum, or the treatment they could dish out to unruly kids.

Hearing all of that, Moriarty wanted no part of it. Life then wasn't easy. Returning to society from Vietnam, he recalled, was confusing, and plagued by more questions than answers. "It wasn't like it is now," he said, "where even if you don't support the war in Iraq, everybody is at least showing their support for the troops. When I returned from Vietnam, that wasn't the country's situation. It was more of a, well, it didn't matter which aspect you played in the Vietnam War, *you* were *part* of the problem."

This unwelcoming sentiment was unsettling to Moriarty. It troubled him. He had given three years of his life to the military. He had seen friends and fellow soldiers wounded and killed. He could have almost died himself. Now people were saying he was wrong for standing behind his country.

After a few years, Moriarty decided he needed to find a career path. He wasn't getting any younger. He wanted to get married someday and start a family, but still hadn't settled on any one particular vocation.

Then one day, Moriarty said, it happened. "I saw an ad in the newspaper for the Akron Police Department, applied and became a patrol officer."

At the time Ed Moriarty had stumbled onto what would become his life's passion, Northeastern Ohio was in a state of social chaos. It was May 4, 1970. Tensions between student demonstrators at Kent State University and the Ohio National Guard, who had been called in to control the escalating situation, were getting out of hand. People were screaming. Throwing things. Yelling insults at government and school officials. Taunting National Guardsmen. What inspired the quagmire, some later suggested, was an American invasion of Cambodia President Richard Nixon had launched a few weeks earlier. Nixon had made the announcement during a televised presedential address five days later. Since then, a group of Kent State students had become outraged. In the end, four students ended up getting shot by National Guardsmen and the day went down as a turning point in American social history.

As Moriarty's career with the Akron Police Department (APD) took off, "I gotta tell ya," he said, chuckling humbly, "I was always in the right place at the right time. It seemed from that very first year, my law enforcement career went from one desirable assignment to another."

It took on a fast track, in other words.

"After two years in patrol, I was transferred to the traffic bureau as an accident investigator. It was at this [point] when I received the schooling and training that gave me the foundation for all aspects of police investigation."

He was then assigned to the solo motorcycle unit, where he was given the responsibility of escorting celebrities, politicians and any other dignitaries that came into Akron.

"That was a real good situation to be in."

Moriarty's next move was undercover, in vice and narcotics, where he stayed for about ten years.

"I liked it because most police work is responsive—

whereas, in vice, you initiate the work. Undercover work means that you seek it out."

A point Moriarty wanted to make clear was that throughout his career, police work was never about individual police officers.

"Police work is the combination of a lot of people working *really* hard toward one goal."

By 1991, he was promoted to sector sergeant, which put him back in uniform. Things were rolling for Moriarty. He had found his place in the community and loved going to work, even though he was given the dreaded midnight-to-eight shift. "Every shift is set up in four sectors," he explained, "and there are usually four cars in a sector, which can give you anywhere between seven to eight law enforcement officers you're responsible for during your shift. Like any police department, we were often shorthanded, so I had, sometimes, two sectors, fourteen officers, to look out for."

All cops have that "one case" they can recall without even thinking about it. It's generally an investigation where all involved shake their heads for years afterward, talking about it over beers at the local pub. For Moriarty, that case took place one day when he and a team of detectives had answered a domestic violence call. When they arrived at the home and walked in, they found the suspect had cut his wife's head off, placed it in a bucket and left it on the premises for everyone to see.

"Incredible, really," Moriarty said, looking back. "We just couldn't believe this guy had actually cut his wife's head off and put it in a bucket. You never know what to expect on any give day of police work."

3

During the early-afternoon hours of June 16, 2001, Sergeant Ed Moriarty was sitting at his desk doing what most cops hated: paperwork. Mounds of reports in front of him that needed his attention. In charge of a unit that investigated everything from homicide to home invasions, Moriarty had been at the office on a weekend because it was, as he called it, "*his* Saturday." He and the other sergeants rotated weekends.

The detective's bureau of the APD is on the sixth floor of the Harold K. Stubbs Justice Building in downtown Akron, just across the block from the university. The sixth floor is a rather plain-looking office space, stretched along the entire distance of the building, with whitewashed walls on one side and police blue on the other. Standing, looking beyond the desk that greets you as you walk off the elevator, it seems like nothing more than another cubicle farm. Detectives sit in four-by-four-feet areas in front of computers and wait for cases.

After a rather calm morning of normal calls, a "SIG 33"—white-male shooting victim—came in. There was a problem with a middle-aged man with white hair at the BJ's Wholesale Club warehouse fuel pumps over at Home Avenue in North Akron. A white male, in his forties, had been found slumped over in his SUV, but nurses and doctors on scene at the time of the crime had pulled him out of his vehicle and were now working on him by the fuel pumps.

When the call came in, dispatch asked one of the 911 callers (there would be several), "Where is the victim?"

A man at the scene said, "He is in his car at the gas station. A motorcycle [driver] drove up and shot him apparently, I did not witness this. . . ."

A few more questions aside, the man continued—"I don't know," he said frantically, "here, talk to this lady." He handed the telephone off to a woman standing near him.

She said, "Hi."

Details were important at this tenuous stage. They were fresh in each witness's mind. The astute dispatcher knew what questions to ask in order to pull imperative information out of each caller. "What color was the motorcycle?" the dispatcher asked the lady. When she didn't get an answer right away, she asked again, slower: "What. *Color.* Was. The. *Motorcycle?*"

"Green and black, hon," the woman said with a bit of Southern hospitality in her voice, adding, "that new limey green color." Listening, one could almost see the woman waving her hands in the air as she talked.

"Lime green and black?" Dispatch wanted to pin her down.

"Yeah."

"One driver and a passenger? Or just *one* driver?" This was important. Good question.

"Just a driver, hon. It was one of those hot rod crotches, you know those—"

Dispatch cut her off. "Like those Ninja type?"

"Yeah," the lady said excitedly, "those Ninja-type ones, hon."

Then they discussed the driver. He or she was wearing a helmet with a face shield. Dressed all in black. He or she shot the guy and took right off. It was quick. Everyone in the area ran toward the sound of the gunshot.

Three more calls came in within the next two minutes. Each described the same set of circumstances. One said nurses and doctors had pulled the victim out of his vehicle and was giving him CPR.

When Ed Moriarty heard what had happened, he sent several detectives to the scene immediately. Police officers from the neighboring town of Cuyahoga Falls were already arriving.

After being notified of what had taken place at BJ's, monitoring the situation and assigning units, Moriarty thought, *Son of a bitch. Not BJ's*. A Saturday afternoon at BJ's was as busy as a flea market on Sunday morning. *Damn. All those people.*

Moriarty, a commanding, thin figure at six-two, in solid shape, was Irish to the core. Flushed-red complexion. Straight hair, parted in the middle, cut conservatively around his ears and neckline. He exuded authority and handled situations in a calm manner.

"You didn't want to piss off Ed Moriarty," said one former underling. "Great detective. Awesome person. One of the best people I know. But damn, he could snap—it's that Irish temper, you know—at any moment. And you didn't want to be near Ed when he lost his temper."

After sending several units to the scene, Moriarty grabbed his radio and car keys and ran into the elevator himself. A routine Saturday morning of paperwork had turned into a possible homicide investigation. There weren't many in Akron. But when they came in, a flush of excitement enveloped detectives like Ed Moriarty and on came that bursting adrenaline rush.

A killer was on the loose. It was time to get out there and begin the hunt.

4

Somewhere between fate and self-fulfilling prophecy, destiny—that sometimes shallow, if not horrific, place some say is paved with self-interest—waits patiently for its next victim. When forty-four-year-old Jeffrey Zack left his house that Saturday morning, he was dressed in a white T-shirt, checkered shorts, a black leather belt. Jeff, along with his wife and son, lived in an unassuming raised-ranch-style home in Stow, Ohio. Tan siding with cranberry shutters and a redbrick face, the Zacks had a nice little comfortable piece of suburbia. From the outside, the only thing missing was the white picket fence and a barking dog.

Before leaving his home in the Temple Trail neighborhood just outside downtown Stow, about six miles north of Akron, Jeff and his wife of many years, Bonnie, got into a bit of an argument on the morning of June 16. For Bonnie and Jeff, the arguments had become more frequent lately. Jeff was "on edge," Bonnie later told police, "all the time." He and Bonnie had a thirteen-year-old son, *Ashton*, but their life together had become a tangled mess of alleged affairs, fights and threats of divorce.

Jeff's mom, Elayne Zack, had called. It was the morning before Father's Day. Jeff had been gone for a few days and had just gotten home the day before. Bonnie had a list of things for him to do around the house. Ashton was on the couch, just waking up. It was around 9:00 A.M.

Jeff was "agitated," Bonnie recalled to police later, from the moment he opened his eyes. He asked Ashton to help him move the kitchen table. He needed to get at a light fixture above it and make a quick repair.

When Ashton didn't move on Jeff's cue, Jeff started yelling at the boy. When that didn't work, Jeff yelled some more. Ashton, upset, went up into his room.

With no one around to fight with, Jeff screamed at Bonnie. "I don't know what your problem is," she quipped back. "Geez, Jeff."

Bonnie went upstairs and started cleaning. Jeff went downstairs and jumped on the computer.

Sometime later, Jeff came back upstairs and, as Bonnie later put it, "started stomping around" nervously.

Something was going on with the guy. He hadn't been home but for a few days and here he was yelling and screaming at everyone the first chance he got.

"You know, just . . . let's not have a fight," Bonnie pleaded. "Let's just settle down. Let's go shopping or something. I want to get some stuff done because everybody's coming over tomorrow. Let's just have a *nice* day, because you've been out of town."

Jeff walked toward Bonnie. "Get out of my way! I found something better," he said sharply, as if he meant it this time.

Bonnie walked out of the room in a huff.

"I got to go take care of my vending stuff," Jeff said grumpily.

"Fine, Jeff. You go do that, then."

By now, it was about 11:30 A.M.

Besides a vending machine business, which included about one hundred machines Jeff had scattered throughout the Akron region, which he generally serviced on weekends, he had any number of different jobs. Construction work. Landscaping. Sales. Helping illegal aliens obtain visas. A recycling company. Brick mason. Anything, it seemed, where he could earn a buck. On Saturdays, though, Jeff always took Ashton with him to help restock his vending machines. Jeff loved his son, no doubt about it. His pride and joy.

This day was different, however. As Jeff prepared to leave, he decided against taking Ashton with him.

Before Jeff left, he started in with Bonnie one more time. As they fought, Ashton, who was still in his room, heard his father scream, "I'm leaving and moving out and not coming back!"

"Settle down," Bonnie said.

"I'm outta here and getting a divorce."

Ashton knew his father would never go through with it. The kid had heard it for years. "My dad always said things like that," Ashton told police later, "when he was mad, but I knew he would never leave us."

"Be calm, Jeff," Bonnie said, trying to talk some sense into her husband.

"You'll see what it's like when I'm gone. You won't know *what* to do without me. You need me to . . . do *everything* around here." Jeff was animated, waving his hands in the air. Huffing and puffing. Pacing. Nervous. Agitated.

In any event, after arguing with Bonnie and "shoving" her out of his way a second time, Jeff grabbed his sandals, "stomped" down the stairs, and walked out of the house. Bonnie was watching him get into his SUV from the upstairs bedroom window. "I saw him throw his shoes in the back of [his SUV] and speed away," Bonnie reported later. It was unlike Jeff to not wear shoes out of the house. "He was very much definitely in a hurry."

Before heading down to the Akron BJ's to gas up his Ford Explorer and purchase supplies for his vending machines, Jeff stopped at a neighborhood yard sale right around the corner from his Temple Trail house. Later, the APD's crimes against persons unit (CAPU), fronted by Ed Moriarty, speculated that a man or woman on a black-and-green Ninja-style motorcycle was waiting down the street from Jeff's house, possibly by the yard sale, waiting for him to leave his house.

5

As Ed Moriarty and his team headed to BJ's, Jeff Zack lay on the ground by the fuel pumps, fighting for his life. He had a single bullet wound through his head, which had entered his left cheek and exited just underneath his right earlobe. It was a good shot. Perfect placement. As Moriarty was about to learn, Jeff was not the most likeable victim the APD had come in contact with. In fact, in many ways, Jeff's dark blue Ford Explorer SUV was a symbol of the type of person some later said he had become: overbearing, arrogant, pushy, guarded. Such a big truck, with its oversized tires, high bumpers and gas-guzzling engine. Jeff was a hulking six-five, 232 pounds. Fluent in several languages, he had brown eyes, concrete gray-white hair, and dark black eyebrows. Many said he was a pain in the ass, always making accusations against people he did business with. Someone was always ripping Jeff off, or giving him a problem. He was paranoid. Jumpy. Vulgar toward people. Bullying some, while threatening others.

Did one of those disgruntled friends or colleagues (former or current) finally have enough of Jeff's foul mouth and tough-guy tactics? Apparently, from the look of things at BJ's, someone surely had it in for Jeff Zack and had followed through on a desire to see him dead.

Pulling in, Moriarty realized his earlier instincts were going to be his first problem. BJ's was packed with cars. But the crowd gathered now wasn't preparing to make a run on some special sale; people were curious about the guy on the ground—still breathing, according to the doctor and nurses treating him—who had blood all over his shirt and a bullet wound in his head.

"What the hell happened?" asked one guy standing by, looking on. The local Cuyahoga Falls Police Department (CFPD), which had sent a series of officers to the scene, had managed to fend off curious bystanders and rubber-neckers. It wasn't every day a man was shot on a Saturday afternoon in the parking lot of BJ's in Akron.

"Is he alive?" asked another.

"Dunno," said a guy standing by, looking on.

"Did someone shoot him?"

No one knew.

Moriarty got out of his car and approached a few uni-formed officers who had gotten there within seven min-utes of receiving the first 911 call at 12:09 P.M. By now, they had secured the scene with yellow crime-scene tape, keeping onlookers at a distance. There were a lot of wit-nesses, Moriarty was informed right away. Officers sepa-rated everyone and explained that detectives would soon be asking questions.

"No one leaves," Moriarty barked at the officers circling around the scene, "until they have given us a statement."

Uniformed officers said they understood.

"Good," Moriarty told one of his detectives when he heard how many witnesses were willing to talk. "We need every statement we can get."

Insofar as a homicide investigation is concerned, one

statement can make all the difference, sometimes even months or years down the road. Moriarty knew this. He didn't want to miss the opportunity. "It's amazing how witnesses can be so contradictory," Moriarty recalled. "You still need that, however. It's incredibly important. Some like to embellish. Some want to withhold. Some just talk to hear themselves talk. And you have to be able to sort through that kind of thing. But every single statement is relevant. And most people try their best to give accurate accounts."

Walking around the scene, Moriarty lit a cigarette and began thinking about what the CAPU had. What struck him first was the accuracy of the shooter. Jeff Zack's attacker had taken one shot, apparently, and that one bullet—a money shot if there ever was one—had hit Jeff in the head. *It was a well-placed shot,* the veteran cop thought, standing to the driver's side of Jeff's truck, looking at the path of the bullet.

Moriarty noticed next that both windows of Jeff's truck had been shattered by the bullet, which meant they had a potential piece of evidence on the scene if they could locate it.

"There's a bullet fragment out there somewhere," Moriarty mentioned to one of the detectives standing by his side. "Let's find it." He threw his cigarette butt on the ground and twisted it out with the sole of his shoe.

"That's one of the things I knew I wanted to have right away," Moriarty commented later, "that projectile. No matter what."

As detectives combed the area looking for any type of evidence, Moriarty began to consider what kind of crime they were dealing with. Many different scenarios ran through his mind as he talked it over with detectives. The crime scene itself, for example, might make the attack appear to be a random act. You have a large SUV and, according to the 911 calls, a Ninja-style motorcycle involved. Perhaps Jeff Zack pissed off some young kid on the road, cut him off or something, and the biker decided to get back at him.

The key to it all was the fact that there was only one shot fired.

The other possibility, Moriarty surmised, was: "Did they know each other and was this an ongoing feud of some sort?"

Moriarty had worked in the organized crime unit for years. He, along with several undercover officers from Akron and Cleveland, were responsible for one of the largest organized crime busts of the past twenty years in Ohio. Standing, sizing up the scene, the thought occurred to him—and how could it not have—that someone had perhaps sanctioned a professional hit on Jeff Zack.

But then the question became "why?"

As members of the CAPU continued questioning witnesses and collecting evidence, having been involved in over one hundred homicide cases throughout his career, Ed Moriarty knew for certain that what had started out as an otherwise peaceful Saturday afternoon of pencil-pushing and bean-counting had been interrupted by one of the more intriguing whodunits the APD had been involved with in quite some time. And as witness statements began to roll in and the APD started to unravel Jeff Zack's life, the case would only become that much more disturbing and unique. As the CAPU would soon learn, it wasn't going to be a matter of finding out who killed Jeff Zack, but rather how many different people had a motive.

Or, as Ed Moriarty later put it, learning "who *didn't* kill Jeff Zack."

6

By 12:31 P.M., Jeff Zack was on his way to Akron City Hospital, fighting desperately for his life. Before they left, paramedics told Ed Moriarty that Jeff Zack had likely pulled into BJ's for the last time. He had lost too much blood. One of the doctors at the scene tending to him had mentioned something about hearing "gurgling noises" as he performed CPR, which meant Jeff's lungs had taken in blood.

Not a good sign.

Akron Emergency Medical Service (EMS) paramedics worked on Jeff best they could during the fast three-minute trip to Akron City Hospital. When they arrived, Jeff was rushed to the emergency room, where doctors, after trying to revive him several times, pronounced him dead at 12:46 P.M. One of the doctors who had traveled with Jeff from the scene and worked in emergency told detectives when they arrived right behind the ambulance that "for all intents and purposes, [Jeff] Zack was dead when he arrived at the hospital."

After being informed of the circumstances surrounding Jeff's death, Summit County's chief medical examiner (ME), Lisa Kohler, ordered an autopsy, which she said she was planning on conducting herself the following morning.

Back at BJ's, Ed Moriarty and his CAPU team of detectives were searching the scene for any evidence left by the shooter. If nothing else, it appeared to be a clean hit-and-run type of murder—at least on the surface. The bullet, of course, was going to be important. Moriarty wanted everyone to focus on finding that one projectile. It had to be somewhere. Jeff's killer had obviously not stopped to pick it up.

"Find that damn bullet," Moriarty snapped.

Experience told Moriarty that the media was going to show up any moment and start asking questions. As sergeant in charge of the investigation, it was his responsibility to give them some sort of statement, a little bit of a crumb to nibble on while the CAPU sorted out best it could what had happened. On that note, in case there had been, in Moriarty's words, a "sinister plot" behind Jeff's murder, he decided to put the case out into the public as a road rage crime. The idea was to make Jeff's killer feel as comfortable and secure as possible during the opening moments of the investigation. Moriarty knew it might throw him or her off balance enough to make that one mistake to point detectives in the right direction. In other words, if the killer was home now, pacing, waiting, preparing his or her next move, if he or she believed cops were looking for a road rage incident turned bloody, it might give him or her not only some relief from worrying about being caught, but time to regroup and figure out his or her next move.

Exactly what Moriarty wanted.

Standing beside Jeff's Ford Explorer, looking in the direction of where the bullet could have possibly traveled after leaving Jeff Zack's head, detectives thought the concrete wall about one hundred yards northeast of where the bullet exited the passenger-side window of Jeff's vehicle was the best place to start looking. It was a good bet a bullet fragment was somewhere in the vicinity of that wall.

During the preliminary stage of any homicide investigation, every aspect of the case becomes a thread—some sort of fact gleaned from nowhere, a continuous collection of circumstances that cannot be hidden by a suspect, for which eventually, with some luck and solid gumshoe police work woven through, lead to his or her arrest. Call it karma. Fate. Hard work. It doesn't matter. Experienced cops know the technique, pay attention to the need for patience and dedication to detail. In time, most homicides *can* be solved. Initially, every point of fact matters because there is no telling which one will be that gem at the end of a case.

Another part of the immediate investigation for Ed Moriarty and the CAPU was gathering all of the videotape surveillance footage from BJ's. Like most fuel stations, BJ's had continually looping videotape cameras watching over the entire area. It was a way to ward off the bump-and-run fuel snatchers, who felt the need to leave without paying, and also robbery attempts. With any luck, the cameras had caught a few frames of the shooter pulling in and racing out—or, perhaps, maybe even committing the murder.

"When we thought about it later," Moriarty said,

reflecting back on the case, "we knew the killer was a bit ballsy for shooting Zack in the middle of the afternoon, in front of all those people, with cameras all over the place. It was that, or we were dealing with one stupid son of a bitch."

Inside BJ's, the retail store itself, detectives started talking to employees. It seemed anyone who had worked at the store for a time knew of Jeff Zack and had some sort of memorable encounter with him, especially female employees.

Detective John Bell spoke to one of the store's managers, who said he knew Jeff, "Because he had frequently shopped at the store."

"What can you tell me about him?" Bell asked.

"Well," the manager said, "from viewing him in the store, I could tell he was very egotistical, arrogant, and was always trying to pick up my female employees."

Other employees, two cashiers in particular, said Jeff Zack never came into the store without saying something sexually charged. He was always asking the girls out on dates. And one female, a rather good-looking underage cashier, said whenever she noticed Jeff had entered the store, she closed her register and ran in the back, scared he was going to say something inappropriate or harass her.

After a few more questions with several employees, Detective Bell moved on.

By 12:45 P.M., Detective D. E. Parnell had arrived to help out. His first assignment from Ed Moriarty was to assist Bell in an interview he was conducting with a woman who had come face-to-face with the suspect on the motorcycle.

"Get with her and Bell," Moriarty suggested, "and find out *exactly* what she saw."

Parnell stood as Bell asked the woman for a complete, detailed version of what she witnessed. "He was riding a motorcycle, lime green in color, with black trim," the woman said stoically. She appeared frightened. Shaken by coming so close in contact with a purported murderer. It was the fifth or sixth report of a "lime green" or fluorescent green motorcycle. That was a good sign. Several reports of the same description meant it was probably true. "I was standing," the woman continued, "very close to the man, but I could not see his face because he was wearing a full matching-colored helmet with a dark visor on it, which was completely covering his face."

It was a man, Moriarty was convinced, simply because of the way in which witnesses described the suspect's build. Stocky. The way he walked. Cocky. Muscular, like a weight lifter. He was white, too, they knew, because he wasn't wearing gloves—the only section of his body where skin was exposed—and the woman saw his hands. Caucasian hands.

"Take it slow," Bell said, trying to calm the woman down. "Relax. It's OK, ma'am."

"I, well, I think he was a young man."

"What makes you say that?"

"His frame and build. He wasn't fat, but firm, you know, like he was in shape."

Parnell looked at Bell and asked him, "Is there anyone else we need to interview?"

Detective Bell said, "Can you go and talk to the general manager?"

"I'm on it."

The general manager told the same story just about everyone else had: when he heard the shot, he ran for the pumps and saw Jeff Zack slumped over in his truck and someone on a Ninja motorcycle speeding away.

"Lime green," the manager said, describing the motorcycle. "I'm *sure* of it."

Parnell then caught up with Moriarty. "We need to find that bullet," Moriarty said again. He was getting impatient, several detectives later said, recounting the scene as Moriarty took control of it. He wanted that bullet.

"It is likely here within the area," Moriarty explained, pointing to a taped-off paved section of the fuel station. Heading around the corner of the parking lot, a cement landscaped wall was holding back part of the parking lot's embankment.

There was an identification (ID) unit scouring the scene with metal detectors. Detective Parnell joined them. At first, they focused on the grass field south of the pumps. Perhaps the bullet had passed through the passenger-side glass window and whizzed up into the field. Passersby were lucky. No one else had gotten hit. A woman in a minivan full of kids heading to a Little League game could have been driving by at the same time. In one sense, Moriarty mused, they were fortunate they were dealing with only one death.

After a careful search of the field, Parnell met with Moriarty and told him they didn't have much luck.

"Nothing?"

"No, Sarge, sorry."

"All right," Moriarty suggested, "let's get some uniforms over here, form a line and walk the entire parking lot in that area over there." He pointed to the northeast, a large paved area with several utility poles. The concrete wall was in the same direction.

It didn't take long. As they swept the area, Parnell

came up with what looked like a bullet fragment. It was sitting on the ground on the sidewalk in front of the concrete wall. There was a fresh chip in the concrete wall directly above it. Looking back toward Jeff Zack's truck, Parnell could see that the bullet had traveled perhaps across the parking lot, hit the wall and had fallen on the pavement.

"Over here," Parnell told someone from the ID unit, "mark this with a placard and photograph it."

Then he walked over to Moriarty. "We found it."

"Great."

"I secured the area. I'll canvass the surrounding-area business employees for other possible witness statements."

"That bullet was extremely important to us," Moriarty recalled later. "That was why we put so much time and effort into finding it. I was thinking ahead. Finding a projectile for a possible future match to a weapon, beyond knowing what type of weapon was used, even if you never recover the weapon . . . it's one of the very important bits of evidence."

The next order of business was going to be the most daunting part of the investigation at this early stage: notifying Jeff Zack's immediate family. It was the knock on the door no cop wanted to make. Not to mention that Jeff's wife had to be viewed as a suspect. Yet as Moriarty gathered a few of his detectives together to have them head over to Stow and notify Bonnie Zack that her husband had been murdered, he could have never imagined the Pandora's box of potential suspects and motives he and his team were about to open.

"Not in my entire career."

7

Like sections of Akron, Stow is a wonderland of middle-class, hardworking people who like to go about their lives in an unassuming manner. According to the 2000 census, some thirty-four thousand people had chosen Stow as their home, making it the third largest city in Summit County. Stow's community profile claims the "city has long recognized the benefits of a diverse tax base and a balance between residential, commercial and industrial development . . . [and] is committed to providing an environment where citizens may safely raise their children and businesses can thrive."

Traveling around town, you get a sense that Stow is no different from any other American town. People go about their business without bothering one another too much, feeling as if they've managed to carve out a little slice of the American pie.

When Detective Bertina King arrived at BJ's, Moriarty asked her to first drive over to the hospital, meet with the medical examiner and get a report regarding the actual cause of Jeff Zack's death. While at Akron City Hospital, King met with Investigator R. Riggins, who took some of Jeff Zack's clothing for evidentiary purposes. Then she found Lisa Ellis, a nurse who had taken several Polaroid photographs of Jeff, and asked her to give the photographs to another detective there at the hospital. With that all done, King took off for Jeff Zack's house in Stow to notify his family about his death.

During the ride over, King contacted the Stow Police Department (SPD) to let them know what was going on, requesting, as a procedure, an escort to Bonnie and Jeff's house.

When they arrived, it appeared as if no one was home. The garage was closed. The house looked dark. Empty.

So King walked up to the front door and knocked.

No answer.

Then she placed her business card in the doorjamb.

"Let's try around back," she suggested to the Stow officer and medical examiner tagging along.

No luck again.

As they walked toward the front of the house, however, King heard a car pulling into the driveway. As they came around the corner of the garage, a black Cadillac made its way up the pavement and pulled into the garage. A woman was driving. When she got out of the car inside the garage, King came up from behind and introduced herself, asking, "Are you Mrs. Zack?"

"Yes, I'm Mrs. Jeff Zack," Bonnie said, a bit surprised and, obviously, quite startled.

King then explained the reason for their visit, letting Bonnie know the circumstances surrounding her husband's death.

When Bonnie heard, she broke down and needed to be escorted into the house, where she sat at the kitchen table, sobbing and shaking.

King sat with Bonnie for a moment and consoled her. She was obviously distraught over Jeff's death, regardless of the bumpy road their marriage had taken. Still, from an investigative position, Bonnie was a suspect. In time, she would have to answer some hard questions.

"Can you phone my brother and Jeff's mother?" Bonnie asked King after she collected herself. "His mother lives in Arizona."

Apart from notifying Jeff's extended family, King asked Bonnie several personal questions regarding her relationship with Jeff. Through that brief question-and-answer period, Bonnie mentioned something about a strange voice mail Jeff had received a few days before, saying, "I saved it. You want to hear it?"

"Yes," King said.

On June 13, a man had left a message on Bonnie and Jeff's answering machine. Quite stern and serious in tone, at 2:55 P.M. that day, the guy said, "All right, buddy, you've got one more out. You need to start carrying your cell phone, OK? I'll be talking to you."

It could have been anyone. It was clear Jeff had been involved in a bit of questionable activity throughout his life. Knowing the voice mail message might come into play down the road, King made a copy of it. By that time, Bonnie's brother had arrived at the house after stopping at the park to pick up Ashton. After Ashton had a moment with his mother, King took the child aside and began asking questions. He was obviously in shock over the passing of his father. They had fought that morning. Jeff wanted his son's help. Now he was dead. The next day was supposed to be a celebration of fatherhood. What in the world was the boy supposed to do now?

Detective Bertina King stands about six feet tall,

quite eccentric in her appearance and demeanor. She is straightforward and direct when she needs to be, but also quite comforting and soothing when duty calls. There is not one colleague of King's who doesn't respect her work ethic and natural ability to get things done out in the field. Growing up in the inner city, King has many contacts and knows how to work the streets. She exudes professionalism and understands when to push a witness and when to step back. People who meet King for the first time never seem to forget her uncanny display of charisma and charm. A proud African-American, her appearance screams of her energetic manner: she has somewhat short, auburn (maybe even red), kinky, curly hair, like spring coils; a medium yet solid build; and dresses conservatively while on the job. Her long fingernails (probably fake) are one of her trademarks. Except for those dire situations, such as the one she found herself in on the afternoon of June 16, heading into an interview with a boy whose father had just been murdered, it's unlikely you'd catch King without some sort of smile on her beautiful, comforting face.

"She knows everyone from the suspects to the chief [of police]," a close friend said later, "and takes her job seriously, while, at the same time, putting people at ease."

Experience and dedication breed success. King had solved cases on her sheer will and calm conduct alone, understanding that suspects are people, too. They need to be treated with street respect. She was going to be a great asset to the Jeff Zack investigation, which was going to need a tenacious investigator like King. Ed Moriarty knew from the evidence they had already uncovered that the branches of the case were going to spread far and wide. With King knocking on doors, tracking leads and utilizing her boisterous, loveable manner, getting people to open up, Moriarty was confident she'd come up with something significant very quickly.

"It's just the way she works," Moriarty said later. "Tina"—short for Bertina—"is the best. I have never worked with a detective like her."

"There's no one else like her," said another colleague. "She has her own way of getting things done. And she *always* produces results."

Sitting with Ashton, King made the boy feel at ease best she could under the circumstances. There was nothing to hide. She was there to find out information that could lead to catching Jeff's killer. She could sense the boy wanted to help.

"How'd you and your dad get along?" King asked Ashton.

"Great. We have our moments, but only because I don't sometimes listen to my dad when I should." The boy was thirteen, in the seventh grade. He loved his father. It was sad, really, to sit and listen to him talk about Jeff. "He always supported me with my sports. I play basketball. My dad went to all of my practices and games. He wanted me to be very good at whatever I did."

After that, Ashton got up and walked into the other room and returned a moment later with some sort of electronic device he said he wanted King to have. The device would explain a lot, he said. But there were three specific phone numbers the boy said he wanted to give King that were on his dad's cell phone. "Those numbers belong to Cindy George," he said.

King was curious. A name already. "Who's that?" she asked.

"My dad and Cindy were good friends," Ashton said.

He looked disassociated, upset by the comment. King knew there was more to it.

"How so?"

"I know Cindy and my dad had a physical relationship. I know he once spent three days at her house and Ed didn't know."

Ed? Who is Ed? wondered King.

"Ed is Cindy's husband," Ashton offered.

"Let me ask you, Ashton, how would you know that?"

Ed George was indeed Cynthia Rohr-George's husband. And the CAPU—hell, most everyone in Akron—knew who Ed George was. Ed was a wealthy restaurateur, the owner of the Tangier restaurant, bistro, club and banquet facility in downtown Akron on Market Street. The restaurant and its accompanying nightclub has been a staple in Akron since the late 1940s. The Copacabana of Ohio. The one nightclub every major entertainer stopped at during his or her national tour. Ed had made millions over the years. He and Cynthia had seven kids. A gorgeous woman, with long, flowing blond hair, she had been a contestant in the 2001 Mrs. Ohio contest and had, the previous year, finished third runner-up. Cynthia was a knockout. A bombshell. Men were drawn to her like rainwater to a wildflower.

But, as the CAPU would soon learn, Cynthia appeared to have a problem with men.

"I can tell you," said one man in town who knew the Georges fairly well, "you'd need a page of paper to list all the men Cindy has been with while married to Ed George." The investigation, however, would turn up only two such men.

Count Jeff Zack among them.

"Well," Ashton continued to King, "me and my dad

were close. He told me everything. He mentioned this about a month ago."

King asked several more questions about the Georges' relationship with Jeff. How did they meet? How long had Jeff known Cynthia and Ed?

Ashton said he had first learned of the Georges about six years ago. He was seven at the time. Jeff was a handyman at the Georges' mansion in Medina County, a wealthy suburb of Akron where the upper echelon in the community built homes the size of warehouses. Ed and Cynthia's house was a massive structure, and the joke about town was that the garage attached to the George estate was bigger than the house where Cynthia had grown up.

Jeff Zack's son knew the George mansion because he had been there with Bonnie, Jeff, and both of them together, many times. The Georges had even been over to his house, he said. They had spent Christmases and Thanksgivings with one another. He liked the George kids and recalled playing with them throughout his childhood.

King had a sense she was onto something. There was a fine line, though, between pushing a kid to dish on his father's affair and writing it off as part of a murder investigation. But Ashton seemed fairly forthcoming with information, as if he had wanted to talk about it, so King didn't stop him.

"My mom didn't like the relationship between my dad and Cindy," Ashton said.

"What makes you say that?"

The boy described an argument he had heard his mother and father having about six weeks ago.

"My dad wanted Cindy to come to the house to talk to my mom. My mom said, 'I don't want to see her. . . . She's not welcome!'"

8

Ed Moriarty had a man shot at point-blank range in his vehicle, a bullet wound through his face, the fragment of a projectile, and several stories that told him Jeff Zack wasn't the most well-liked man in Akron. There were any number of possibilities that could have taken place, any number of people who could have wanted Jeff Zack dead. Moriarty had spent just about his entire adult life as a cop. He was slated to retire in a matter of months. Now this. As morbid as it sounded, or maybe even as disrespectful as it seemed (which it wasn't), Moriarty was excited about showing up for work again. There was a homicide to investigate. It kept things fresh. Police work could get awfully monotonous. Having a new case kept things interesting. But this one, Moriarty could smell from the beginning, had the hallmarks of an extensive, detailed investigation that would take months, if not years.

"We knew it was either going to be cut-and-dry, or a long, drawn-out investigation that would put us to the test," Moriarty said later.

Finding the bullet was a critical starting point. Also,

Moriarty found out that evening, the black-and-white videotape surveillance from BJ's had picked up a man on a motorcycle flying out of the parking lot at 12:01:21 P.M. The image was grainy and diluted, but nonetheless proved each witness had been accurate with his or her description of the suspect and his motorcycle. "The only thing that videotape really told us," Moriarty explained, "was that yes, we had one individual involved in this, the time it occurred was documented, and there was no doubt that this individual was on a motorcycle. So we knew that was all true. Many times, when you get a lot of witness statements, you cannot put a whole lot of credence in them. But in this particular case, that videotape helped us establish that the information we were getting was pretty much on point."

Having the videotape back up what witnesses were saying was enough for Moriarty to put out a detailed description of the motorcycle—which was going to cause an entire new set of investigative difficulties.

Still, as Moriarty worked back at the department putting his team together and rationing different jobs, Bertina King was about to uncover an important piece of information. Back at Bonnie and Jeff's house, King continued asking Ashton about Ed and Cynthia George. What else did Jeff's son know about the relationship Jeff had with Cynthia and Ed?

Ashton explained that while he and his dad had watched ABC's *20/20,* a news magazine show, one night a few weeks back, Jeff said something startling. The show was about a man who had hired a hit man to kill someone he knew. While they were watching the show, Jeff turned toward his son and uttered, in a soft and serious voice, a profound statement that, knowing what had occurred at BJ's, Ashton had a hard time writing off as a coincidence. "If anything ever happens to me," Jeff Zack told his son as they sat on the couch watching the show, "tell the cops to look at Ed George. He's got a lot of money and can afford to hire someone."

A consummate professional, King was able to contain any excitement she might have felt. Having a thirteen-year-old boy come out with such a powerful accusation made it even more profound. Kids tend to overexaggerate things to an extent without trying, and perhaps forget details, overlooking the obvious. But for a kid to come out with a story such as the one Ashton was telling, basing it on the memory of a television show, it was extremely credible on face value alone.

No sooner had Ashton given up Ed George, however, did he complicate matters by involving two other potential suspects, whom Jeff had had a run-in with recently.

"You think your dad had any other enemies?" King asked.

"No," said Ashton, "except for [two guys the family has known for quite some time]." One man by the name of *Carl* was a "family friend." The other, *Seth,* helped coach Ashton's peewee football team. Carl and Jeff had been good friends at one time. But a siding job Carl and Seth were supposed to do for Jeff had turned into a situation over the possible theft of a $6,200 check that, Ashton said, the two guys had taken for a job they never did. They had even possibly forged Jeff's signature in order to turn the paper into cash. Seth was the one who had gotten especially heated one day when he and Jeff were talking. They were out behind Stow High School. Ashton was there. He said he heard Seth say, at one point during the argument, "I'll rip your throat out with a hot butter knife."

"No kidding," King said. "He said that?"

"Yeah. I remember."

After a few more inconsequential questions, King thanked Ashton for the courage he displayed talking about his father so shortly after hearing probably the worst news of his life. The investigation, only a few hours old, was moving along. Although King knew there would be more questions for Ashton down the road, she was energized by what the child had to say this early on.

"You take care, OK, Ashton," King said. "Call me if you need anything."

"Thanks."

John, Bonnie's brother, sat with King next. He was obviously disturbed by the news of his brother-in-law's death, but, by the same token, knew there were major problems between his sister and Jeff. John had lived in Arizona for most of his life, but he had been back in the Akron area for the past year.

"I last saw Jeff on Thursday night," John offered. Two days ago. "I stopped here around six P.M. to pick up Ashton. Jeff was sitting at the table eating something."

"How'd you get along with Jeff?"

"We were, you know, on good terms. Sure."

"Ever seen your sister and Jeff argue?"

"No. She's always told me that they got along good, but of course had some stressers."

"What about Cindy George?"

"Those rumors have been circulating through the family for years. Everyone had speculated. I heard once that Cindy and Jeff were seen riding bikes together."

"This is helpful," King said. "What about any enemies, you know of anyone that might have wanted to see Jeff dead?"

"If I had to speculate about who killed Jeff, I'd say

Cindy George had something to do with it, or either Seth or Carl, because of that aluminum-siding deal that went bad. Jeff told me he was going to send someone to jail over it. But he never said he was fearful of either of them."

As they spoke, John shook his head. No one could believe it had come to this. Further along, he explained how Jeff had told him one night that he wanted to set both Seth and Carl up. His plan was to have them come over to the house and admit how they were scamming people out of thousands of dollars. Jeff was going to have an undercover cop in the house with him to hear it all. But as the CAPU would soon learn, it was just another elaborate plan of Jeff's that had never materialized.

"He had been receiving strange calls lately," John said next. "I know that."

"What types of calls?" King wanted to know.

"Derogatory and threatening in nature."

"No kidding."

"I don't know who they were from."

Same as she had with Ashton and Bonnie, King took copious notes as John spoke, and later wrote about the conversations, using pointed detail in her report. In just a few hours, the APD's list of potential suspects had grown with each person detectives spoke to. While he sat and talked, John added another suspect to the pool. He said someone was messing with several of Jeff's vending machines, moving and smashing them. Jeff was extremely angered by this, John suggested. He could see how perhaps Jeff might have waited one night for someone to vandalize one of his machines and from that a feud might have developed, which later escalated to murder.

Jeff himself had raised the eyebrows of most of the people in his life the last four weeks, John explained. Jeff was generally known inside the family circle as hotheaded, mean, even nasty at times. For some reason, over the past month or so, he had been acting "extremely nice." Everyone in the family had noticed it.

"It was like," John said, "he was trying to make amends or something."

Just recently, Jeff had flown out to Arizona to visit family members. Jeff's sister and mother both noticed the change; for the first time since anyone could remember, Jeff was actually nice to everyone during the visit. He didn't argue. He didn't put anyone down. He was polite. Caring. Quite the change from the arrogant SOB family members had known Jeff could be at times.

John believed Jeff's murder had something to do with the threats he had received recently, saying, "Jeff never told me who he thought was doing it. He never acted like the threats scared him. But I knew they *bothered* him."

King was thrilled by what John had to say. The CAPU had plenty to go on. It appeared as though the best place to start was with Jeff Zack himself. Take a look back into his life over the past year or more and try to track his movements through the people he knew.

John had one other important comment to make before King concluded the interview. "I felt like," he said before pausing, "I felt . . . he was making amends with everyone the last month, because he was so nice, like he *knew* something was going to happen to him."

When King left Bonnie's, she called Ed Moriarty and told him what Ashton and John had said.

"Good work, Tina. Looks like we'll have to go out and pay Ed and Cindy George a visit."

9

Tips drive the fluidness of any homicide investigation. Law enforcement rely on them as a normal process of elimination to help cross off suspects and add new ones. With Ed Moriarty releasing the road rage story to the press, watchdogs all over the state of Ohio started calling in, all of whom claimed to have seen the now-infamous "lime green Ninja-style" motorcycle sometimes called a "crotch rocket."

Each tip had to be checked out. It didn't matter how much credence was put into it by detectives. One call in particular from an anonymous female at first seemed promising. "Me and my husband have seen a motorcycle driving by our home that matches the one in the newspaper." Upon further talking to the woman, however, detectives learned that some people have a hard time paying attention to even the most obvious details.

"What color was the bike you saw, ma'am?" asked one detective.

"I'm not sure of the colors, but I think it was red, white and green."

Nonetheless, the CAPU did a cross-reference check and located all of the woman's neighbors: each one checked out. None had anything to do with Jeff Zack's murder.

Ed Moriarty sent two detectives to the Summit County Medical Examiner's Office at 10:30 A.M. on Sunday morning, June 17, to attend Jeff Zack's autopsy. Although they felt confident in knowing the cause of Jeff's death, the autopsy could yield some useful information. Detectives found rolling papers and a small amount of marijuana in Jeff's pocket. If he smoked pot, it was possible he had taken harder drugs, which could lead to different scenarios, and the autopsy would bear that out. Who's to say Jeff Zack hadn't liquored himself up, taken a handful of pills and hired someone to shoot him in the head? He had made a point of spending the last month telling family members how sorry he was for the chaos he had been causing. He was distraught, a source had come forward and claimed, over an alleged breakup with his longtime (nearly ten years) mistress, Cynthia George. He had, said this same source, spent the morning of his death on the computer searching for Cynthia's new telephone number. She had apparently broken off their relationship several weeks before his death, changed her cell phone number and told Jeff she never wanted to see or hear from him again. Several people reported how upset and depressed Jeff had become over the breakup—and that he had been possibly harassing Cynthia.

As everyone had surmised, the bullet that killed Jeff had entered his left cheek and exited just underneath his right earlobe. What the medical examiner was quick to confirm was that the bullet had traveled through the roof of Jeff's mouth and the base of his tongue. Both of his lungs had filled with blood. The bullet had not hit any major arteries. By all accounts, Jeff would have survived the gunshot wound if he hadn't drowned in his own blood.

When detectives started to learn about Jeff Zack's life, within their list of growing suspects, no one in particular stood out. Moriarty had known Tangier owner Ed George for a number of years. Perhaps he had snapped, Moriarty thought, and hired someone to kill his wife's lover? "Because the obscure cannot be understood," so says a Latin proverb, "[it] does not mean that the obvious should be denied."

"I called this case," Moriarty remembered later, "once we started to learn about Mr. Zack's life, one of the longest-running suicides in history. Zack was involved in things that could have brought somebody out to harm him. As a result of that, not only did we have to find out who did it, but we had to eliminate, for prosecution purposes, several other suspects."

And that's where all of the work stood as the second day of the investigation commenced—in the minutia. Those minor details that could bring forth a tangible suspect, not just a person who looked good on paper.

Moriarty had a practical way of viewing suspects and making sure that when one of his homicide cases was sent to the prosecutor's office, he was sure they had the right guy. For Moriarty, what made him realize how important it was to be certain his team wasn't putting the wrong man in prison was a trip he once took to the infamous Mansfield Reformatory, a prison. He and several of his law enforcement colleagues had put together a softball team and went in to play the inmates in an exhibition game. "After that experience, having never quite seen anything like it, I was determined in my career that no one I investigated would end up in prison unless I knew one hundred percent they were guilty. I didn't want to be responsible for having somebody in *that* kind of a situation who may have been innocent."

Along with Deputy Chief Paul Callahan, Bertina King and Captain Elizabeth Daugherty, Moriarty headed out to the George estate in Medina County on Sunday afternoon to speak with Ed and Cynthia George regarding the comments Ashton Zack had made to Detective King the previous day. The Georges lived in an 8,100-square-foot French-style monster of a brick house that Ed George had built from the ground up in 1992. Located in Medina County, Ed had purchased nearly 130 acres of land in the late 1980s and built the house for his rather large family of Cynthia, a housekeeper and seven kids. "Ed George Manor," if you will, was located about fifteen miles west of BJ's, near the Bath Nature Preserve, approximately twenty miles south of Cleveland. When you look at it from the street, Batman's Wayne Manor comes to mind. It is an immense piece of property, the home quite contemporary. Located a foot or two from the road is a rather direct, albeit small, neon yellow sign with black lettering: "POSTED: PRIVATE PROPERTY . . . VIOLA-TORS WILL BE PROSECUTED."

Ed and Cynthia George wanted to be left alone.

Driving up from Bath Road, taking a right toward the blacktop road leading to Ed's home, the enormous structure, equipped with a garage larger than many of the homes in the surrounding neighborhoods, stood tall and wide. Castlelike, and surrounded by so much land, it was hard to believe a family of nine alone lived there. The house was a far cry from the humble condominium Ed and Cynthia had lived in before building the house. Ed George told an *Akron Beacon Journal* reporter the year work was completed on the mansion, "My wife says she needed room to breathe. We're going to have a lot of room to breathe now."

And for years—at least on the surface—that so-called "breathing room" had existed inside the George household without complication or disruption. Cynthia had grown so accustomed to her life of luxury and quasi-celebrity status, Ed hired a nanny to help with their rather large family. After all, Cynthia had other business—mainly, being the glamorous wife of a millionaire. She needed to work out in order to stay fit and trim for her appearances with Ed and walks down the runway of the Mrs. Ohio America pageant. They had the money. Why not free up her afternoons so she could come and go as she pleased? At five feet four inches, extremely petite, Cynthia wasn't as tall as a supermodel, but she could certainly hold a candle to any of those women walking the runway. Born on July 8, 1954, Cynthia was forty-six in the year 2000 when she not only entered the Mrs. Ohio America pageant, but finished as third runner-up. With her captivating blue eyes, dazzling and engaging, her flawless porcelain skin, she was still a "wow" type of looker heading into her late forties, a woman who had given birth to six children (she and Ed adopted one) and spent the time necessary to keep that baby weight off. Several of her pregnancies, she later admitted in interviews, were wrought with problems, which had kept her confined to bed for months at a time and had sent her spiraling into a depression. When she wasn't held up in bed dealing with her pregnancies, Cynthia loved bike riding, especially down into the Cuyahoga Valley National Park area, not too far from the Tangier. She'd even met Jeff Zack down there countless times and rode the bike trails for miles and miles. After all, she and Jeff were friends, like buddies. They adored each other's company. Cynthia said later she helped Jeff deal with life, as any friend might.

Regardless of the woman she was, or the status Ed's money afforded her, Cynthia and Ed were going to have to answer a few questions. Someone was accusing Ed of hiring a hit man. At the very least, the Georges needed to give an alibi to the CAPU.

Moriarty rang the doorbell after he, Callahan, Daugherty and King made their way up the long, exotic entranceway to the home.

The nanny answered.

"Can we come in?" Moriarty asked.

Cynthia was standing in the lobbylike entryway of the George home. She didn't look thrilled, but nonetheless invited the detectives in.

It was odd, Moriarty noticed right away, that here it was the end of June and the Georges still had most of their Christmas decorations up in the house. Secondly, with all the expensive furniture and furnishings inside the home, not to mention a kitchen larger than most condominiums Moriarty had set foot in, the Georges had cages of animals sitting on the tile floor near the sink.

After explaining why they were there, Moriarty asked Cynthia if Ed was around. "At the restaurant," Cynthia said. She seemed standoffish, like she didn't want to say much.

Where else would Ed be? Tangier had been in the George family for the past fifty-plus years. Ed had taken it over some thirty years ago and seen the establishment through good and bad times. But the one constant in all of it was Ed George's time away from home and his utter determination to see the business work. The restaurant had sucked any free time Ed had away from the family. But Ed still found the time—when Cynthia was off doing her own thing—to drive the kids to dance rehearsal, soccer practice and any other extracurricular activities they had. He was a super father, many later said. As for his workaholic ways, Cynthia knew the deal when she married Ed. Still, she likely had no idea how much it would actually affect their marriage—that is, until she lived it.

Walking around, scoping out the place, Moriarty was curious. There was a cockiness about the detective. Although he tried, he had a hard time shaking it off. So he used it instead to his advantage when questioning witnesses and suspects. Moriarty wanted to know where Ed George was the previous day. It was a simple question.

"Ed was in Akron," Cynthia said. Now she seemed nervous and broken. She was uncomfortable talking. "He was with the City of Akron Health Inspectors." There had been a sewer backup in the restaurant and Ed had to close the place until the problem was resolved. "He left around eight-thirty A.M. I didn't see him until about one-thirty P.M. that same day. I met him at St. Vincent's Church on West Market Street (right down the street from the restaurant). I had spent the entire morning getting the children ready for a wedding we attended."

Moriarty shook his head. He later said he had a sense that Cynthia was hiding something, holding back, and was going to throw them out of the house as soon as possible.

10

While Ed Moriarty, Captain Daugherty, Bertina King and Paul Callahan continued questioning Cynthia George, Detectives John Bell and Vince Felber were busy tracking down BJ's employees that possibly had more information about Jeff Zack. One woman claimed she had met Jeff several times, not by her own volition, mind you, but by Jeff's pushy, sexually explicit talk and behavior. "I helped him find stuff in the store, or return things. He always asked for me. It was about two months or so ago that he started making sexual advances."

Within a day, detectives learned that Jeff Zack had quite the reputation. There was one time when Jeff walked into BJ's, one of the clerks reported, and "teased" her about "running away" with him. "Come on, baby," Jeff had said. "I'll take you to Lima." After that, he described all of the "*things* he wanted to do to [her] sexually."

The woman was disgusted by it and felt threatened.

"After that day, whenever I saw him come into the store, I would take off for the office and hide."

A second cashier came forward and told detectives basically the same story. Being a bit young and naïve, the girl had given Jeff her telephone number. But one of her coworkers, when she heard what her friend had done, told the girl's parents and the relationship ended before it ever got started.

Back at the APD, detectives brought in potential suspects who had been seen or stopped riding motorcycles similar to the one described by BJ witnesses. After questioning several, even subjecting one man to a gunshot residue (GSR) test, all were cleared and released.

The first full day of investigating Jeff Zack's murder had ended. Moriarty and the CAPU were a bit closer to a major lead (they could sense it), but still hadn't turned over the stone with a golden ticket under it. The ebb and flow of any investigation is a seesaw of ups and downs; yet the first twenty-four to forty-eight hours, any experienced detective will say, are crucial. It is within that time period when the most valuable leads make themselves available. Good police work involves carefully combing through the litany of interviews and the physical, circumstantial and forensic evidence to locate a common denominator. Yet in the case of Jeff Zack, it appeared as though his murderer had done quite a professional job. As the hours went by, Moriarty, for one, knew the case was going to hinge on, perhaps, a mistake. Maybe not by the killer, but by someone who possibly held on to that one important piece of the puzzle.

The key was finding it.

11

By Monday morning, June 18, Bonnie Zack had a little over a day to collect her thoughts and begin to mourn the loss of her husband. That said, there was an intense homicide investigation under way and any information Bonnie could provide was going to help further facilitate that probe. From the APD's perspective, thus far there was nothing definitive to prove Bonnie could be checked off the APD's list of potential suspects. A Realtor by trade, Bonnie didn't have a solid alibi for the time period in question. And when a guy with Jeff Zack's extramarital history was murdered, his wife was, of course, one of the first people at whom detectives took a look. "Every homicide," Ed Moriarty recalled later, "is worked from the inside out—you go to those closest to the victim and work your way through." In other words, a homicide investigation is the target (the bull's-eye) and each family member, friend, lover and spouse is a latent suspect (a ring around that bull's-eye).

Moriarty, Bertina King and two colleagues drove back over to Bonnie Zack's house that morning to ask Bonnie several follow-up questions. King and Moriarty sat down with Bonnie and started at the beginning. "How long have you two been together?"

Bonnie had a gaze about her, Moriarty said later, one that made them feel as though she could get lost in space, daydreaming or ruminating. She was a thinker. Not someone to just rattle off answers. Bonnie analyzed what she said before she said it.

Moriarty wondered about this odd characteristic he had rarely seen. *Is Bonnie hiding something?*

"Fifteen years," Bonnie said, as if it were ten too long. She dropped her head. She couldn't believe it. After all she and Jeff had been through, he was gone. They had problems, sure. They fought and threatened each other with divorce. But somewhere inside all that impaired marital bliss was the Jeff Zack of long ago that Bonnie had fallen in love with. She had met Jeff back in 1986 in Phoenix, Arizona. They were married two years later. From Phoenix they moved to Colorado. ("We just got sick of the heat," Bonnie said.)

In many ways, Bonnie was her own person; she had never depended on Jeff to be the breadwinner. For the past six years, Bonnie had worked as a real estate agent. She enjoyed the work. It got her out of the house. She was always meeting new people, traveling to new places. She worked hard. With shiny red hair, a nice shape and a pretty face, Bonnie could have had any number of men herself. But she had made a promise to Jeff and kept it. Their son, Ashton, was the bond between them.

"Tell me about yesterday morning," Bertina King asked in her gentle manner. King was Moriarty's ace in the hole, he later said. He knew King's calming demeanor and garrulous way of getting people to open up would be an asset to the case as it began to unfold. King had been with the CAPU since 1997. She had questioned hundreds of witnesses and suspects throughout her career.

"We were all at home," Bonnie explained. "Jeff had a brief argument with Ashton about moving a table. He left the house [after that]."

"Where was Jeff going?"

"He usually checks his vending machines on the weekends. He doesn't have a particular schedule, but checks them regularly—I can't believe this. I don't know where his accounts are exactly, but Ashton would."

"Do you have any idea who would want your husband dead?"

Bonnie winced. She seemed taken aback by the question. But it was fair, considering the circumstances. "I don't know," she said. "I'm not sure if he had any enemies, but I don't think he did."

Moriarty knew the statement was either a stretch, pure naïveté, or a flat-out lie. By now, Moriarty and King knew enough about Jeff Zack to know that Bonnie wasn't being completely forthcoming.

They talked about the strange voice mail Jeff had received, the one King had recorded. Bonnie said it was odd that someone would call Jeff on *his* telephone number—they had two separate lines in the house, one being Jeff's private "business" line.

"Ashton or me never answer that line." It rolled over, Bonnie explained, to Jeff's cell phone whenever he left the house. "He was constantly using his cell phone."

Moriarty and King needed to know what Bonnie was doing on the morning—specifically the time—her husband was murdered. It was a tough question, but one that needed an answer. Bonnie had no trouble answering. "I was at the house most of the morning," she said. "Then I dropped Ashton off at the Putt-Putt Golf and returned here. I cleaned up a little. I then went over to [a friend's] for about fifteen minutes. Ashton called me for a ride. I took him and his friend to the pool at Maplewood Park. I then stopped back at home and then went to my office." She never hesitated. Never backed up and said, "Wait, no, I think I . . ." Instead, Bonnie whipped off her morning as if she had written it down and memorized it. This was important to Moriarty as he listened. It told him that Bonnie was telling the truth. People who lie, Moriarty knew from experience, stumble, vacillate and have trouble locking themselves down to a story. Bonnie had to know they'd go back and check out every step she took and she didn't seem to care one way or another as she spouted details.

When she returned home to retrieve a telephone number for a client she had been dealing with, Bonnie added, she ran into Bertina King as she walked from around the backyard toward the garage. Bonnie said that was the first she'd heard of Jeff having been murdered.

Again, without maybe realizing it, Bonnie created a time frame for herself. But, as Moriarty put the times together and added things up while sitting there, it occurred to him that, following along the window Bonnie gave, aside from the fact that she was on the road for a good part of the morning, it allowed her enough time to zip over to the Chapel Hill Mall and plug Jeff herself. But then, where did the motorcycle fit in? And, could Bonnie have actually straddled a motorcycle and shot her husband? It seemed unlikely. ("But it still didn't mean she didn't hire someone to do it," Moriarty said later.)

Bertina King asked, "How was your relationship with Jeff?"

"Everything was fine. Jeff had just returned from a bike trip to West Virginia on June thirteenth. He went with a friend. He was also in Arizona for a time near Mother's Day. Look, I need more time. . . . I can't do this."

Bonnie got up and walked toward the kitchen. In not so many words, she was asking King and Moriarty to leave. It was all too much. She needed space.

Moriarty and King weren't satisfied with what Bonnie had given them. They needed some background, maybe a few names to go on. They weren't leaving. "Start when you met Jeff," King pressed. "How did you guys meet?"

12

As Bonnie explained it to Bertina King and Ed Moriarty, her life with Jeff Zack had not always been a cacophony of arguments and extramarital affairs, as others would tell the CAPU in the coming weeks. There had been good times. There was a time when they were young and in love. For Bonnie, it was her second marriage; she had wedded a guy in 1980 and divorced him three years later. Three years after that, she met (and fell in love with) Jeff. As a young and attractive woman, Bonnie was working for a cable television company in Phoenix at the time. Jeff was a headhunter then, someone who put together résumés and found jobs for people. Bonnie was tired of her job, so she hired the company Jeff worked for with the hope of finding something new. By the time they were married, they had settled in Boulder, Colorado.

"We liked Boulder," Bonnie recalled.

Jeff was able to get a transfer to Denver within the company he worked for, so they moved again. Denver offered more opportunities. It was a bigger city. More action. Soon after, Jeff managed to get his Series 7 stockbroker's license. Fulfilling a dream, he was now a licensed stockbroker. For the next few years, he learned the ins and outs of the stock market and seemed to have found his calling. Then, Bonnie announced she was pregnant.

"Jeff, at about this time, got an offer to work with L. F. Thompson, a brokerage firm in San Diego, so we moved," Bonnie recalled as Moriarty and King listened.

Whether Bonnie realized it then or not, Jeff had initiated a precedent into their lives: whatever Jeff wanted, Bonnie was seemingly forced to go along with. Life for Bonnie became, quickly, all about Jeff's dreams, aspirations, feelings, *his* goals. Jeff was, others said later, focused on that one "big" score to set him up for the rest of his life. He worked hard, but his energy centered on hitting it big.

"Bonnie was difficult," Moriarty remembered later. "When we were finding all sorts of things in Jeff's background, we couldn't rule her out because Jeff was so blatantly mean to her. . . ."

After they uncovered it, one of the things that stood out to Moriarty and King was how at one time Jeff had threatened to take Ashton away from Bonnie. He hung it over her head, teased her with it in a threatening manner. He used the threat, Moriarty believed, as a means to control her.

"I want a divorce," Bonnie had shouted during one of her many arguments with Jeff shortly before his murder.

"You do that," Jeff warned, "and I'll take Ashton and move to Israel." Jeff had spent some time in Israel when he was young. He had told friends he dreamed of returning one day.

This, Moriarty assumed during the early days of the

investigation, was a motive for Bonnie to kill her husband. It had to be taken seriously. What's more, before Jeff and Bonnie were married, Bonnie's father hired a private investigator to conduct a background check on his future son-in-law. It seemed that Jeff had been involved in a little more than finding new jobs for people. With a simple background search, the investigator—a cop Bonnie's dad knew—found out Jeff had been arrested and charged with pandering, which, legally speaking, in Jeff's case, turned out to be basically acting as a middleman between a prostitute and a john. In his defense, Jeff had told several people the CAPU later interviewed that he didn't know what he had been involved in.

As Bonnie continued to talk to Moriarty and King about her life with Jeff, she explained that as they lived in San Diego during the late 1980s, she and Jeff started to make trips a few times a year out to Ohio to visit her mother. Around 1991, Bonnie's mother became "very sick." So, "Me, Jeff and Ashton moved to Ohio because of my mother's illness."

Stow, Ohio, didn't present quite the exciting, exotic atmosphere Denver and San Diego had offered Jeff's manic, boisterous personality; in downtown Akron, however, he soon found the action he craved.

Jeff became a fixture at Ed George's Tangier nightclub and other hot spots around town. The environment catered to Jeff's talkative, free-spirited attitude; he loved being around the clinking of the glasses, the lights, loud music, cabaret-style décor—and, of course, the women. All those luscious, adorable, single (and married) women. He adored their company and fell victim to it—which summed up Jeff's character fairly well: he was outside himself and didn't really care what anyone thought, obviously, including his own wife. But still, according to others, Cynthia was Jeff's ultimate catch, the woman he had fallen in love with. How they met showed Jeff's deep, indigenous attitude toward life and how he had perhaps took advantage of every opportunity, even when it meant hurting the people who loved him. According to what Bonnie later told police, one night Jeff brought her out to the Tangier for dinner. They were sitting, enjoying what should have been a peaceful, romantic night together. Ashton, three years old then, was at home with a babysitter. As they ate, Jeff noticed a woman sitting at the bar. His eyes were fixed on her hourglass figure, blond hair, apple red lipstick, long, painted fingernails and seductive smirk. Bonnie later described the woman to Moriarty and King as "looking really flashy."

"Boy, she looks good," Jeff said to Bonnie as they sat and ate. He was totally taken in by the woman. He had a hard time focusing on his meal—or Bonnie.

Bonnie was curious, so she turned and looked. "Huh," she said smartly, sipping her water, "that woman wouldn't have *anything* to do with you, Jeff."

It was said in jest, not as a challenge, so to speak. Here was Bonnie's husband checking out the blonde hanging off the bar. It was not only disrespectful, but it seemed to Bonnie that nothing else mattered to Jeff after the moment he laid eyes on this woman. Bonnie became a prop, a fixture, someone there to keep Jeff company while he looked for something better.

"Oh, yeah," Jeff said, responding to Bonnie's chiding remark. "Watch this."

Jeff got up, walked toward the bar and approached the woman.

"And started talking to her," Bonnie recalled with a

touch of remorse and disgust in her voice. King and Moriarty were surprised by the anecdote. It told them a lot about Jeff's personality, and who they were dealing with as a victim.

The woman Jeff became mesmerized with was Cynthia Rohr-George. She looked dazzling that night, a gorgeous thirty-seven-year-old mother. Just by looking at her, Cynthia embodied status and affluence, understanding perfectly how the wife of a wealthy, celebrity restaurateur should act. Cynthia was an ornament, a piece of eye candy for patrons to stare at while they spent money inside Ed's establishment. Some beautiful blond bombshell to hang on Ed's arm when he attended social events. The Tangier was booming at the time. Money was rolling in as if printed in the basement. Cynthia played the part of rich wife well, wearing long gowns, expensive jewelry, hanging around the nightclub like Rita Hayworth or Kim Novak.

"From that day on," Bonnie told King and Moriarty, speaking about the moment Jeff saw Cynthia for the first time, "I was *nothing*."

13

As it turned out, the brokerage firm Jeff Zack worked for in San Diego was nothing short of a scam operation. The company's owners, according to Bonnie, had been conducting fraudulent business practices for years. But Jeff had nothing to do with any of it, she insisted. In fact, after an investigation, feds arrested the owners and charged them with a host of white-collar crimes. Jeff was interviewed several times—and cleared.

About six weeks after they moved to Ohio, Jeff started working for a scrap metal company in Hudson as a salesman, selling scrap-metal-recycling machinery. As he started along this new career path, he became paranoid that the investigation back in San Diego was going to put him and Bonnie on the IRS's radar. He saw huge income tax "issues" in his and Bonnie's future. Jeff sensed the feds were going to scrutinize his income and maybe come down on him because they didn't have anything to nail him on during the initial investigation.

"So Jeff put all of our assets into his parents' names." For Moriarty and King, that answered the question as to why Jeff's Ford Explorer—the SUV he was driving on the day he was killed—was in his stepdad's name. But there were plenty of unanswered questions looming. Bonnie needed to continue talking about Jeff's career path and the plight of their marriage. "Please continue," Moriarty suggested, stopping every so often to take notes and study Bonnie's reactions.

By the time they put all of their assets in Jeff's parents' names, Bonnie said, she and Jeff had purchased a house and several cars, not to mention all of their personal belongings. So there was a lot at stake. They needed to provide for Ashton, keep a roof over his head and prepare to put him in a good school. Yet unbeknownst to Bonnie, while they were making sure their financial security was in order, Jeff was secretly communicating with Cynthia George on a weekly, if not daily, basis. "Friends," Jeff told people who started asking questions. "We're just friends."

Indeed, Jeff Zack explained to the people in his life that he had found his soul mate, but then insisted that he and Cynthia were nothing more than "good friends." She understood him. She had kids. Ashton had new friends. Bonnie could even get to know both the Georges. They could all hang out together.

By putting all of his and Bonnie's assets in someone else's name, Jeff felt a small sense of security. But that didn't stop him from dabbling in the stock market, winning and losing, Bonnie said, thousands of dollars over the course of several years. By 1995, Jeff was once again looking for a new job after a falling-out with his boss at the recycling manufacturer. Tall, good-looking, with a fast-talking, charming deportment, Jeff had always been known as a ladies' man. So as the economy blossomed during the mid-1990s, using those skills he'd developed wooing women, Jeff had no trouble getting work within his new field. He found another job immediately—but with one catch: the main office was based in South Carolina. Bonnie and Ashton wouldn't have to move, but Jeff, who was now selling junk car-crushing equipment, said he was going to have to start traveling all over the world.

As the years went by, Jeff became unhappy with his new job. The company had been bought out and Jeff had a difference of business opinion with his new bosses. Yet throughout his years selling products related to metal, he believed he had an insider's feel for the industry. So he took a reported $150,000 of his and Bonnie's money—although Bonnie said later it was likely "two or three times" more—and dumped it into metal management stocks.

For the first few years, the stock did well, but Jeff got greedy. Instead of cashing out, he let it ride. And before he knew it, the metal market crashed—and with it, all of Jeff and Bonnie's money disappeared. They were completely broke, she said. "Jeff lost everything. And when the stock fell apart," she added, crying now, "*Jeff* fell apart."

He eventually left his new job. Discouraged with the metal industry altogether, he started working a series of jobs he lost as quickly as he found. But it wasn't the economy thwarting Jeff's vocational opportunities; he spent much of his time, according to Bonnie, "goofing around" while at work, hitting on many of the women he came across throughout his workday, which didn't sit well with his employers.

At this point, Jeff began doing odd jobs, anything at all to make money: landscaping, roofing, aluminum siding, deck work. Blue-collar jobs mostly. And then he started working for Ed George around his mansion, inside the restaurant at times, and any other odd jobs Ed needed done. The relationship between the Zacks and the Georges picked up, too. Soon they were spending holidays together. Celebrating birthdays. Having dinner parties. And throughout the entire time, Cynthia and Jeff were sneaking around, having sex, talking for hours a day on the telephone, and taking bike rides throughout the Cuyahoga Valley National Park.

Bonnie was emotionally exhausted by this point in the interview. She was visibly upset, knowing, of course, that the punch line to her hour-long diatribe regarding Jeff's history was that his behavior may have finally caught up with him. She needed a break to compose herself. So Moriarty and King told her to take five and regroup. Have a glass of water. Relax. "We've got plenty of time, Mrs. Zack."

14

There was one pressing issue CAPU detectives couldn't scratch from their growing list of suspicions. Tangier owner Ed George, according to his somewhat evasive wife, Cynthia, claimed he was dealing with sewer problems at the restaurant before heading off to a wedding with Cynthia and the kids late Saturday morning. The time frame Cynthia had given Moriarty and his colleagues when they interviewed her on that Sunday morning after Jeff's death fell right in line with the crime's timing. Looking at Ed George, a proportionately slim, rather tall, foreign-looking man with stringy gray hair, he did not seem the type to dash around town on a Ninja motorcycle looking to put a bullet at point-blank range in the head of his wife's lover. Not to mention that Ed George was a personality in town; he had built a reputation for affluence, standing in the community, access to Ohio's more glamorous and important social circles, with a pipeline into some of the country's most famous celebrities. On the walls of the Tangier, Ed had photographs of himself standing, arm in arm, with the likes of Joan Rivers, Redd Foxx, Slappy

White and Buddy Greco, alongside Charo and many others. Lola Falana dedicated a photograph to Ed, writing, *With great and fond memories, always.* Doc Severinsen penned how he had *[a] great time!* at the Tangier when he appeared. *Thank God for the restaurant . . . [but] your golf stinks,* PGA professional Fuzzy Zoeller wrote.

Ed George wasn't the easiest man to get along with, some claimed. Yet as others sharply pointed out, he didn't come across as a man who would likely kill anyone—especially a con artist and womanizer like Jeff Zack. And who said he knew about the affair Jeff Zack was having with Cynthia, anyway?

All the same, Ed George's star credentials didn't rule out the suggestion that he could have hired someone to do the deed for him. It was no secret that Jeff Zack and Cynthia George were, at one time, an item—that they had been fooling around under Ed's nose for the better part of ten years. In fact, a murder-for-hire scenario lent itself more to the professional nature of the crime and Ed's standing. If the CAPU could pinpoint Ed knowing about the affair, they might have something to go on.

Late on Monday morning, June 18, detectives tracked down the environmental health official who had allegedly been with Ed around the time of Jeff Zack's murder. "I was with Ed George," the man said when he was questioned, "on Friday night, from four P.M. to seven P.M." Further, he said, he had met with Ed and several other men at the restaurant to assess a few sewer problems. Once he had a good look at the main problem, he informed Ed that the restaurant was going to be shut down until repairs were made. This riled the restaurateur a bit, but Ed understood the health concerns a sewer backup posed a business centered around food and drink. The main reason Ed was so upset was that someone from the restaurant was going to have to stay overnight on that Friday with a crew of workmen to see that the problem was fixed by the following morning. Saturday was a busy day and night for the restaurant, banquet hall and nightclub. It was imperative the place be open. The environmental official told Ed to call him when they were finished so he could come back, inspect it and clear the restaurant for reopening.

"What about Saturday? Did he call you?" asked one of the CAPU detectives interviewing the environmental official.

"Oh, yes. About ten-thirty A.M. He said the corrections would be done around noon." With that, the guy said he then picked up his partner and headed over to the Tangier. They arrived "shortly before noon," he remembered. The Tangier's "fiscal manager" was there with several other young men, said to be Ed George's nephews.

According to a police report, Ed George didn't show up on the site of the inspection until somewhere between 1:00 to 1:15 P.M. The inspector said he was under the impression, however, that Ed had been in the restaurant for the entire duration of the inspection, just not in the section of the building where the problem was located.

After giving the restaurant a passing grade, the two inspectors left somewhere around quarter to two. "When we left, Ed George was still there."

Detectives wanted to know if Ed had made or received any telephone calls while in their presence. "Not that I know of, not that I can recall," said one of the inspectors.

In theory, Ed George had somewhat of an alibi in

place for the time of Jeff Zack's murder. Yet detectives still believed he could have been involved on a mastermind level, and no one, by that point, could say where he was definitively between 11:30 A.M. and about 1:00 P.M. on Saturday.

The more witnesses detectives spoke to regarding Jeff Zack's life, the more it appeared as if there were not enough adjectives available to describe Jeff's attitude toward women—his wife, Bonnie, in particular. Calling Jeff a ladies' man was an understatement. If anything, Jeff Zack was a chronic womanizer—that much was clear as friends, relatives and acquaintances began opening up.

When Detective Mike Shaeffer caught up with Bonnie's other brother Robert Boucher, on Monday afternoon, the middle-aged man was quick to brand Jeff "erratic, volatile, crude, obnoxious, hot tempered, and *very* secretive."

After hearing that, Shaeffer stopped to reflect. The guy was dead and yet still being talked about in an unsavory manner. Shaeffer was concerned by this. "People hated that guy," Shaeffer commented later. "This made our job that much tougher."

"Yeah, Jeff was very verbally abusive to Bonnie and Ashton. . . ." They had discussed divorce, Robert Boucher claimed, as far back as ten years ago. "They've had their ups and downs since then, but have been trying to maintain a family."

"They ever seek family counseling—a marriage counselor?" Shaeffer had a way about him. He wasn't involved in the investigation on day one only because he was at sniper training. A former U.S. Marine, father of five, Shaeffer was solidly built, yet spoke softly, in a soothing manner, so as not to overstep his boundaries as a detective.

"I don't know," Robert said. He seemed a bit unnerved by Jeff's death, although not at all shocked by it.

After explaining a bit of Jeff's work history, Robert brought up Ed and Cynthia George, saying, "Jeff is a friend of Ed and his wife, Cindy."

"How'd he know them?"

"I guess he did some work for Ed a while back. Bonnie, however, told me that Jeff had an affair with Cindy. But Jeff went to her a few months ago and told her that Cindy and him were no longer friends."

By now, it was apparent that Jeff hadn't been a faithful husband. So Shaeffer asked Boucher about any other women Jeff might have slept with over the years. Any female Jeff had had relations with, at this point in the investigation, could be a potential suspect or witness. There was a chance detectives would be knocking on doors for the next two weeks, tracking down any female Jeff had come into contact with. But Boucher couldn't recall seeing Jeff with any other women. It was Cynthia, he said, all the time, adding, "Jeff lived a separate life from his family. He wouldn't let them get involved in any part of his life."

After explaining to Shaeffer that Jeff often lied to Bonnie about the "bike trips" he took with a friend of his, Robert brought up a "conflict," as he called it, Jeff had with someone he thought had been messing around with Jeff's vending machine business.

Robert admitted that he rarely had a one-on-one conversation with Jeff. It was only during family functions, with everyone around, that he had spoken to him on any real personal level. And even then, all Jeff ever talked about was, well, Jeff Zack. "[He] mostly bragged about his accomplishments, being a paratrooper in the Israeli Army, his possessions, the yard work he did."

It was becoming clear to the CAPU that Jeff's murder was perhaps prompted by his own behavior—that someone had obviously had it out for him and followed through with threats Jeff had been receiving via telephone and in person for months leading up to his death. It didn't make it right, or justify killing the man. But detectives needed to look at the murder from the point of view of the perpetrator and get inside his or her mind. Shaeffer was a sharp interrogator; he knew how to get people to loosen up. Part of that skill, he said later, was how, as an interviewer, you always make people feel as though you're on their level. "For example, you would never stand and interview a witness or suspect if he or she was sitting. Regardless how you perceive it, they feel inferior to you, which makes them uncomfortable."

With the theory playing out in his mind that Jeff had brought on his own demise, the next question Shaeffer had for Robert Boucher became: "What is your opinion of what happened to your brother-in-law? Who do you think is involved?"

Robert thought about it. Then, "I think a *woman* was involved."

"No kidding?" Shaeffer said, shaking his head.

"I don't believe it had anything to do with Jeff's vending business. Jeff's been keeping himself scarce lately," which, Robert intimated, seemed a bit alarming. "It was like he was hiding from someone."

Then something else came up. Those two business partners of Jeff's, Seth and Carl, the two guys he'd gotten involved with while doing an aluminum-siding job on his house, and recently had a falling-out with—they worried Robert Boucher. "I believe that it might have been [Seth] who left that message on Jeff's answering machine," Robert said. "[Ashton] said he recognized the voice as Seth's. Someone likely followed Jeff when he left the house that morning and then phoned the person on the motorcycle. . . . Jeff was mad when he left."

After giving up a few more details, Shaeffer thanked Robert, saying, "Listen, here's my card. If you think of anything else, hear something, or have any new concerns, please give me a call."

Robert Boucher held the card out in front of himself. "Yeah," he said. "I'll do that."

15

When Jeff Zack played back that ominous message left on his answering machine on Wednesday, June 13, he became irritated and squirrelly. It had obviously unnerved him greatly. Somebody was, in a not-so-subtle way, intimidating Jeff. But he didn't want his wife to know how bothered he was by it.

When Bonnie sat with Moriarty and King and described the message for a second time, Moriarty later said, "She became really upset." Bonnie had approached Jeff that day about the message and asked him what the hell was going on. In her view, things were escalating. Routine threats had turned into recorded messages that seemed fairly serious in nature. Should she be worried? What about Ashton? *Talk to me, Jeffrey . . . tell me what's going on here.*

"Don't you worry about it," Jeff raged. "I have it taken *care* of."

Just a few weeks ago, Bonnie said, Jeff told her he was taking off for Arizona to visit family. It was near Mother's Day. Worried later about the message, thinking about his trip, Bonnie asked Jeff how things went out in Arizona, demanding to know if he had actually gone to Arizona to begin with. She sensed something wasn't right. He was acting strange. Anxious. Worried. Had something happened during the trip?

"I drove up to the Grand Canyon," Jeff shot back angrily. "I slept in my car for the night."

"Did he go there?" asked Moriarty. He was watching Bonnie carefully as she spoke. He studied her body language, which spoke of a woman who never believed for one minute her husband had gone where he said he was going.

Bonnie dropped her head and started shaking it. "I couldn't be sure he was *ever* telling the truth anymore."

On June 8, Jeff and a friend had allegedly taken off to West Virginia on a bicycling trip, which Jeff enjoyed immensely. Bicycling kept his large frame in somewhat good shape. When they were together, he and Cynthia had gone biking probably three times a week; Cynthia nearly every day.

"When did he return?" Bertina King asked.

"June thirteenth." It was the day, Bonnie remembered, Jeff received that threatening message. "But who knows . . . ," Bonnie said next. "I couldn't be sure if Jeff did what he said he was doing."

"How so?" Moriarty wanted to know, chiming in. He asked Bonnie for an example. One scenario, even if Bonnie believed it was insignificant, could break the case. Everything mattered now. Where Jeff stopped to get his morning coffee. Where he traveled throughout his day. Who it was he spoke to on a regular basis. But Bonnie was being pushed away from Jeff further and further as their marriage went into a dramatic decline over the years.

"Well," Bonnie said, "I received a call from Las Vegas

recently from a friend of ours who spotted Jeff in Vegas." She stopped and "rhetorically," Moriarty explained in his report of the conversation, looked at him and Bertina King and asked herself what was an extremely pertinent question: "What in the *hell* was Jeff doing in Las Vegas?"

Bonnie said she had no idea he had even gone.

After a short spell, while fidgeting with a tissue in her hand, Bonnie said, looking at Moriarty, "See, I never knew *what* he was doing. He kept *everything* from me."

16

There was a part of her husband's life Bonnie Zack had a hard time discussing. Ed Moriarty and Bertina King knew from observing Bonnie's mannerisms, and listening to her voice crack as she spoke, that Jeff's relationship with Cynthia George was probably going to be off-limits. Yet, as Moriarty and King pressed, Bonnie opened up about it.

Moriarty asked Bonnie if Jeff knew the George family as well as he knew Cynthia.

Bonnie replied, "Yes."

Moriarty wasn't satisfied. "What do you mean by that?" he asked. He could sense there was more to it, but also, he recalled later, the bitterness oozing out of Bonnie's pores as she began to step back in time. There was so much more to talk about. Patience, Moriarty understood, was essential when dealing with a witness or suspect like Bonnie. Don't push too hard. Let her sort things out and come to terms with how she feels. What was surprising, however, especially as Moriarty and King started to put pressure on Bonnie, was that she never once pulled out the lawyer card and said she was done talking. And she could have, at any moment, asked them to leave and work through her attorney from that moment on.

"That told us," one of the detectives working the case later recalled, "that Bonnie wasn't worried about getting caught up in having to explain herself. She was guarded, sure. But she was also forthcoming with information."

Bonnie explained how Jeff met Cynthia that night at the Tangier while they were having dinner. "From then on," she added, "Jeff and Cindy started doing all kinds of things together. They were calling each other several times a day. Jeff made no secret about their relationship, and did a lot of things right in front of me."

Incredible, thought Moriarty. *The guy was shameless.*

Bonnie was furious about Jeff's lack of respect for their marriage, not to mention the values he was teaching their child. "How dare you!" Bonnie said one night after Jeff got off the telephone with Cynthia. Bonnie had been standing on the opposite side of the wall, adjacent to the room Jeff was in. "Right in front of me?"

"We're just friends, Bonnie," Jeff swore. "She's my confidante. My counselor."

A while later, Bonnie said, she heard Jeff "on the phone making a date with Cindy." This time she was standing around the corner. It was as if he didn't care. He must have known Bonnie was in the house, yet he still carried on. "Let's meet at the Sheraton," Bonnie heard Jeff tell Cynthia. "The one in Cuyahoga Falls [a suburb of Akron and Stow]."

Bonnie decided, even though she was terribly upset by the call, she wasn't going to say anything. Instead, she arranged for a babysitter on the night Cynthia and Jeff were rendezvousing and headed out to Cuyahoga Falls herself.

As Cynthia and Jeff walked into the hotel lobby, Bonnie followed them from behind, like a spy. Then she slipped behind a picture in the lobby and waited for the right moment.

As Cynthia and Jeff smiled and stared into each other's eyes like young lovers on a first date, frolicking right there in the lobby, Bonnie stepped out from behind the picture and, she explained to Moriarty and King, "surprised them."

"What happened next?" Moriarty asked.

Taking the high road, Bonnie didn't say anything. She stared them down for a moment and just walked away. This told Cynthia and Jeff that Bonnie knew what was going on. She was not some ignorant, naïve wife, overlooking the obvious because it made her life less complicated. She was in their face.

As Bonnie exited the lobby and walked out into the parking lot, she started to break down in tears because Jeff didn't even get up and try to talk to her. He kept on doing his business with Cynthia. He never even acknowledged that Bonnie had caught the two of them. No Hollywood moment of running after his wife and apologizing. No telephone call later on that night. Just coldhearted silence.

"What was it like at home after that?" Moriarty wanted to know.

"He didn't come home until four A.M. the next day."

"While she was relaying this information to us," Moriarty recalled later, "Bonnie would at some points cry, and at others get a faraway look about her." Moriarty knew that reliving the experiences crushed her.

After getting through the hotel story, Bonnie took a deep breath, held up her index finger and, through a multitude of tears, said, "I have another story, much worse."

She remembered the year as 1998. It was a vivid memory. She was in the master bathroom getting ready for bed. As she was doing her business, Jeff walked into the room—obviously not realizing she was in the next room—and called Cynthia. "Cindy, that you?"

Bonnie recoiled and got a bit closer so she could hear. After a brief pause, Cynthia got on the line. They talked for a bit. Then Bonnie heard Jeff say, "I can't get enough of being inside of you."

After that, she went "blank."

Collecting herself, Bonnie walked into the bedroom and confronted Jeff. Enough was enough. "What the hell do you think you're doing?" She was crying hysterically. It was one thing to understand that an affair was going on behind her back. But for Jeff to throw it around so freely in her face, adding insult to injury by saying hurtful things, was too much. He'd taken it too far.

"What do you mean?" Jeff shot back.

"I heard you."

"I didn't say anything like that. You didn't hear me say that."

"Yes, I did, Jeffrey."

"It wasn't Cindy, anyway."

Jeff never admitted talking to Cynthia and certainly not to saying anything sexual. So he and Bonnie walked away from each other in a huff and tabled the subject.

Moriarty asked Bonnie about Jeff and Cynthia's relationship over the past few months. Was there something significant she could offer? Ashton had mentioned the relationship was over.

"I would hear him on the phone with Cindy recently," said Bonnie, "but things were different. He would yell at her and use foul language. He was very abusive toward her."

"What can you tell us about the Georges?"

"Over the years, me and Jeff have been to the Georges' house in Medina. Numerous occasions. . . . We were even at the house before they finished building it."

"How was Cindy?" Meaning, was she cordial to you? Had she always been pleasant and polite?

"She was always nice to me."

What a strange world the Zacks lived in, Moriarty and King thought as they sat listening to Bonnie talk about this bizarre relationship the two families had. The guy had apparently carried on an affair with Ed George's wife for years—and through it all, they remained friends.

It was getting late. Bonnie looked over toward the clock on the wall and told Moriarty and King she needed to get ready for Jeff's funeral. She was still "very upset," Moriarty wrote in his report of the interview. She needed some time by herself to prepare for the burial. "I have to get ready to leave," Bonnie said.

"We understand. I'll be back, though, likely tomorrow, to continue this conversation. OK?"

Bonnie shook her head.

Driving away, Moriarty looked at Bertina King with a bit of amazement. "Can you believe what we just heard?" he said as they pulled around the corner of Bonnie's house.

"Incredible."

"We were collecting all of this information," recalled Moriarty, "and Jeff Zack's family is trying to push us down the Ed George road—that Ed had had something to do with this murder. That's their major contention. And it's sort of playing out as possibly true, because there *is* a connection." Moriarty, as he often would when he explained something, stopped for a moment to catch up with his thoughts, then added, "We understood that *clearly*."

That connection, however, still didn't defuse the situation Jeff and Bonnie Zack lived in. And Bertina King and Ed Moriarty, as they headed back to the sixth floor of the APD, couldn't get it out of their minds that for months leading up to Jeff's murder, Bonnie had been put through so much turmoil in her marriage, they wondered if it all just got too much for her to take. Had she snapped? Hearing Jeff talk to Cynthia about how good it felt to be "inside of her" had really stirred Bonnie up. King and Moriarty could see that from the way she reacted when telling the story. It could have been, they considered, a reason for Bonnie Zack, pushing her to go out and hire someone to kill her husband.

"Let's keep an eye on her," suggested Moriarty as they headed up the elevator. "Let's allow her to bury her husband and then turn up the pressure."

17

Detective Mike Shaeffer was busy tracking down people who could further explain Jeff Zack's complicated life. Shaeffer wanted a better understanding of the negative information coming in about the guy. Bonnie's father, Bob Boucher, had hired what the APD thought at first was a private detective to investigate Jeff before he and Bonnie were married. But it turned out that the guy was an Arizona police officer, a friend of Boucher's.

Shaeffer was the type of detective that allowed information to resonate inside him for a time before he made any judgments. He treated everyone he spoke to (witnesses and suspects) on a level playing field. His job—and he did it well—was to gather information, study it and make determinations (based on evidence) that further facilitated the investigation. Follow the evidence and see where it led. Law enforcement hadn't always been in Shaeffer's blood. He wasn't born into it, like a lot of cops. After high school and some college, Shaeffer got a job working for Ohio Bell, a telephone company, as a sales representative. Eight years into that, he was bored beyond belief and yearned for a change. Instead of simply switching jobs within the company, though, at twenty-seven years old, Shaeffer, a husband and father, decided to join the U.S. Marine Corps. But several years into his military career, he ended up hurting his back and was discharged. Back at Ohio Bell, feeling as though he had gone in a complete circle, he spotted an ad one day in the local paper: the Akron Police Department was looking for recruits. Out of five thousand applicants who took the test, Shaeffer scored in the top two hundred, and a future in law enforcement presented itself. It had always been hard for Shaeffer to sit still; he embraced vocational challenges. Although he didn't know it then, police work would offer him that perfect mixture of excitement and ambiguity, never knowing what the job was going to bring from day to day. ("Don't limit yourself," Shaeffer told me later, speaking about life in general.)

Indeed, he spent two years as a patrol officer. Then, in the early 1990s, as the crack cocaine boom infested the streets of Akron and many other cities across the United States in epidemic proportions, he was offered a job with a new fifteen-person uniformed unit designed to frustrate crack dealers hanging around street corners. "Our job was to go out there and be proactive instead of reactive," Shaeffer said. In the chief's words, Shaeffer added with a laugh, "Get out there and legally harass those dope dealers."

Shaeffer spent nine years working that detail, along with becoming a member of the swat team as a sniper and, in 2000, landed a job as a detective with the CAPU. He learned the ropes and felt comfortable in his new role as an investigator. When Shaeffer said not to limit yourself, he drew those conclusions from experience.

Never, he said, assume the obvious, because the obvious is often the least likely conclusion to come out of a homicide investigation.

Bonnie's dad, Bob Boucher, lived in a nondescript apartment building in Barberton, about a thirty-minute drive south of Stow. A rather pleasant man, well-groomed and seemingly peaceful, he had misgivings about his deceased son-in-law, which were obvious the moment Shaeffer knocked on the door and introduced himself. For all the CAPU knew, Bob Boucher could have hired someone to kill his son-in-law after watching the guy mistreat his daughter for the past ten years. What father didn't want to protect his daughter? What was clear to Shaeffer from the get-go was that Bonnie and other members of her family were stuck on the notion that Ed George had had something to do with Jeff's death.

As Shaeffer walked into the senior Boucher's apartment, he asked, "Can we talk a little bit about Jeff Zack?"

"Sure, come on in and have a seat."

Mr. Boucher seemed more than willing to help. Right off the bat, his description of Jeff was no different than most others: "pushy, outspoken, ballsy," he said. "He pissed people off. People in the family. So I assume he pissed off *other* people outside the family, as well."

Shaeffer learned that it wasn't a private investigator, after all, that Bob Boucher had hired to look into Jeff's background when he and Bonnie became engaged. Mr. Boucher admitted he had a friend who was a Mesa, Arizona, cop at the time. As for the prostitution and pimping charge Jeff had on his record, Mr. Boucher confronted his son-in-law with the allegations when he found out. Jeff denied knowing anything about what was going on, saying, "All I did was drive the girls around."

"We tried talking Bonnie out of marrying him," Mr. Boucher explained to Shaeffer, shaking his head. "But she obviously didn't listen."

Shaeffer wasn't all that surprised by what he heard. Every rock he and his colleagues had turned over thus far exposed another level of Jeff Zack's corrupted character. Depending upon whom they spoke to, Jeff was a brute. Charlatan. A filthy liar who seemed to take what he wanted when he wanted it. There was one time, Mr. Boucher explained, when Jeff followed one of Bonnie's sisters into the bathroom during a family gathering. Once he was alone with her, he, purportedly, exposed himself while he urinated.

Incredible, thought Shaeffer, shaking his head, taking notes.

Jeff had always talked about his time in the Israeli Army as a rather secretive, sensitive security matter. He had routinely bragged about the level of importance he played in the Israeli government's military. Stories circulated about him being involved in covert, undercover operations for the Israeli government that made him out to be some sort of Jewish James Bond. On that note, Mr. Boucher had his own theory. "His status," Bob Boucher said, "was that of an equivalent to our Navy SEALS."

"No kidding," remarked Shaeffer. A jarhead himself, Shaeffer felt a connection, but based on all the information he had collected about Jeff Zack, he didn't quite believe Jeff had been involved in the Israeli military.

"Yeah," continued Bob Boucher a bit confused, "he also worked for Air Israeli, I believe, as a security officer. He'd board planes with a briefcase dressed as a passenger. Inside the brief case was an Uzi. His responsibility was to intercept terrorists on the plane."

Were these campfire stories Jeff was telling family members, or actual facts? Shaeffer made a note to have Jeff's military background checked out thoroughly. If he had been in the Israeli equivalent to the CIA, the job increased the suspect pool substantially.

Apparently, according to what Jeff had told his father-in-law, he was given a lifetime membership into the local Jewish Community Center for his service in the Israeli Army. "But Jeff was not an active member of the synagogue."

In Mr. Boucher's view, Bonnie didn't find out about Jeff's affair with Cynthia George until 1998, when she heard him on the telephone. Before that, she believed Jeff was *friends* with Cynthia and had worked for Ed George at times. "I've seen Jeff out with other women," the elder Boucher said. "Ed George and Jeff used to be tight. But they had a big falling-out over Cindy. Two weeks ago, Jeff told Bonnie that he and Ed were no longer friends."

Jeff had told his father-in-law that Ed said the "Tangier was starving . . . and [another company] was making all the money." Ed seemed disturbed and upset by this. The other company, for the most part, provided jukebox entertainment and other music services to restaurants, bars and nightclubs throughout Ohio. One of Ed George's brothers owned the company. Moriarty later said that through his years of working in the organized crime unit of the APD, it was well established that the company had "a reputation." But that was a long time ago. The company was certainly legit and no one connected to the company on a management level had ever been charged or prosecuted.

Bonnie's father seemed to be a wealth of information, opening up several new avenues for investigators. And then, near the end of the conversation, Shaeffer heard something that further piqued his interest. "Three weeks ago," Mr. Boucher said as Shaeffer prepared to leave, "Jeff took Bonnie to the basement of their house and showed her something."

"What was that?" Shaeffer asked.

"He had all these cabinets with records inside. He called them his personal files." Apparently, while showing Bonnie the files, Mr. Boucher indicated, Jeff looked into her eyes, as if he were a character in a Hollywood thriller, and said quite stoically, "If anything ever happens to me, here are all the records."

If anything even happens to me . . .

Shaeffer noted Mr. Boucher's concern with that conversation, asking, "So what's your opinion of why this happened to Jeff?" It was obvious the older man had a theory that he wanted to express.

Mr. Boucher thought about it momentarily. "It might be an insurance deal, or something with Cindy and Ed George. I don't believe it had *anything*"—he shook his head—"to do with his vending machine business, or even any of his former employees." Then, in a theory lending itself more to Ed Moriarty's hypothesis after studying the crime scene, Mr. Boucher mentioned that it could have been a simple, random act of road rage violence. "Jeff drove like hell. Very fast. He may have cut someone off and then pissed them off, you know. He had a knack for doing that. Your road rage theory"— he said he had seen the newspaper article about it— "might not be too far off."

"You'll call me, Mr. Boucher, if you think of anything else?"

"Sure. But I think I covered everything."

Shaeffer turned to leave.

"One more thing," Bonnie's father said as they walked toward the door. "That rabbi, um, um . . . Sasonkin, that's his name, the one who was talking to Bonnie and [Ashton]. He . . . he told her that Jeff had come to him five years ago with 'a problem.'"

"What was it?"

"I don't know. I never heard what it was."

"Well, thank you for your help," Shaeffer said, shaking Mr. Boucher's hand. "Call me if you think of anything else."

"Will do."

18

   Late Sunday afternoon, June 17, an episode that was going to propel the investigation into yet another tailspin took place inside the Akron Police Department. It was a little over twenty-four hours into the case. If Ed Moriarty and his colleagues didn't have enough to contend with already, the murder of Jeff Zack was about to get even more complicated.

   Moriarty and Bertina King wanted to speak to Ed and Cynthia George. The George name had been popping up all over the place. Cynthia had made it clear when Moriarty, King, Daugherty and Callahan showed up at the George mansion earlier that day that she wasn't about to talk to police without her husband present, and all but kicked them out of her house. That was fine. They understood. But a telephone call Ed George had made to the APD in early 2001 seemed extremely vital to the current situation the Georges now found themselves in. Deputy Chief Paul Callahan had taken Ed's call that day. "Can you give me some advice in dealing with a problem my wife, Cindy, is having?" Ed George asked Callahan.

"What is it, Ed?" They weren't friends, but like many public officials in town, Callahan knew Ed George.

"She's being harassed by some man. He's following her and bothering her." Ed sounded genuinely worried about his wife. In his report of the call, Callahan said he could sense the concern in Ed's voice. There were plenty of nutcases around. Add a wealthy family to the mix and those types of people seem to come out of the woodwork and cause problems.

"Has Cindy made a complaint report with us?"

"No, she hasn't," Ed replied.

"Listen, Ed, the first thing she should do is file an incident report so we can begin to establish a paper trail, in case the suspect continues to harass her," Callahan suggested. It was good advice. "Have you confronted the guy? Do you know him?"

"I have not confronted him," Ed said. "Yes, I *do* know him." Ed wouldn't give Callahan the man's name.

"Since you know him, Ed, you can confront him and tell him to stay away from Cindy."

Ed didn't say anything.

"Do you want to file an incident report?" Callahan asked a second time. "We'd need that before we can investigate the allegations."

"I'll think about it and get back to you."

A week before Jeff Zack was murdered, Ed George left Callahan a voice mail: "Can you get back to me, Paul? I want to talk about the man harassing my wife. He's still bothering her. Maybe you can come out to the restaurant for lunch one day and tell me about my options."

Callahan, for one reason or another, never called Ed back.

Now that random telephone call, together with the voice mail Ed left, could possibly play into the APD's current investigation. It had stuck with Callahan. He was thinking about it as Ed and Cynthia George were being discussed around the department as possible suspects and potential witnesses. Ed George's wife had an affair—a very *long* affair—with the victim, which, on paper, had given Ed George a motive. It was clear Ed George was unhappy about the affair, as any dedicated father and husband might be. When Moriarty and King interviewed Cynthia briefly that Sunday morning, according to them, she remained evasive and didn't want to talk. While they were in the house, Cynthia pulled Bertina King aside and asked if she could speak to her alone. King said sure. "Let's go over there."

They walked into the dining-room area of the house, away from everyone else. "How did you hear about Jeff Zack's murder?" King asked, trying to break the ice between them and get Cynthia talking.

"Ed read me the article earlier this morning."

According to Moriarty and King, Cynthia said Ed hadn't read the newspaper to her as they romantically sat by the window and had eggs Benedict and coffee, but had rushed into the bedroom as she was getting up and threw it on the bed. "You see that," he ranted while pointing at the front-page article detailing Jeff Zack's murder. It was obvious to Cynthia, at least she expressed as much talking to King, that Ed was being facetious and patronizing.

"I'm confused about what happened," Cynthia explained to King that Sunday, "and I don't know what to do."

King was confused, too. What was Cynthia trying to say? So she asked, "Was Jeff Zack the man who was harassing you?" It seemed obvious.

"Yes, he was."

"Why would he be harassing you?"

Cynthia shrugged her shoulders and mumbled.

"Was Jeff Zack a lover, Mrs. George, or someone from the restaurant who started bothering you?"

She wouldn't answer. Then, "He was just harassing me. I can't get any more specific than that."

The CAPU began to wonder why Ed George would run upstairs in a huff and throw the newspaper on the bed, announcing Jeff's murder. There was some obvious animosity there between the three of them. Ed's actions spoke to that clearly. Now, just a few weeks ago, Ed had called in a *second* report of his wife being harassed. In lieu of this information, the pieces, if not entirely juxtaposing, were beginning to fit. "We had gone out to the George house once already," Moriarty recalled, "and Cynthia was *very* elusive. We thought there was something to the information we had, but she wouldn't talk without her husband there." Moriarty had even sent King and another female, the captain of the unit, Elizabeth "Beth" Daugherty, in to talk with Cynthia that same day. Because the situation was so volatile, possibly opening up an ugly vein of her marriage, Moriarty hoped Cynthia might feel more comfortable speaking with female officers. "But she was no more forthcoming with them—besides describing that newspaper incident to Tina—than she was with us," Moriarty added. "That told us something. Why was she being evasive? What purpose would it serve her unless she and Ed had something to hide?"

Moriarty had broadcast a "road rage" theory on Saturday so the press would get off his back for a while, or at least until detectives could come up with something tangible to feed them. The road rage ruse, however, quickly turned into a "fiasco," Moriarty later said.

"Once big names come out, you have a problem. The press wants to know. They'll keep hounding you. They make it pretty difficult for us to investigate leads and theories."

On the following Monday morning, June 18, Paul Callahan, thinking back to the telephone calls from Ed George, called Ed George in an attempt to set up a meeting with members of the CAPU. It was time Ed and Cynthia came down to the APD and made themselves available for questioning. Ed was concerned that bad publicity would fall on him and Cynthia regarding meeting with police. If the press found out they were being questioned with regard to the death of Jeff Zack, people would speculate, not knowing the truth, and it could mean trouble for the Tangier. The restaurant hadn't been doing all that great to begin with over the past few years. Negative publicity could have a detrimental effect on business. Ed didn't need any of that right now. He had seven kids to feed, a wife, a mansion on the hill, bills piled on top of bills, a reputation that was, for the most part, pretty damn good around town. Why get involved in a homicide he'd had nothing to do with?

As soon as Ed got on the telephone, he said, "Can you believe this?"

"Was Jeff Zack the man harassing Cindy?" Callahan asked, referring to their previous conversations.

"Yes."

"We need you to come in for an interview—you and Cindy."

"I understand," Ed said. He seemed more than willing. "Let me check with Cindy and I'll call you back later this morning."

Callahan felt Ed and Cynthia were going to meet with detectives at the police department at some point that afternoon. This way, they could get in and out without anyone knowing what was going on—especially the *Akron Beacon Journal*, located only a few blocks down the road from the APD.

Callahan understood the predicament Ed found himself in. He wanted to help him through it. In fact, keeping his word, Callahan didn't tell Moriarty about the potential meeting. He, like his colleagues, would find out when Ed and Cynthia showed up.

According to an *Akron Beacon Journal* source, a court reporter for the newspaper received "a tip" at some point during the afternoon that Ed and Cynthia George were going to be interviewed at the APD in relation to the Jeff Zack murder. That source claimed the *Journal* had no idea who had called in the tip, but it seemed sensible to send a reporter down there to check it out, anyway.

The *Journal* had published an article about the Jeff Zack murder that morning, basically establishing the case as a whodunit. Cops were baffled. A hit man, maybe? Had a disgruntled neighbor, the article suggested, perhaps taken out Jeff Zack because he had threatened one of his neighbors, the guy's kids and wife? Any and all possibilities existed. "Police are looking for the driver of a tri-colored, Ninja-styled motorcycle," part of the *Journal*'s article read.

As the *Journal*'s reporter wandered around the lobby area of the APD down on the first floor, he or she saw Ed and Cynthia George walk into the building. Something was up. The anonymous tip was accurate. Why else would Akron's golden couple be heading into the APD accompanied by Ed George's flashy lawyer?

Indeed, walking alongside Ed and Cynthia was the highly touted, much respected and hugely expensive Akron attorney Robert "Bob" Meeker, who had been Ed George's personal and business legal representative for years. Meeker was a tough lawyer to tangle with, many of the detectives working the Zack case agreed. He had been with Ed George through thick and thin and protected his interests. He was respected. Detectives knew that Meeker was going to advise Ed and Cynthia to keep quiet.

According to what detectives found out later, when Meeker spotted the reporter, he became incensed and steamed upstairs to the sixth floor with Ed and Cynthia in tow. When a person exits the elevator on the sixth floor, where the CAPU is located, there's a long, chest-high front desk, to the right, with a waist-level saloon-style swinging door into the cubicle farm that makes up the unit off to the side. Meeker and the Georges, according to sources there on the day they arrived, had a "major hissy fit" standing by the front desk.

Moriarty, who was down at his desk, walked out into the foyer near the front reception area; as soon as Meeker saw him, he got an earful. "You set the Georges up," Meeker said, referring to the reporter downstairs. "This is ridiculous." He threw up his hands and walked around in circles for a moment.

That one variable, which happened to be nothing more than a rare happenstance (or was it?), Moriarty later concluded, set a precedent for the relationship Ed and Cynthia George were now going to have with the APD. Robert Meeker would see to it that if the APD wanted to speak to Cynthia or Ed, they were going to have to go through Meeker and his rather powerful team of lawyers at Blakemore, Meeker & Bowler Co., a staple in the Akron legal community since the late 1960s. No more, Meeker warned, could Moriarty and his investigators just pop up unannounced at Ed's restaurant or home. If they did, they had better have a warrant or court order.

"This is disgraceful!" Meeker said as he, Ed and Cynthia walked into the elevator and headed back downstairs to leave.

For the CAPU, they had no motivation whatsoever to telephone in the tip to the *Journal*. In fact, they had every reason *not* to. Their goal was to speak with Ed and Cynthia George. Why would a cop tip off the local newspaper, letting them know that the Georges were on their way down to the department? It didn't make sense. With only the lieutenant, Ed, Cynthia and Ed's attorney knowing, it wasn't such a far-fetched theory to come up with the source of the leak. They thought they knew who did it—and better yet, why.

"The Georges could appear to us like they wanted to talk," said a source from the APD, "but, by the same token, get out of it."

As a practical matter, regardless who called in the tip, CAPU detectives now knew the cat was out of the bag. With that, they had other business to tend to at the present time—before it was reported that Ed and Cynthia George were being questioned about the death of Jeff Zack. More important, a suspect could be at Jeff's wake, which was set to take place later that same night. So Moriarty sent several detectives to the funeral home to scope it out, advising, "See what you can come up with and get back to me as soon as possible."

19

As Ed Moriarty woke up the following morning, he sat and thought about the case. *It's going to be a productive day,* Moriarty thought as he got ready to head into the office. Cops sometimes get a sense that the next lead they uncover will be that inevitable smoking gun. One superficial or seemingly insignificant piece of information can turn a complicated murder case into one that is easily solvable, even during those crucial early days of the investigation when information is coming in so fast it's hard to keep up with.

While Moriarty drove into work, sipping from his cup of coffee, it occurred to him that finding Jeff Zack's killer was going to come down to checking people—a *lot* of people—off the APD's growing pool of suspects. However subtle it may have seemed, the weather, Moriarty noticed as he pulled into his parking space along the street in front of the APD, was certainly going to help on this day. It was clear in town, the sky as blue as Caribbean seawater, with comfortable, moderate temperatures in the high 60s, a dew point hovering around 54 percent by 8:00 A.M. Those numbers wouldn't change too much throughout the day, forecasters promised, which would, in turn, keep detectives and potential witnesses rather calm and at ease. There was nothing worse than heading out into the day with humidity levels hovering at 90 percent and the mercury capping out at 100. It made people miserable and uncooperative, certainly less willing to be accommodating to invasive questioning.

The CAPU didn't have staff meetings every morning, but when the situation warranted it, they all got together so everyone could compare notes and sketch out the days ahead. "You have to understand," Moriarty recalled, "inside the unit, everything else didn't stop when Jeff Zack turned up dead. We still had to work other cases as they came in."

With the Zack case now branching out in so many different directions, however, Moriarty put up a large board on the wall in one of the conference rooms and scribed Jeff Zack's name in the middle, with each possible suspect flanked out around him. Time and again, the George name was coming up, Moriarty considered as he stood and he looked at the board. Neither Ed nor Cynthia could be eliminated. Not because they were acting suspicious, but because Bob Meeker was making contact between the APD and the Georges nearly impossible. Every time Moriarty and his colleagues stopped to talk to Ed George, somehow Meeker knew about it and called to break up the meeting, ripping into Moriarty over the telephone. Moriarty had even stopped at the Tangier a few times, as did other detectives, but Ed would only say, "Look, my attorney says I shouldn't be talking to you." A comment, incidentally, that by itself alarmed Moriarty. "When somebody tells me that their attorney won't let me talk to you, that signifies to me that you have something that you want to say."

After the morning meeting, Moriarty walked over to his desk, sat down and took out a copy of the *Akron Beacon Journal.* And there was the headline staring back at him: SHOOTING AT BJ'S STILL A MYSTERY, DETECTIVES SUSPECT ROAD RAGE IN STOW MAN'S DEATH.

At least they're still buying it, thought Moriarty, sitting, looking at the newspaper. Reading the accompanying article, Moriarty realized the CAPU still had time before the press totally caught on to what the investigation was fleshing out. There was a saying around the unit about Moriarty that he could talk to reporters for fifteen minutes and not say anything. He had a knack for spinning. This morning's article proved as much.

"Moriarty said investigators are considering whether road rage prompted the incident," *Beacon Journal* reporter Dave Ghose's article read in part, "but have no proof yet of such a cause."

Moriarty took a pull from his coffee and snapped the fold of the newspaper to see it more clearly. *Here it comes,* he thought, *let's see what I said:* "'It's probably the most obvious thing that stands out,'" Ghose quoted Moriarty. "'But we are looking at all possibilities. We really don't know the motive at this point.' Moriarty said Zack was shot after he pulled up to the pump. He had yet to purchase any gas. 'To our knowledge, he never got out of the car.'"

Not bad. I'll take it.

By midmorning, scores of new tips came in. After getting together and discussing the case briefly, Callahan and Moriarty considered it might take weeks, if not months, to check out every man or woman who had owned and operated a Ninja-style motorcycle in the

Akron-Cleveland area. Every neighbor, disgruntled lover, family member, friend, stranger and so on, who had ever come in contact with or been annoyed by the chainsaw-like whine of a Ninja-style motorcycle had called in to report it. Moriarty and Callahan were forced to utilize dozens of officers to check out every tip. They knew 99 percent of the leads were going to yield nothing, but integrity drove them to have it done, nonetheless. Even so, how could they know, without checking each tip, that one of those Ninja owners *wasn't* the shooter?

20

The youngest of four children, Dave Whiddon was born and raised in Akron. He had been a police officer with the APD since 1992 after taking the test and scoring high marks. The year before, Whiddon met his future wife, Laurie, who was working as a triage nurse in the emergency room of the local hospital. "We both got out of bad relationships," Whiddon recalled later, "and we hit it off from the start. She is the greatest woman I have ever met and has a special gift in dealing with sick children."

Whiddon's name carried an air of respect around the APD. His great uncle, Harry Whiddon, was the APD's chief of police for nearly twenty years (1958 to 1976). Uncle Whiddon was a tough, no-nonsense type of leader. He knew his police force and, even better, had the respect of his officers. All cops spoke of Harry Whiddon in the highest regard.

By pure luck, Dave Whiddon joined the police force at the right time. There were a lot of officers set to retire in the coming years, which of course opened up many different opportunities within the department.

Whiddon was a college man, a book person. He had studied history and, at that time, wanted to get his Ph.D. and teach high school or college. Besides his uncle, he was the only one in his family to enter law enforcement. He soaked up the city during those early years, making contacts on the street and putting his heart and soul into his work. Within five years, Whiddon took the test for sergeant and, by 1997, was promoted as one of the youngest officers to ever make the ranking. The job didn't come without a few dirty looks from some of the other officers, or a bit of skepticism on the part of some who thought he'd fail as a supervisor. But Whiddon worked for the respect of his officers and, over time, earned it.

For the next three years, Whiddon worked as a patrol sergeant. During that time, he took the test for lieutenant. When the results came back, it was no surprise that he finished near the top and was put on the list to be promoted once again. "The only problem," Whiddon said later, "was that I *hated* being off of the street and not doing actual police work. . . . My wife did not want me to take the promotion because I currently had holidays and weekends off. She did not understand that it was driving me crazy not to be doing actual police work."

In December 2000, not quite knowing where he was going to end up, Whiddon found out a lieutenant's job had opened up in the detective's bureau of the CAPU. "I always wanted to work in the detective bureau," Whiddon added, "especially investigating homicides. But I also knew that this unit was in shambles at the time. Also, this was an exempt position and one not based on seniority. It meant that the deputy chief and captain could choose who they wanted for the job, regardless of seniority, unlike most of our positions."

Fellow officers warned Whiddon about Ed Moriarty, who had a reputation in the department as a raging firebrand. Don't mess with Moriarty, Whiddon was told. He'll tear your head off.

When Whiddon showed up on the sixth floor to begin his new job, Moriarty pulled him aside. "Hey, kid," he said, "I heard a lot of people in the department want to see you fail." From Moriarty's standpoint, the department was not in the best shape at that time. There were many internal problems. The negativity alone was enough to bring anyone down, he said. Whiddon was walking into a hornet's nest. Moriarty knew there were some who would cheer at the idea of Whiddon failing.

As Moriarty talked, Whiddon listened closely. He had respect for Moriarty, whose reputation as a tenacious investigator with a quick temper followed him, but also as someone who never gave up on a case.

"I'm retiring soon," Moriarty continued, "but I'm going to do everything I can before I go to help you out and show them all that you're definitely the right person for the job."

Moriarty believed in Whiddon. Many wrote off the relationship before it started, saying the moment would come when Whiddon and Moriarty went at each other's throats. But Moriarty never saw it that way.

As it turned out, Moriarty's attitude was comforting to Whiddon, who found the work on the sixth floor—especially out on the street—stimulating. One of the things Whiddon did was refuse the private lieutenant's office that came with the job. He instead chose to sit among his unit in a cubicle. With a solid, stocky build, entirely barrel-chested, Whiddon looked more like a fullback for the Ohio State Buckeyes—his favorite football team—than an investigator working the streets of Akron. He wore his dark hair shortly cropped and had a comforting disposition about him that worked well out in the field. Although his size might have been intimidating to some, he also showed great poise and delicateness that supported the psychology behind what he did for a living. Ever since Whiddon joined the team, as he had promised, Moriarty took him under his wing and taught him the things only a detective with decades of experience could.

Moriarty gave Whiddon a lead in the Jeff Zack case that had just come in, telling Whiddon to get with another detective and check it out. Then he organized and dispatched several additional investigators to follow up on some of the telephone calls they had received overnight and into the morning. Mike Shaeffer went out and spoke to a young girl who said Jeff Zack had been involved in apprehending a man who had caused an accident years ago that killed her girlfriend. Jeff had followed the driver of the car who had caused the accident. After stopping him, Jeff sat with the young girl until an ambulance arrived. He was a kind man, who had done a Good Samaritan act, the girl suggested. The driver of the other car was later sentenced to a year in prison for vehicular homicide. With all the other theories piling up, Shaeffer knew that being responsible for putting a guy away in prison for a year was as good as any other motive they had. Maybe the dude got released from prison and developed a resentment against Jeff and finally built up the nerve to get back at him. It was worth a look.

The reason the girl had called was to say she believed

Jeff Zack had followed someone. "And maybe that other driver shot him."

Shaeffer wondered about the guy Jeff helped put in prison.

"After his release," the young girl told Shaeffer, "the guy developed diabetes and died."

"Thank you, ma'am," Shaeffer said, a bit frustrated. "If you think of anything else, call us."

Another promising lead that amounted to nothing.

Although Jeff Zack had worked many different jobs, he was, at the time of his death, an "employee" of Accurate K Flooring Systems. He had worked there on and off for the past five months. Sixty-four-year-old Zahi Kakish, an immigrant from Jordan who had been living in Akron as a United States citizen for decades, was Jeff's boss at Accurate. Dave Whiddon pulled into Accurate with Russ McFarland, another CAPU detective. McFarland had spent thirty years of his life with the APD, twenty-one of those as a patrol officer. His brother was a cop, and McFarland looked up to him and the "good guy" role he played in society. McFarland had gained some weight over the years, but it did little to dampen the decades of law enforcement experience he had on many of his colleagues. Like Moriarty, McFarland had spent some time in Vietnam, one year with the First Cavalry Division Helicopter Repair outfit. Married, he had a nephew in the APD, a son who was a North Carolina trooper, another who was a JAG attorney in the military, two other kids, five grandchildren and two on the way. With a growing family and decades in the department, one might think McFarland was ready to hang up his badge and spend the rest of his days drifting aimlessly in a boat on a lake, fishing away his life. But none of it fit his style. "You know,"

McFarland said in his soft voice, "I still look forward to and like coming into work every day."

On the Monday afternoon after Jeff Zack's death, Whiddon and McFarland met with Kakish, and felt he might have some useful information. There was no telling which one of his peers or colleagues Jeff had reached out to and discussed how chaotic his life had become over the past few months.

Kakish immediately explained how distraught he was over the death of his employee—that much was obvious in the way the man acted. Jeff's death had no doubt affected him deeply. As they spoke, it was also apparent that Kakish had a different view of Jeff Zack than most of the people the CAPU had spoken to. He described Jeff as an "OK worker, punctual, who got along fine with his coworkers."

"Was he always here? Did he take a lot of time off?" Whiddon asked.

McFarland slipped into the background of the conversation so he could watch Kakish. One of McFarland's assets was a knack he had for reading people, which is something a good cop develops over the course of a long career.

"No," Kakish said. "The only time he missed work were excused absences. He took some time off in May to go to Arizona to visit his parents. And again, he took off"—Kakish put his hand on his head and massaged his temples, thinking—"I can look it up . . . um, he took off June eighth through the thirteenth, I believe."

Whiddon and McFarland knew without saying that the May dates were the same days others had claimed Jeff had gone away. Jeff's credit card receipts, moreover, backed it up.

"Jeff told me his aunt who lived in Detroit was very

sick . . . on a respirator and she was dying. He said he went up there to be with family when they 'pulled the plug.'" Then, after giving Whiddon and McFarland a list of employees Jeff had worked with, Kakish said, "Jeff never discussed his personal life. I'm shocked by his death. He was good, harmless man. So sad."

Leaving Accurate, Whiddon and McFarland discussed Kakish. He seemed sincere, Whiddon believed. But there wasn't much there. Jeff's coworkers, however, could be a different story. "Jeff was a swindler, a crook and a convicted criminal," Whiddon said later. "That was the impression we were getting."

"He had made a lot of enemies," McFarland added. "That was very significant to us during those early days of the investigation."

Anyone could have killed Jeff Zack.

As they were heading back to the department, Bertina King called Whiddon. "Hey, Bonnie Zack just called in a name—Ben Fluellen."

Whiddon and McFarland looked at each other—the name was on Kakish's list of Jeff's coworkers.

"Bonnie said she just received a call from Fluellen," continued King. It seemed urgent. Bonnie was sure Fluellen could help.

McFarland called him. "Listen, I just came back from Jeff's funeral," Fluellen said. "I'm really upset . . . but I think I have some info that could help you guys out."

"We'll be there right away," McFarland said.

21

Detective Mike Shaeffer hooked up with Ed Moriarty and Bertina King at the same time McFarland and Whiddon headed over to Ben Fluellen's apartment, and drove out to Bonnie's Temple Trail home to interview Jeff's mother, one of his brothers, a friend and, as they were about to find out, another mistress of Jeff Zack's.

For cops, interviewing the mother of a murder victim is not a part of the job they enjoy. Under the normal circle of life, parents aren't supposed to outlive their children. Elayne Zack was going to be beyond distressed and was likely not going to be much help. On top of that, the entire family had just returned from Jeff's funeral. The feeling in the house was docile and dark. A few days ago, Jeff was running around yelling and screaming at everyone, being his old self. Now he was in the ground. The last thing family members wanted to do was ponder Jeff's extramarital life or his past. A stiff drink, a few hours of mind-numbing television, some tears, memories and a good night's sleep sounded more like it.

But Moriarty and his team wanted to find Jeff's killer. Accomplishing that, they knew, would bring some solace to the family, however miserable they felt at the present time.

Elayne Zack lived in Arizona. She was in town to bury her son. Apprehensive at first because she was so knocked down by grief, as Elayne opened up, she began by talking about Jeff's recent trip out to see her and the rest of the family in Arizona during the Mother's Day holiday. "It was a surprise," Elayne told Moriarty, "he said he got a free ticket."

Moriarty and King knew it was one more in a long list of lies—albeit a small one—Jeff had been telling, because they had a Visa bill of Jeff's that showed a charge for plane tickets to Phoenix. That is, unless someone else was paying his Visa bill.

"During the visit, Jeff told me he had broken it off with Cindy," explained Elayne. "And he said he was *very* unhappy about it."

"Why, Mrs. Zack, had they broken up?" asked King. "Did Jeff tell you why?"

"Well, he said that him and Bonnie were 'close now.' He told me Bonnie knew all about the relationship and he flaunted it in front of her because he needed attention."

Elayne and her husband, David, knew about the affair her son was having with Cynthia George. It was disheartening to them both. They hated hearing Jeff talk about it, and were appalled when he paraded it in front of them. In an interview, Elayne said Jeff could be "erratic at times," but at the same rate, he had a "darling personality . . . he was a great salesperson" and "probably had some insecurities, but who doesn't?"

Addressing King once again, Elayne said, "It was very upsetting to my husband, because Jeffrey used to tell us that he was having an affair with Cindy, and I—my husband and I objected to this. So when

Cindy would appear wherever we went, we would get very upset."

On top of that, the telephone calls became a sour subject. When Jeff would visit his mother and stepfather, Elayne remembered, his cell phone would "incessantly ring. It rang all the time and it was *always* Cindy."

The Zacks adored Bonnie, which was one of the reasons why hearing about the affair and seeing it take place when they were in Akron visiting hurt them so much. "We liked Bonnie so much, we felt badly, and we—we didn't want the situation to take place."

As other witnesses the CAPU had interviewed also explained, Elayne agreed that Jeff was "very sweet" to everyone while he was in Arizona, "which was unusual," she added, "since he was usually very aggravating." In fact, during that last trip Jeff took to Phoenix, he had surprised them all with the visit. It wasn't planned. That Friday night, Elayne, groggy and preparing for bed, took a telephone call from Jeff. "I'm in Phoenix," he said. "Do you want me to come and get you?" Elayne asked. She thought he was at the airport. "No, I'm fine. I'm going to have something to eat."

Jeff showed up that weekend and, Elayne remembered, "his whole demeanor was different. I mean, he was . . . he had been angry with [his brother] over [a] ski vacation, and that whole week [he stayed], he was a different person. My husband and I kept looking at each other because, you know, Jeffrey wasn't the most reliable person. He would take my car and show up late. This time he was always on time. . . . He did tell me that he couldn't see Cindy anymore and he was very angry, saddened by it."

Taking a break to collect herself as Moriarty and King comforted her best they could, Elayne said she "worried about Jeff because of his relationship with Cindy."

22

Jeffrey Zack was born on January 20, 1957, in Motor City, Detroit, Michigan. Beyond being famous for displaying the world's largest tire, a Uniroyal out on I-94 near Allen Park, so big it was turned into a Ferris wheel for the New York World's Fair, and the largest stove, measuring an immense twenty-five feet high, thirty feet long, twenty feet wide—during the 1950s and 1960s, Detroit was a melting pot of cultures and races. Like many northeastern cities, it was a haven for Jewish immigrants to find work and affordable housing. Jeff's father was born Alvin Lieberman, and had passed away a few months before Jeff was murdered. Still, the emotional pain Alvin had injected into the boy's life, according to Elayne Zack, took place decades before, when he, she told me later, "left [the family] when Jeff was eight." Jeff had never gotten over the horrible feeling of being abandoned by his father, who wanted "nothing to do with him," even as the years passed and Jeff grew into a man. "Jeffrey hated being rejected," Elayne said.

As a child, Jeff was "very, very close with his biological

father." When his father wanted nothing to do with him, it turned into the ultimate rejection. He lost a sense of himself and whatever self-worth he had developed. "It beyond crushed him," Elayne added. It was as if Jeff had done something wrong to bring about the isolation of not being able to see his dad.

Elayne was never close to her first husband. It was one of those marriages, she said, that she was "forced into" by her parents. "You have to marry him," her mother had told her. "And then when we split up, she didn't speak to me," Elayne recalled. She was nineteen years old when she married Jeff's father. "Very frightened. So I succumbed to the pressure, married him and thought, 'This is my life.'"

Even after they divorced, Alvin stuck around and stayed close to Jeff, but then he met a woman and everything changed. "She was very jealous of Jeffrey and wouldn't allow Alvin to speak to his son."

Jeff's brothers were able to handle the rejection, Elayne said, because they weren't as close to their father as Jeff.

As Alvin's new wife came between Jeff and his father, things between them got worse. Jeff would call and his father wouldn't even answer the phone. Soon the calls stopped and they lost complete touch.

Regardless of the mistakes Jeff made later, Elayne pointed out, "Jeffrey was the most charming person. He never dealt with those issues of his father abandoning him. It distorted his personality. He couldn't talk about it."

Life at Detroit's Southfield-Lathrup High School became almost unbearable for Jeff. Because of the parental disruption in his childhood, the situation affected every part of his life. He wanted desperately to go to a renowned university after high school. Furthermore, a psychologist Jeff was seeing promised him, Elayne said, that he could get Jeff into a good college. But when it came down to it, Jeff just didn't have the grades. So, for a brief term, he studied at Farmington Hills College, a respectable community college in Detroit's north end, near Highland Park. But Jeff always viewed it as a step down; he never accepted that community college was going to bring him much in life. "That psychologist," said Elayne, "led him to believe he was going to be able to get into a great school. It never happened." For Jeff, it was one more rejection. First his father; now, as he went out into the world, the establishment was doing the same thing.

A family member later told police that Jeff had a "very turbulent youth. He was the oldest and his mother was always working. Jeff resented that. He never got along well with his mother, they were like oil and water."

Elayne admitted later that they had their ups and downs and fought. But she loved her son, of course, and felt she couldn't do anything to pull him out of the hole his biological father had thrown him into. "You see, he had this love-hate relationship with me. He blamed me and felt that I did all these things to get rid of his father."

As the social and political unrest of the late 1960s and early 1970s worked its way into Detroit, Jeff watched life from afar, never really taking a stand one way or another. Yet, with his surroundings and the social landscape changing as he faced adulthood, at eighteen Jeff left home one day, but no one knew where he'd gone. "He did not tell anyone where he was going," Elayne recalled. "He was very much against life at a community college, so he ran away. He was angry. He didn't tell anyone. Why he really ran away, though, was because this girl broke up with him and he couldn't face it. Jeffrey could *not* face rejection."

Running away from home was not all that unusual for Jeff. At sixteen, he took off by himself to Jamaica. "If Jeffrey wanted to do something, he was so determined. I couldn't stop him."

When months went by and no one had heard from Jeff, his family began to worry. But Elayne suspected he had run off on one of his excursions somewhere to figure out his life. She checked with the travel agency the family used and soon found out that her son had purchased tickets to Israel. Then the telephone rang one day and Jeff confirmed her suspicion. "Hey, Ma, I'm living in an Israeli commune called a 'kibbutz,'" Jeff said.

"Kibbutz?" answered Elayne. "What?"

In retrospect, subscribing to life in the kibbutz was an interesting choice for Jeff Lieberman. According to a condensed version of Britannica's Encyclopedia, the kibbutz is an "Israeli communal settlement in which all wealth is held in common and profits are reinvested in the settlement." The first kibbutz was established in the state of Palestine somewhere around 1909. The breakdown of everyday life is strictly controlled—and maybe that's what attracted Jeff to it. Adults live in "private quarters," while "children are generally housed and cared for as a group." All meals are "prepared and eaten communally. Members have regular meetings to discuss business and to take votes on matters requiring decisions. Jobs may be assigned by rotation, by choice, or skill. The kibbutz movement declined dramatically in the late 20th century. But kibbutzim continued to play [an] important role in the tourism industry in Israel, attracting students and other short-term residents, mostly Jews from overseas seeking a link with the past."

Taking the way the group operated into consideration, it appeared as though Jeff wanted to get in touch with his Jewish roots possibly to find out who he was. He obviously yearned for structure and discipline, yet clearly felt the American military couldn't offer it to him. "He was really angry," Elayne said, speaking to that period when Jeff took off. "It wasn't really at me, I knew that. It was at this girl that broke up with him. He couldn't take it. He was tough to be around all the time. He had a very forceful personality."

Elayne wasn't happy that her son was halfway across the world in a new state, living like a soldier and gypsy among strangers. But what could she do?

"How did you end up in Israel, Jeffrey?" Elayne asked.

"I'm in the army here now," Jeff said.

"How did *that* happen?"

"All people in Israel end up in the army, Ma."

Jeff's dream was to be an Israeli pilot, said to be the most regimented and professional in the world. But for reasons he never explained, Jeff wasn't able to do that, so he joined a paratrooper unit instead.

Family members later told police Jeff was "very pro-Israeli." Jeff's stepfather, David Zack, believed Jeff had "dual citizenship—America and Israel."

One thing Jeff liked to do with his stepfather was hang out at a popular cigar shop in Akron. The owner of the place was an Arab. Although Jeff and the guy were "acquaintances," they often argued heatedly about the state of Palestine and Middle East politics. "They had a falling-out once," David Zack explained to the CAPU, "and the guy and Jeff stopped speaking." Even more interesting to detectives when they found out, according to David, the owner of the cigar shop was "connected to" Ed George in some way.

Three years after Jeff's trip to Israel, he returned to Detroit, but Israel hadn't really changed him much. "He had the most phenomenal personality when he wanted," Elayne said, fighting back tears. "But he could be manic, too. He had the potential to do whatever he wanted. He could have been someone, but was, of course, held back by these flaws, fears and things he couldn't face, not to mention the sadness over his dad."

Elayne had married David Zack by the time Jeff returned to the States. David got a job in Phoenix and they were planning to move. Along with Jeff, one of his brothers was adopted by David and took the Zack name, while Jeff's other brother, Ricky, chose to keep Lieberman as nothing more than a personal choice.

What was clear to detectives as they continued to interview Elayne was that she was proud of her son in many ways, but knew—and was honest about—the person Jeff had become. She was totally forthcoming about Jeff, both good and bad points. Jeff had spoken six languages (English, Hebrew, Arabic, Russian, German and Spanish). "He could have done anything he wanted to do," Elayne said that first afternoon detectives interviewed her. *"Anything."*

One of the reasons Elayne gave for her son changing jobs as often as shoes was that she believed once Jeff "conquered a job, he got bored with it and would move on to something else." Most astonishingly, the result of the affair Jeff had with Cynthia George made it seem, at least in the way family members later viewed the situation, as if Jeff had two families, each of whom knew about the other. Elayne and David Zack had been over to the Georges' mansion for parties and get-togethers. Regardless how she felt about the affair, Elayne liked Cynthia. It seemed Cynthia was a good influence on Jeff. She kept him grounded and gave him a sense of worth. "Jeff just adored Cindy," Elayne explained to Moriarty. "Whenever me and David were in town, Cindy would visit us and seemed to follow us wherever we went, to restaurants and such."

Detectives saw this as an awfully awkward situation, yet an understandable motive for murder. The further along they got into Jeff Zack's life with Cynthia George, the more it seemed like the person that could help the investigation the most was the one person who didn't want to talk to them.

23

The APD detective's bureau investigating Jeff Zack's murder was bombarded with leads by the end of the day on Monday, June 18, 2001. Reports and interviews with witnesses were coming in at such a clip that it appeared as though an AMBER Alert had been issued. For detectives, gathering information became a tedious, gumshoe process—that, if patience was applied, could yield results. In fact, in some respects, during the early days of the investigation, the CAPU had too much information to sift through.

The person in charge of keeping track of all those tips coming in was twenty-three-year-old Carrie Stoll, a pleasant, cute, absolutely dedicated CAPU secretary. Many of the detectives in the unit went out of their way to say Carrie was the absolute "heartbeat" of the office. Without her, they would be lost in a mountain of paperwork, telephone messages, reports and minor details that would ultimately keep them cooped up behind a desk and off the street, where the true magic of any investigation occurred. "Carrie is, well," Dave Whiddon said later, "she's great. Without her, we couldn't run this unit. She's our eyes and ears. We don't know how she does it, but Carrie keeps everything in front of us and never lets us forget what we're working on."

More than that, Carrie took many of the calls coming into the CAPU. She transcribed all the tape-recorded interviews and telephone calls. She was in charge of keeping a list of every detectives' assignments and all of the tips piling up. Initially she kept a database of the tips that came in on motorcycles that matched the description of the one leaving the scene of the homicide. "I also assisted with the telephone records (trying to find subscriber information and identifying the numbers)," Carrie said later.

Late that Monday afternoon, Carrie received a call that would, in effect, throw the investigation into an entirely new direction. A secret Jeff Zack had been keeping from mostly everyone around him was about to be unearthed. It was a fact so incredibly unbelievable, it was going to take a court order to prove, once Moriarty and the CAPU felt their hunch might be true. But before that, it was back to sorting through Jeff's life. Police work—the old-school way—was going to get to the bottom of any type of international conspiracy or mafia hit behind Jeff's murder. In truth, the CAPU felt confident the mafia or an international group of radicals was not behind Jeff's murder. However, they took the insinuations seriously and checked out every lead or tip that led them in that direction.

As they did that, however, and Jeff's family continued to talk, one name kept coming up. "Jeff had once told me," David Zack explained to the CAPU, "'If Ed George ever finds out about [my affair with Cynthia], he'll kill me.'"

Ed and Cynthia George. No matter what parties the

CAPU spoke to, where they looked, the investigation routinely led them back to the Georges. The only problem was that the Georges were still refusing to talk.

While detectives interviewed Jeff's brothers inside Bonnie's Temple Trail home, David Zack, looking on, came up with an idea that might change that situation. "Why don't we have Elayne call Cynthia?"

The telephone call was a good suggestion. Maybe Elayne could get Cynthia to say something. Cynthia liked Elayne. She surely wouldn't hang up on her.

"If that is a normal thing for Elayne to do," one of the detectives said to David Zack, "then we would not be opposed to it. If she does talk to Cindy, however, we would be interested in knowing what the conversation consisted of."

"I'll ask her," David said, walking into the kitchen, where Elayne was sitting.

"One minute, though, Mr. Zack," a detective said, stopping David. "Do you think Elayne would object to us recording the phone call?"

"No, of course not."

David went out to the kitchen and grabbed Elayne.

"Yes," she said enthusiastically, walking into the living room. "I'll call her and you can record it."

Lieutenant Dave Whiddon and Russ McFarland were at Benjamin Fluellen's apartment discussing the last days of Jeff Zack's life when Fluellen brought up an important point. An African-American, Fluellen said he and Jeff had become "close friends" throughout the final few weeks of Jeff's life. So close, in fact, Jeff's death had impacted the thirty-four-year-old in a way he had not expected. "I had never," Fluellen said, "gotten that close to a white man before." Fluellen wasn't thrilled to have McFarland and Whiddon in his apartment, but said what he knew overshadowed any concern he might have regarding his uncertainties about cops.

"I appreciated Ben's honesty about his feelings toward whites, and especially white police officers," Whiddon said later. "He first told Russ and I that if it wasn't for Jeff, he wouldn't even have let us in his apartment. I know he really admired Zack and looked up to him. I got the sense that he was someone who would believe everything that Jeff told him."

That aluminum-siding job Carl and Seth had supposedly "burned" Jeff on became a topic and motive for murder once again. As Fluellen explained it, after allowing McFarland and Whiddon into his apartment, right up until the last time he had seen Jeff, he said, Jeff was extremely "pissed off" about the deal and he believed Jeff wanted to see Seth and Carl pay for what they had done to him.

"How so?" asked Whiddon.

"Seven thousand dollars. Jeff lost seven grand," Fluellen said.

"He was upset about that, huh?"

"Wouldn't *you* be? Hell yeah, he was upset about it—but also the threats."

"What threats?" McFarland asked.

"Jeff told me [recently] that he was getting death threats from one of those two guys."

"No kidding."

"Last Friday, Jeff told me he filed an insurance report . . . because one of those two guys had forged his name and cashed a check. The death threats were supposed to keep Jeff from going to the cops about it."

"Did he mention what was actually said?"

"What bothered Jeff most was that the threats included his family. Oh, man, that really got to him." Fluellen came across sincere and truthful. He was simply telling it the way he heard it, which was all Mc-Farland and Whiddon wanted. "Jeff really *loved* his wife and son. He was afraid something was going to happen to them."

"Anybody would be," Whiddon said.

Later, Whiddon observed, "The more I talked to Ben, the more I actually liked him. I kind of felt sorry for him because he was really devastated when Zack was killed. I think he and Zack were *that* close."

As Fluellen explained, Jeff was supposed to help him on the Saturday he was murdered. They were going to fix a floor at Fluellen's girlfriend's house. Jeff was eager to help. He told Fluellen that all he had to do was check several of his vending machines and then he could meet up with him to help with the floor. Fluellen, however, overslept and called the job off at the last minute.

"You know any other jobs Jeff did?"

"Vending business."

McFarland asked Fluellen if he knew where Jeff bought his merchandise. Although subtle, it was an important question. The killer certainly knew.

"I don't know for sure," Fluellen responded, "maybe some place in . . . Arlington?" He shrugged. "Not sure."

"Did you know Jeff had ladies on the side?"

"Huh? No way. He never got into his personal life, like if he had a girlfriend or not. I would have never guessed, though. Especially the way he loved his wife and son. He took that kid everywhere."

"You've been helpful. Thanks."

"You know," Fluellen said as they concluded the interview, "I think someone followed Jeff."

"What makes you say that?" McFarland asked.

"Jeff wasn't a 'f- - - you' type." What Fluellen meant was, if someone had pissed Jeff off on the road, he believed Jeff would have more or less ignored it. He wasn't a vengeful driver, Fluellen said. He knew this because he had driven with Jeff plenty of times. "It wasn't road rage," Fluellen added. "No way."

"You don't think so, huh?" Whiddon asked.

"Nope."

"What do you think happened, then?"

"One of those two guys"—Seth or Carl—"that ripped him off for that check. That's my bet."

"Thanks a lot, Ben. We appreciate this. If you hear anything at work, give us a call."

24

When Elayne Zack agreed to call Cynthia George and have the CAPU record it, the prevailing notion was that the telephone call might allow detectives a closer look into the relationship Cynthia had with Jeff. Or, more important, what caused the split. As an added bonus, maybe Cynthia, without knowing it, would say something damaging about her husband's potential role in Jeff's demise. Any way they looked at it, the telephone call could help.

Ed Moriarty fixed the cassette tape into the recorder and pressed play and record, saying, in his deep baritone, "There's about to be a phone call made from Elayne Zack to Cynthia George and this tape will contain that conversation."

Then, pointing at the telephone, Moriarty looked at Elayne, who was standing, waiting for the signal from Moriarty to dial the numbers. Walking toward him, she said, "I think I should do it privately. I'll be more natural."

There was another detective standing with Moriarty. "We can leave if you want, Mrs. Zack?" he said.

It seemed like a good idea.

After a few tries, Cynthia picked up. "Cindy, it's Elayne."

"Hi, Elayne. Hold . . . hold on one second, OK?"

"Cindy, please." Elayne was a bit impatient. She wanted a moment of Cynthia's time. Considering the circumstances, it wasn't all that much to ask.

"Hold on a second, *can* you?"

"Please, please talk to me, Cindy." Elayne sounded frazzled and panicked. She assumed Cynthia was trying to blow her off.

"I don't know what . . . just hold on, Elayne, OK?" Cynthia sounded as if she were thinking, *Enough already, lady, just wait a damn minute.*

Then a pause.

"Hello?" Cynthia said.

"Cindy, Cindy," Elayne said fast, "what happened to Jeffrey, he was killed?"

"I know," Cynthia said. She sounded saddened by the remark.

"Cindy, weren't you his best friend? He *loved* you."

"I know," said Cynthia. But then changed the subject quickly, saying, "You know what, I didn't know whether to call . . . I . . . you know, I tried calling once."

"Cindy, I cannot believe you weren't at the funeral and I can't believe I didn't hear from you." Elayne was finding her comfort zone. Emotion was still raw, but she sounded sincere. "I thought he loved you so much, what happened?"

"I was afraid Bonnie would be mad at me."

"Cindy, what happened?" Elayne asked again. "Why? What happened between you? He was so hurt by you. *What* happened?"

Cynthia was at a loss for words, or didn't want to broach the subject of the affair. It was an odd circumstance for her to be in: the affair was common knowledge among the Zacks. Bonnie knew, Elayne was sure of it. However, no one really talked about it—the proverbial white elephant.

Finally Cynthia said, "Uh . . . I . . ." and then went silent.

"Please *tell* me, Cindy. I *have* to know."

A mother had just buried one of her sons. She felt she deserved an explanation regarding what went wrong in the relationship, seeing that Jeff had expressed on numerous occasions to his mother the love he felt for Cynthia.

"You know what, I don't, I don't know. I just *don't* know. At the end of, he was just . . . I don't know if he was . . . I don't know . . . I don't know if he was on drugs or what."

Elayne was taken aback by the comment. *Drugs? What a lame excuse,* she thought. Jeff Zack wasn't into drugs. He was—many who knew him later said—against drugs. Detectives had found a small amount of marijuana in his pockets when they went through his belongings after his death. Although pot wasn't considered the same as methamphetamine, cocaine or "hard-core" substances, it proved Jeff Zack did take illegal drugs of some sort from time to time. So Cynthia, whether Elayne knew it or not, was speaking from experience.

"Drugs!" Elayne shot back. "Jeffrey never would take a drug, you know that, Cindy. He came to Arizona, he was so calm, but he told me he was so hurt by you and he wouldn't tell my why. What did . . . what happened? Please tell me." Elayne paused. Despite the secretive nature of the telephone call, she sounded genuinely upset. She was Jeff's mother now, not some witness trying to get Cynthia to open up. "I *have* to know."

"I know that—"

Elayne interrupted, "Please tell me, Cindy." Her voice was pleading.

"It's like, I, I didn't, I . . . I was so worried about Bonnie. I called there and I just, I . . . I . . . I . . . I . . . thought well, you know, maybe that you'll call me or something."

"I had to call you, because I know he loved you so much."

"I know . . . I know—"

"You were his best friend and he was so hurt by you. I could tell when he came to visit. . . . He said, 'Mother, Cindy hurt me so much, I miss her so much.' And then he was distraught when he got back home and . . . Cindy, why would someone murder him?"

"I don't know."

"*Why?*"

"I don't know. I, he said something, I don't know exact—"

"What? Why?"

"I don't know. I don't know. I don't know."

Elayne continued to question Cynthia about the breakup, asking at one point, "Did Ed suspect something between you?"

"No. No."

"No?"

"I mean, he just, he just wasn't acting right. I mean, and he, I, I know he said something about having to go and get away and—"

"But he said he wasn't 'allowed' to be your friend anymore."

Cynthia continued to say, over and over, "I don't know." She sounded confused and bewildered. Like there were no words to describe how she felt and how her relationship with Jeff had ended. The tone of her voice would have led one to believe that Jeff's murder was something she had never expected. Not what she wanted by any means. She was as surprised by it as everyone else.

They talked about Bonnie for a time, Cynthia explaining how she wanted to attend the funeral and call the house, but she didn't want to impinge on Bonnie's pain, making her grief any worse. Elayne brought up Ed again, but Cynthia ignored the mention of her wealthy husband and focused on why she didn't attend the wake or funeral.

"He was distraught," said Elayne, "and why someone would murder him—"

Cynthia cut in. "I don't know, I don't know, I don't . . . ," she said, trailing off. Then, "I mean, I, I was supposed to be in the [Mrs.] Ohio pageant and I didn't even go. I mean . . . everything was ready in the program and everything, I . . . I . . . couldn't go. I just couldn't go. I can't . . . I just can't say that he was acting so strange lately."

Elayne Zack was getting tired of hearing "I don't know." With a more stern voice, quite out of character, she asked, "I want to know *why* he wasn't allowed to be your friend! That's what I'm curious to know, because I know that"—she hesitated for a moment—"he used to come to Phoenix and call you like every five minutes."

After another round of "I know . . . I don't know," Cynthia went back to saying how sorry she was for not stopping by the house or going to the wake. "I was just afraid of Bonnie, you know, what she would think. . . ." In the same breath, however, not being able to make the Mrs. Ohio pageant that year seemed to bother Cynthia more than missing Jeff's funeral. While talking about Jeff, she added, "I had sent all my money in and . . . and been through the whole thing." It was a waste. All that time. The application and interview process. Fixing her hair. The clothes. Exercising. For what?

Nothing.

"But why didn't you go?" Elayne asked. "Because you were upset about Jeffrey?"

"Yeah, I mean, I, I couldn't, you know . . . I just . . . he, he . . . I wanted to go over there . . ."

"But didn't your husband ever suspect that something was maybe going on between you? Didn't he wonder?"

Cynthia went silent.

25

When Cynthia decided to speak again after a short pause, she said, "Well, he, you know, I always like, you know, a lot of time he would call, he, and just be upset about anything or whatever. It just seemed like I was the one that he always, you know . . ." She trailed off, apparently lost in thought.

Elayne was confused: "Who, Jeffrey or Ed?"

Cynthia didn't answer at first. Then she digressed yet again and carried on about Jeff's various jobs and how he had perhaps got hooked up with people on crack cocaine. It was a shock to Elayne that Cynthia would say such a thing.

Crack cocaine? Jeffrey? Come on.

Elayne countered by saying he would *never* take that type of drug. Cynthia ultimately agreed. They were going around in circles. Elayne kept dangling the Ed George carrot, but Cynthia wouldn't take it.

After talking a bit about how members of the CAPU were at her house the previous Sunday asking questions, Cynthia sounded exhausted and even more confused, talking in brief sound bites that made little sense to Elayne, who kept pressing, asking about the relationship and what could have happened to Jeff.

At one point, Cynthia went on the offensive. "I know my husband did not hurt Jeffrey! I mean, if that's what you're implying."

"No, I just, I know he didn't, either. He wouldn't have done it purposely himself."

Cynthia changed the subject and asked about Ashton, saying at one point, "It's a tragedy."

And it was. Regardless of the type of person some thought Jeff Zack was, he had been a dedicated, loving father to his son. The boy was going to suffer the most. He would bear the brunt of the media's coverage as the case developed. The more skeletons that came out, the more Ashton would begin to question things.

"It *is* a tragedy," Elayne agreed. She was hurt. There was no need to pump up that emotion. What could be worse than losing a child?

Cynthia blamed the end of the relationship on extenuating circumstances, explaining that there was something else going on in Jeff's life that weighed heavily on the two of them, which ultimately became a problem within the dynamic of the relationship. In describing that, she seemed to suggest those problems were too overbearing and the relationship wasn't worth the trouble it was causing. What would become important to the investigation later, Cynthia made no mention of any type of sexual or physical abuse as a reason for her ending the relationship. To the contrary, she blamed the breakup on the problems it was causing for both their marriages.

Still, Cynthia was very vague, not locking herself into what, exactly, had caused the demise of the romance. Elayne wanted specifics. She was determined to find out precisely what, as she later put it, the "final straw" had been. She said she wanted to "understand" what happened so she could have some closure. It was going to help her during the grieving process. As Jeff's mother, didn't she deserve as much? "I'm not accusing anybody," Elayne finally said. "I'm not implying *anything*." She sounded strong and organized in her thoughts.

"No, no," said Cynthia.

"I'm just curious to know why you wouldn't see him anymore?"

It was awfully strange to Elayne that they had dated for nearly ten years and only weeks after the breakup Jeff ended up dead.

"It . . . it didn't have anything to do with that," Cynthia said.

"He never told you what it was?" asked Elayne after Cynthia went on about "something" that was bothering Jeff.

"Um . . . ah . . ."

"He probably confided in you more than anybody else."

"The last thing I . . . the last thing he said [to me] was, 'They're investigating me at work.'"

"Cindy," Elayne said, sounding as though she were rolling her eyes, "I saw his boss. There's no way."

"That's the last thing that he told me," Cynthia said sharply. She meant what she said.

"There's no way."

"I don't know . . . I mean, you can ask, I don't know. But that's what I, that's what he *told* me. Something about . . . uh . . . you know, Phoenix and—"

"Oh?"

"Of, if, uh, and the, um, he was just, you, you know if you, the way that he is or was . . . he was acting like that all the time." According to Cynthia, when she was around Jeff during those final weeks, he, too, was calm and apologetic. Much different from the norm.

"So you told him that he couldn't see you anymore?" Elayne wanted to pinpoint Cynthia down to some sort of concrete story.

"No, I just, I just, I said, 'I don't know what you're, what's going on or what, you know, but, you know, you know, I can't, I can't have, you know, it's, it's, you know . . .'"

It was getting ridiculous. Cynthia would start to say something, but then stop herself.

"No more fun," Elayne said condescendingly.

Ignoring that, Cynthia came back with, "He said, 'I got to get out of here. I gotta, I gotta get out of here.'"

Elayne didn't know what to make of the statement.

"I don't know what kind of trouble he was in," Cynthia said.

Elayne pounded home the point that it was nearly impossible for her to believe that between all the time Cynthia and Jeff spent together that Ed George never questioned the relationship. It was inconceivable.

Cynthia agreed. What else could she say? Elayne wasn't some deranged mother, filling her days with *The Young and the Restless*, ignorant to what was going on in the world. She was an educated, intelligent woman. Cynthia had better not underestimate her.

"It was a problem here and a problem there," Cynthia said.

Elayne didn't answer.

"But he, he really, he didn't care," added Cynthia.

They continued to talk about how distressed Jeff seemed recently. Then Cynthia dropped the Arab card, saying that she knew Jeff was doing some work for an

"Arab family," adding, "I don't know if he owed money [to] them."

Elayne was still puzzled by the fact that Ed George didn't make more of a stink about the relationship, saying, "I mean, if my husband saw me on bike trips and being with another guy, he would have wondered and said something. I had to call and ask you that, and I'm not accusing anybody and I know that he had nothing to do with it, believe me, it was the guy probably Jeffrey cut off."

Cynthia responded immediately: "Pardon me?"

"The guy that murdered Jeffrey," Elayne said harshly, trying to shift the conversation into the reason why she agreed to make the call. "Jeffrey probably cut him off, had a fight with him, because he left here angry on Saturday morning. He probably had road rage somehow. I'm not, I know Ed had nothing to do with it. But I never could understand and I, I just need to *know*."

"Yeah," Cynthia said, "that, that [meaning road rage] happened a lot. . . ."

This theory of Elayne's seemed to calm Cynthia down. She started talking about what she was doing on the day Jeff was killed. She mentioned the wedding she and Ed had attended with the kids. Then she said the police had scared the kids by coming to the house on Sunday to ask questions.

Then the conversation went back to Bonnie. "Bonnie never gets mad at anybody," Elayne said.

Cynthia disagreed, claiming that Bonnie had screamed at her a few times.

For the CAPU, the telephone call wasn't going to obviously produce anything of investigatory value other than—as Ed Moriarty explained it later—proving that Cynthia and Jeff had an active extramarital affair going on for quite some time. It was significant for the reason that Cynthia herself, on tape, was admitting to it.

"Ed kind of accepted that we were friends . . . ," Cynthia said near the end of the conversation.

Cynthia and Jeff had told people their relationship was a platonic friendship—that Cynthia knew Jeff better than anyone and had been, as she tried telling Elayne, "consoling" Jeff on the problems he had in life.

To that, Elayne said, "I have to be honest and tell you that he did, he, he did tell someone that, 'If something happens to me, it's because of Ed George.' Now, that could be Jeffrey's drama."

"Yeah," Cynthia said quickly, seemingly unaffected by the comment.

"You know Jeffrey was very dramatic."

"Right."

26

Detective Melissa Williams caught up with the guy Jeff had supposedly taken a bike trip with to West Virginia between June 8 and June 13. No sooner had Williams flashed her badge and explained why she was at the guy's work, then he came clean and said he and Jeff never took that bike trip. "It was just a cover so Jeff could go to Las Vegas and see this girl."

Detective Williams, just to be sure, asked Jeff's friend if he was talking about the same woman everyone else had been.

"No, this is not Jeff's mistress, who he has been seeing for ten years."

So the question became, then, how in the heck did Jeff know a woman in Las Vegas? How many girlfriends did the guy have?

Apparently, while Jeff was on his way out to Arizona to visit his mother for Mother's Day—that weekend every-one had said he was not himself, making amends and apologizing for his previous behavior—he met a woman on the plane ride out there, sweet-talked her, and ended up not only sleeping with her, but spending a better part of the week with her.

Williams took notes, prodding. "Tell me about this 'mistress,' as you call her."

"All I know is that Bonnie knew about her [Cynthia George]." They were standing in a warehouse. It was noisy. Machines buzzing. Loudspeaker. The guy asked Williams to step into the lunchroom, where it was quieter, adding as they entered the room, "And so did the woman's husband."

"What did Jeff say about the husband?"

"That he was in the mafia."

"Was Jeff concerned?"

"I don't think so. It had been going on for so long and nothing happened. Jeff really didn't think it was a problem." Then the guy explained that Jeff and "his mistress" had recently split up.

"You know why—did Jeff ever say why?" Williams asked.

"I believe Jeff wanted to make things better with his family."

Bonnie Zack had given Ed Moriarty and the CAPU several photographs of the George family Jeff had either taken himself, or Cynthia had given him. One of those photographs had struck Moriarty as particularly strange ever since he saw it that first time. There was something different about the photo, no doubt about it. Not the image itself, a simple family portrait: Ed, Cynthia and their seven children standing in rows on the stairs of their home like grammar-school kids on a podium posing for their class picture. From the image, the Georges appeared to be a happy, close family. But it was one of the kids, Moriarty thought. Five of Cynthia and Ed's children looked alike—with the exception of one, a child they had adopted. Yet the seventh child, born just recently, didn't quite match up with the other children, who were all dark-skinned and dark-haired, obviously taking on the bulk of Ed George's Lebanese genes.

Moriarty called several of his colleagues together and asked, "Do you see anything in that photo that seems significantly inconsistent?"

Everyone agreed. That one child, the youngest, looked remarkably different from the others.

But what did it mean?

By June 21, Detective Williams was able to find Jeff's Las Vegas lover. After speaking with Jeff's friend, the one who had unearthed the Las Vegas connection, in a smart piece of police work, Williams figured Jeff had likely called the woman from his cell phone. So she went through the long-distance calls Jeff had made during that time period—June 8 through June 13—and found several calls to a number with the name *Lisa* scribed in the cell phone's directory. But when Williams called the number, she got a voice mail message: "Hi, this is [Lisa], I'm not available right now. . . ."

So she left a message.

A short while later, the woman called back.

"It is my number," Lisa said. "I'm in [another state] with my aunt. She's sick." Lisa, who lived in Arizona, sounded beaten, like, *OK, you caught me.* She had been anticipating the call, she admitted.

"You know why I'm calling you?"

"Yes, I do."

"Do you know that Jeff Zack has been killed?"

"Yes, I heard."

"I'm going to have to ask you some questions about your relationship with Mr. Zack—" Williams started to say as Lisa interrupted.

"I know. I understand. I've already decided to be open and forthcoming about it all. But it will be difficult."

Williams was curious. "Why?"

"I'm married. My husband doesn't know a thing about my relationship with Jeff."

"Can you give me your full name and address, Social Security number and date of birth?"

Lisa gave Williams her address and name, but declined to give up her Social Security number or date of birth. She was worried. It was in her voice. Her entire world—which she had kept hidden from her husband—was about to collapse. How many lives an affair could ruin—but people still felt the need to do it, rather than divorcing and moving on.

Jeff and Lisa had hooked up on that flight Jeff took to Arizona. She was on her way home from a business trip. They talked, she said, and bonded instantly. She believed after spending just a few days with Jeff in Phoenix after the flight that she had "found [her] soul mate." Isn't that always the case? The inevitable life partner—the adultery excuse of the twenty-first century: *I met my soul mate. I couldn't help it.* A spiritual connection, one that her husband wasn't giving her.

After the flight, she and Jeff exchanged business cards. "Call me," she said.

"I will," said Jeff, smiling.

The next day, Jeff called and asked Lisa about purchasing some of the equipment she sold.

"We became inseparable after that," Lisa explained to Williams over the telephone. "We spent every day together while he was in Phoenix visiting his family. I had never done anything like that in my life, but I had no control over it. I was devastated by Jeff's death when I heard."

When they parted in Phoenix, Lisa told Jeff about a business trip she had planned for Las Vegas a week and a half later. Jeff was thrilled. He said he'd meet her there.

"When you were in Vegas together," Williams wondered, "did you guys talk . . . I mean, did Jeff open up about his life?"

"Sure. We talked about *everything*. He told me about his affair with Cindy."

"He did. What did he say about it?"

It was shocking that Jeff was honest with his new lover about his affair with Cynthia—yet he hadn't been truthful in respect to the details of it. "He said he and Cindy ended it about two years ago. He said it had been on and off for about ten years."

It was a lie. Cynthia had told Jeff it was over about a month before he was murdered. Jeff never ended it.

"What can you tell me about Cindy? What would Jeff say about her?"

"Her husband, I know, was older. Jeff said he was very wealthy and he and Cindy were hoping maybe he would die soon so they could be together. Jeff also mentioned that Cindy had seven kids with her husband."

Williams could tell from Lisa's voice she knew more—that she was perhaps holding something back, especially when the conversation turned to Cynthia's kids. Although she had no proof and it was just a hunch at this point, Williams took a wild shot: "One of them kids was Jeff's, huh?"

Silence.

"Yes," Lisa said. *"Ruby . . ."*

"Isn't she the youngest?"

"Yes."

"Did Bonnie know about the child?"

"I think so. I think Jeff told her during an argument one night in the heat of it, you know what I mean."

"Sure. But let me ask you, did Ed George, Cindy's husband, know?"

"I don't think he did."

This was substantial to the investigation. So many possibilities had now opened up. The Ed George motive had gone from a simple, however complicated, extramarital affair to Jeff Zack possibly fathering one of Cynthia George's children. Was there a better motive for murder? News that Jeff had fathered one of Ed George's kids could destroy the man's reputation. Maybe Jeff even threatened Ed, the CAPU considered, and tried extorting money from him to keep quiet. Who knew at this point?

Later, while Ed Moriarty was in the office musing over the new information, he couldn't help but think of something Jeff Zack had said to Bonnie one day regarding Ashton: *"I'll take the kid and move to Israel if you even try to divorce me and take him away."*

Had Jeff said the same thing to Cynthia? Had Ed George found out about the child and, not realizing Cynthia was even having an affair, snapped? Once again, the more the CAPU learned about Jeff Zack, the more complicated the case became.

"A true-to-life whodunit," Moriarty said later. "This was it."

Detective Williams was only a half hour into her interview with Lisa and she had truly put more on the table in the form of relevant information than any of the dozens of witnesses the CAPU had interviewed over the past few days.

Still, as Williams continued pumping Lisa for information, Lisa would drop yet another bombshell.

27

There was no doubt in Ed Moriarty's mind that Bonnie Zack had more information to share with police. For all he knew, Bonnie could have suspected that Jeff fathered a child with Cynthia and, fed up with being treated like "the other woman" for the past decade, had her husband killed. If true, it wasn't too incredible to ponder, considering the circumstances of Jeff Zack's life and how he was killed.

Moriarty headed over to Bonnie's Temple Trail address late on Tuesday afternoon, June 19. She'd had a few days to deal with her emotions and allow Jeff's death to settle on her. In no way did Moriarty believe she had gotten through the initial impact of it all. But her mind was still fresh with details. It was important the CAPU continue to put itself in a position to allow Bonnie to talk.

"Hi, Bonnie," Moriarty said pleasantly, walking in.

Bonnie shook her head, but didn't say much. It was obvious she was still in a lot of pain.

"There are a few things we need to go over. You OK with that?"

Bonnie said, "Come in. Yes, sure."

After going through a bit of Jeff's financial history, Moriarty asked, "Listen, what do *you* think happened to Jeff?"

"I just don't have a clue. I don't know. Jeff was *so* secretive. He was always telling me that I didn't need to know what he was doing and he would take care of everything." She stopped and thought about it. "I can tell you this—I know it's not road rage," Bonnie said, shaking her head, "like everyone else is saying."

"What makes you say that?"

Bonnie took a moment. She had tears in her eyes. This was difficult. Looking squarely at Moriarty, she managed to say, "Jeff told me Ed George was getting sick of the relationship he had with Cindy. *This* is what's behind his death."

Moriarty had to be careful. He felt Bonnie was sincere. But he had to keep his objectivity in check. Bonnie was still a suspect—a prime suspect at that. There would come a time, he knew, when he would have to ask her to take a polygraph.

"Is there any other reason you can think of that might have led to Jeff's murder?"

"I don't know. Maybe that whole thing with [Seth and Carl]. I didn't like [Seth] the first time I saw him."

Money. That worked, too. But it didn't seem to fit here. Jeff had burned people in his life before. Why now? Why *this* time?

For the next few minutes, Bonnie explained all she could about Jeff's youth in Detroit. But, she admitted, it was hard for her to believe anything Jeff said because he had told so many lies over the years. "He did say that his time in the Israeli Army was the best time of his life."

"Did he ever talk about being in combat?"

There was that Arab connection Moriarty couldn't abandon. A few of Jeff's friends thought for sure there had been a hit put on Jeff by someone with a link to the Middle East. It didn't make sense to Moriarty, but he needed to explore it and, if anything, cross it off the CAPU's list.

"He said he was involved in some combat, but again," Bonnie said, shaking her head, more in disgust, Moriarty felt, than sorrow, "I don't know if that was true or not."

By this point, Bonnie was quivering so violently from head to toe Moriarty couldn't write it off as pure stress. It wasn't out of fear, he thought, but emotional bondage. She was scared of talking, sitting there weighing the past ten years, the life she'd had with the guy, and how it all had turned out. Ashton was going to grow up without a father. When the toll of Jeff's death hit the boy, it was going to devastate him—same as it had for Jeff, perhaps, when his own father left him. Bonnie knew that. Trying to hold back the tears best she could had internalized it all. Moriarty understood. He had interviewed scores of witnesses under the same duress. "You don't know what that emotion is like or what it can do to you," he said later, "until you've had to go in and tell a father that his only child is dead and he falls into your arms, holding on, hugging you and crying his eyes out. . . . Until you've gone through that, you don't know how extended victims are in one murder."

After allowing Bonnie a few minutes to collect herself, Moriarty asked, "Do you know how long Jeff was in the Israeli Army?"

"If he did tell me, it wouldn't mean anything. One year. Two years. Three. Who knows?" she said, throwing up her arms. "I'm not really sure."

"Just a bit more of your time, Bonnie," Moriarty said. He could sense she was getting uncomfortable and wanted to stop. "Jeff ever mention any problems with the Arab community because of his service in Israel?"

Bonnie shifted a bit, noting the seriousness of the question. Looking down at the floor, then up toward the ceiling, she said, "Jeff told me he was involved in the Mossad. But he said I didn't need to know any more than that. Listen, I'll say it again. Jeff led a *very* secretive life." She stopped herself. Then, getting up, "I'm done with this for now."

According to the Israeli Secret Intelligence Service, the Mossad is an "institute for Intelligence and Special Operations . . . appointed by the State of Israel to collect information, analyze intelligence and perform special covert operations beyond its borders." In other words, the Mossad is Israel's version of the CIA. Jeff had mentioned to several people that he was an agent for the Mossad. He couldn't talk about it, he claimed, because his work was top secret. Some believed him, others didn't.

Moriarty wasn't sure what Bonnie had implied by mentioning the Mossad, or if she was covering up something for Jeff. Nevertheless, it was time to send a few investigators back out to track down anyone who could tell the CAPU about the Mossad and the possibility that Jeff got himself caught up in an international conspiracy that ended in his death.

"It was a long shot, sure," Moriarty said later. "But that is what we were dealing with. We had to check out every possible lead and connection. In the end, when we found out who was responsible, none of it mattered. But we didn't know it then."

28

Over the course of the first week of the investigation, there were more suspects than witnesses; more open-ended questions than answers. At times, Ed Moriarty was overwhelmed by the scope of the potential suspect pool. Yet when he sat down and thought about it, some suspects seemed more important than others. Between June 20 and June 23, for example, detectives interviewed nearly a dozen more potential suspects. Many were brought in and immediately released, for one reason or another. One seventeen-year-old girl called and thought maybe her father had shot Jeff because Jeff had harassed her. She had worked at BJ's. One day, Jeff came in to buy a cell phone and introduced himself. When she brushed him off, he followed her around the store and ended up with her phone number after watching her throw a receipt in the garbage for something she bought on her break. According to her, the next day Jeff called seven times, trying to get her to go out with him. The eighth time he called, the girl's father answered the telephone and told Jeff she was only seventeen, raging, "Do not ever call her back again."

Jeff called a couple more times—and saw her at BJ's on another day—and then left her alone. It was the first week of June, she explained to detectives.

But that lead, like many of them, turned up nothing. A father wasn't going to shoot a guy in the head because he had called his daughter a few times. It seemed possible, but not all that practical.

Other suspects, reportedly seen driving lime-green-and-black Ninja-style motorcycles, were still being brought in, questioned and, quite quickly, released. The APD crime scene unit (CSU) had lifted a sample of rubber from the motorcycle in question at the scene. The murderer had driven over a curb and cut through a parking lot, but had to slow down to miss a car, before he or she then took off at a high rate of speed, leaving a rubber mark behind. The CAPU had a sample of the tire. Although it was a very common rubber, it was still possible to rule out several brands of tires.

So it was back to good old-fashioned police work—and learning all they could about Jeff Zack. Many of Jeff's problems later in life, according to one of his brothers that Detective Mike Shaeffer interviewed, were manifestations of his upbringing. Marc Zack basically repeated what Elayne Zack had been saying all along: Jeff couldn't take rejection. As far as Jeff's other brother not attending Jeff's wake or funeral, investigators learned that Jeff and his other brother often got physical with each other throughout their relationship and never really got along, "but not to the point of fighting," Marc said. Even so, the reason he hadn't attended Jeff's funeral turned out to be a clash of circumstances. He was out of town camping and wasn't notified until late on Sunday night. He couldn't get into town in time.

"Jeff always lived on the edge," said a source. "He was a risk taker. He always seemed to seek others' approval."

Rejection was such a major issue for Jeff that when a girlfriend once broke up with him—it was right after high school, shortly before he left for Israel (he and the girl had planned on getting married)—he went over to the house she lived in and moved all of her belongings into the apartment they had rented together.

David Zack had initiated Jeff into the scrap-metal-recycling business when Jeff returned from Israel. They worked together, but it didn't last long. David found out Jeff was going back into the scrap metal yard at night, stealing metals and selling them. When David realized what Jeff was doing, he "threw him out of the business."

Few in the family trusted Jeff. There were times, Marc Zack said, when years would go by without Marc and Jeff talking, solely based on the way Jeff had treated Marc and his wife. Jeff was rude and offensive when he didn't get his way. Often verbally abusive, Marc said, to his wife over the telephone. That's why it seemed so strange to Marc and the rest of the family when Jeff showed up in Arizona for Mother's Day and began apologizing to everyone in the family for the problems he had caused, even going so far as mentioning specific episodes where Jeff admitted he was out of line. "He acted strange and had a peculiar look in his eyes [that weekend]," Marc told Shaeffer. "He looked as if he was afraid of something . . . extra nervous. I felt he was hiding something and running from someone."

It wasn't only Marc who noticed this. Elayne and David also saw a different Jeff Zack that week. "He knew something was going to happen to him," Elayne said later.

Whereas Jeff never mentioned his affair with Cynthia to friends and coworkers, Marc claimed Jeff had no trouble bragging about it to him. "Jeff was hurt by the end of the affair, I could tell that." While Jeff was in Arizona, he pulled Marc aside one day and told him, "It's over now." Verbalizing it upset Jeff.

"How come?" Marc asked.

"Ah . . . her husband wants it to end. He told me not to come around there anymore, to 'get out of the scenario.'"

Jeff had spoken to Cynthia while he was in Arizona. Marc was sure of it. Add to that the opinion that Ed George had put his foot down about the affair and demanded it come to an end, it seemed Ed had good reason to want Jeff out of the picture. Maybe Jeff and Cynthia didn't end the affair, after all, but only acted like they did to fool Ed and Bonnie?

During that Mother's Day trip, Jeff went out to dinner with Marc, his wife, their new baby, Elayne and David Zack. It was a pleasant time. Yet Jeff seemed to want to hold the small child all throughout the dinner, bouncing the child on his leg, making baby talk, smiling, just having a grand time enjoying the bond between them.

For the family, this was "unusual" behavior on Jeff's part. Marc and his wife, when they got home that night, discussed it. "Maybe Jeff has a baby with Cindy," Marc told his wife. "Maybe . . ."

"And maybe he's unable to see it . . . that's why he was so excited tonight."

Shaeffer asked Marc why he thought Jeff had been murdered. It was the same question detectives had put to everyone. It was important to keep asking. Going over scenarios a second and third time with the same witness could yield new leads.

"It wasn't road rage," insisted Marc. Instead, Marc was with those who believed Seth and Carl were behind it. Covering up for monies stolen from an insurance company, he said, was good motivation for murder. Jeff was determined to get Seth and Carl back for what he believed they did to him. The situation had escalated.

"Nothing else?" Shaeffer wondered. "You don't see any other possibility?"

"Well," Marc said, "it could have occurred due to Jeff's involvement with Cindy."

Marc seemed to know Jeff's last words to Ashton, which, looking back, were quite emblematic of Jeff's life leading up to that final moment. After a "heated" argument with Bonnie and Ashton, Jeff went for the door, according to Marc, turned and, directing his words straight to Ashton, said, "See what's it's like when I'm not here."

29

Earlier in his career, while working undercover, Ed Moriarty got into a bit of a jam. Looking back now, he figured it had somewhat of a connection to Jeff Zack's murder, if only in the substance of what happened. Moriarty was working drug detail, initiating buys and busting drug dealers in the Akron area. The FBI had called the APD one day and warned Moriarty they had information that a "hit" had been put on his life. The hit, claimed the FBI, was sanctioned by a group of Arabs.

"That report," Moriarty recalled, "had come in through [a source connected to Ed George]."

Moriarty was called into his lieutenant's office, who told him about the hit. When the Ed George connection was made and Moriarty later heard that there could be an Arab connection involved in Jeff Zack's murder, he said, "We couldn't rule that out, especially knowing what I knew about [that Arab connection] and the hit that was supposedly put on me years before."

As the second week of the investigation got under way, Moriarty and the CAPU ruled out the possibility that Jeff was murdered by an Arab group. "There were just so many possibilities in this, that the Arab connection didn't fit," Moriarty said. "I mean, at about the same time we found out that Jeff was also involved in [some very shady business] in Phoenix when he was younger. . . . The stock market scams he was involved in. The scams with his various businesses. He was even involved with a credit card scam at some point right before his death. He had his fingers in so many different things. He spoke fluent Russian. We got a tip that the Russian mafia was behind it all because, reportedly, Jeff had somehow scammed them while overseas in Israel. We also had word that he was running drugs in Israel."

None of it, however, as far as Moriarty and the CAPU could tell, turned out to be true. Jeff had bragged about being part of an Israeli intelligence team for Israeli airline El Al. But the APD couldn't confirm or disprove it. To add more seasoning to a melting pot of suspects, it was common knowledge that Jeff and his neighbors didn't get along. Jeff had hit on a neighbor's wife and gotten into several altercations with her husband. But again, the idea that one of Jeff Zack's neighbors had murdered him in an act of revenge or anger—well, it just didn't fit.

When members of the CAPU sat down, compared notes and looked at all the possibilities, the investigation turned to four specific suspects. And so, when they scratched all those potential suspects off the list, one by one, the CAPU found themselves focused on Bonnie Zack, Ed George, and Seth and Carl, the two men Jeff had a gripe with regarding an aluminum-siding job. "When you look at murder," Moriarty observed, "and you've been around murder investigations all your life, you know that it usually comes down to two things—love or money."

When Detective Melissa Williams returned with information from her interview with Lisa, Jeff Zack's mistress from Arizona, the woman with whom he had spent the week in Las Vegas before his murder, at first it cleared up a few inconsistencies that had been left hanging. However, it also invited more questions that the CAPU really didn't need at this point.

It appeared as if Jeff had told Lisa about several threats Ed George had made to him. "But I don't think they happened recently," she had explained to Williams. In any event, the reason Jeff gave Lisa for the end of his relationship with Cynthia, detectives knew, was another lie. Jeff explained to Lisa that Cynthia had been "too controlling." Because of her obsession with having power over the relationship, Jeff claimed, he couldn't "go anywhere—not even on a family vacation—without Cindy following [him] around."

According to many other sources, it was Cynthia who had ended the affair, not Jeff. And it was Cynthia who couldn't go anywhere without Jeff badgering her and following her and begging her to take him back. Jeff had become, in effect, a nuisance in Cynthia's life.

By the same token, Jeff told Lisa he owned several horses. Taking it further, when Lisa asked him where he kept the horses, Jeff stated, "At home. I have a large barn. . . . I have black guys working for me obtaining semen from the horses for breeding." Jeff also told Lisa his vending business was "connected to the mafia."

At one point while they were in Vegas, Jeff wanted to

call Ashton and have Lisa speak to him. "We talked about something more permanent," she explained. Jeff wanted Lisa to get to know his son. When she resisted, feeling as though talking to the boy would be crossing a line, Jeff changed the subject and showed her photographs of his time in the Israeli Army.

During what Lisa described as an "intimate moment" one night, Lisa and Jeff started talking about safe sex. "Great," Jeff said when she asked him about his sexual history, "does this mean I'll have to get tested again?"

"What do you mean by that?" Lisa wanted to know.

"I just upped my life insurance to one million dollars," Jeff said, "and they made me get tested."

Williams wrote in her report of the interview that she had asked Lisa if Bonnie knew about the life insurance. It was critical, perhaps one of the most vital questions to date. If Bonnie knew, it certainly pushed her to the front of what was becoming a smaller pool of suspects.

"I assumed Bonnie knew," Lisa told Williams.

As the interview concluded, Williams realized that as much as Lisa knew about Jeff, most of it was based on fabrications or embellishments. Lisa never knew, for example, that David Zack wasn't Jeff's biological father. Lisa thought he was. Yet, according to Lisa, the most telling portion of their time in Vegas had come during their final night together. Jeff had "concerns," she said, that something was about to happen to him. "He was very intuitive," she added, "and had premonitions that something was wrong." Most of Jeff's worries focused on Ashton. Jeff believed the child was in danger. When they parted ways at the airport, Jeff kissed Lisa and whispered, "I'm afraid that I'll never see you again." He didn't mean that Bonnie was going to find out about the relationship; Lisa felt it was more of a feeling that he knew something bad was about to happen. In fact, on the plane ride back home to Ohio, Jeff had called Ashton from the plane to make sure he was okay.

When Jeff returned, he and Lisa began talking "three to four times a day," she said, and e-mailed each other daily. Jeff set up a special e-mail account that only he could access with a secret password. They communicated right up until that Friday before Jeff was murdered. During one conversation over the telephone, Jeff said, "This is how I got caught with Cindy. Bonnie's coming in the house right now. I have to go."

Jeff called Lisa back sometime later and apologized, saying, "Happy anniversary, it's been one week since Vegas." He was cheerful, upbeat. "I'll e-mail you before I go to bed."

"Just e-mail me in the morning if you're too tired," Lisa told him.

Later that night, Jeff sent Lisa a quick note, signing off, I love you until my death.

When Lisa didn't receive an e-mail the following morning, Saturday, the day of Jeff's death, she said she grew "concerned." At around one o'clock that afternoon, Lisa tried calling Jeff on his cell phone. When a man whose voice she didn't recognize answered—it was one of the detectives at the hospital with Jeff's body— she hung up.

After having a friend call around all day and the next, finally getting through to someone at Bonnie's work, Lisa said she found out Jeff had been murdered.

30

Captain Beth Daugherty was able to obtain a subpoena by Thursday, June 21, for a look into the bank accounts of Ed and Cynthia George. The period the CAPU was most interested in, according to the subpoena, was January 1, 2001, to the end of June that same year. One aspect of digging into Ed and Cynthia's bank accounts was to see if a large withdrawal had been made at some point near the time Jeff was murdered. Another was to try to make any connection they could between Ed and Jeff. "We were looking for moving money," Ed Moriarty recalled. "Before the advent of the Internet and before drugs were really a part of it, murder was more personal, intimate. The first motivator is emotion. The second is money. When in doing a homicide investigation, the money trail can get you to where you want to go. We were looking for the money trail, a personal connection." Anything that could connect Jeff Zack with Ed George. "If someone had been hired to kill Jeff," Moriarty added, "we believed then that it probably would have come through Ed George."

A bit apprehensive and standoffish at first, after the

bank got a look at the subpoena, the accounts manager said it would take at least five to six days before they could fulfill the request.

That was fine. There was plenty of work to do. After an intense search for Seth and Carl, two CAPU detectives finally tracked down where they believed Seth lived. If Ed George wasn't behind Jeff's murder, it was a good bet that Seth and/or Carl had some sort of link, perhaps for the simple reason that, beyond Bonnie and Ed, Seth and Carl had a textbook motive to want Jeff dead: to shut him up.

The residential neighborhood in which Seth lived contained four houses flanked in a cul-de-sac. Detective Russ McFarland and Lieutenant Dave Whiddon went up to Seth's door and knocked. It appeared that no one was home, or, rather, no one had been home in quite a while. Still, Whiddon thought as he approached the door, it was worth knocking.

After several minutes, no one answered.

"Let's spread out and go door-to-door," Whiddon suggested.

After knocking on the doors of Seth's three neighbors, no one seemed to be around. So the detectives left their business cards at each house, hoping someone would call.

By the time they got back into the car, Mike Shaeffer had come up with the name of Seth's neighbor. The guy was a firefighter. He worked up the road at a local firehouse.

"Great, we'll head right over there," McFarland told Shaeffer.

Hopefully, the neighbor could offer some insight into Seth's comings and goings.

"That guy [Seth]," the firefighter said after Whiddon

and McFarland introduced themselves, "has a problem with everyone in the neighborhood. He's very arrogant. Likes to flash his money around in front of people."

It was obvious from the firefighter's terse, emotional response that Seth was not the type of neighbor people invited over for cookouts and parties.

Further along into the conversation, the firefighter said Seth was in the landscaping/home repair business and had a reputation for hiring contractors to do work on new homes and then ripping them off. He said he had seen a moving truck in Seth's driveway "about four weeks ago" and believed Seth moved to Florida with his wife and kids. "But he came back a few weeks later by himself and then left again."

McFarland and Whiddon looked at each other.

"Have you seen him since?"

"Nope."

Whiddon took out a Kawasaki motorcycle brochure with a photograph of a green-and-black Ninja on the cover. "You ever seen one of these at Seth's house?"

The firefighter thought about it. "I've never seen *that* type of motorcycle over there, no."

Whiddon showed him a photograph of Seth.

"Yup, that's definitely him."

Then a photograph of Carl.

"Don't recognize that guy."

The time frame worked. Seth had split to Florida with his family a month ago, then returned at or near the time of Jeff's murder. It was possible he came back to Akron to commit the murder and then bolted back to Florida.

Another guy at the firehouse who knew Seth came forward next. The guy's brother-in-law had lived across the street from Seth in the same neighborhood. "Scum of the earth," he said of Seth. "Someone that never kept a real job. I know he just purchased a car wash, but I guess it flopped and he never made any money and never made any payments on the business."

"What about his house?"

"Several people were interested in buying it, but the thing had so many liens against it that it wasn't worth it."

Leaving the fire department, McFarland and Whiddon headed back over to Seth's neighborhood to see if anyone had made it home. By pure luck, they saw the second fireman's brother-in-law working in his yard. "You got a few minutes?" Whiddon asked.

"No problem." He invited them in. "Sit down, please."

"How long have you lived here?" Whiddon asked.

"Oh, about five years."

"What about your neighbor"—pointing to Seth's house—"over there?"

"He's been there about two or three years."

A homicide detective's life can become cyclical. Many homicide investigations move in a circle, leading investigators back to the same set of suspects and circumstances. A seasoned homicide detective never looks at the obvious. Most of the time, when someone looks too good as a suspect, he or she turns out to be innocent. With Seth and Carl, on paper their guilt seemed like a perfect fit—which was why Whiddon and McFarland were so interested in dragging one of them in for questioning. Whenever you have a potential pair of murderers, it was easier to get one to drop a dime on the other. Human nature and a bit of police ingenuity could work wonders. But the key was getting them downtown together and then quickly splitting them up.

Seth's neighbor said he was known as a "high roller . . .

but most of his money was made through questionable business deals."

"How do you know that?"

"He tried to lure me into some of these deals and often asked me personal questions about my finances."

The man said he and his wife used to be friends with Seth and his wife, but they had a falling-out after Seth went nuts one day, yelling and screaming at some kids playing out in front of his house.

"That was it?"

"He also made sexual advances toward my wife when I wasn't around one day. When I found out, I confronted him. We haven't spoken since."

More interesting to Whiddon and McFarland, the man said Seth routinely argued out in the open with his employees and contractors who worked for him.

"He liked to talk about *The Sopranos*. It was his favorite show."

Whiddon took out the brochure of the Ninja. The man shook his head. Said he had never seen a bike like it at Seth's.

31

Dave Whiddon was able to get Carl's address from another source. He and McFarland headed straight over to his house after leaving Seth's neighborhood that second time. Pulling in, it appeared as if no one was home. Whiddon got out. As he was walking up to the door to leave his card, a gold Ford Explorer pulled into the driveway. From the photograph he and McFarland had, Whiddon could tell Carl was driving. The female next to him, he surmised, was his wife. There were three children in the backseat. "Carl, I'm Lieutenant Dave Whiddon," he said, pulling out his badge, "this is Detective McFarland."

Carl didn't say anything.

"Can we talk to you for a few minutes?"

"Come on into the house," Carl said. He seemed calm. Not scared at all.

Carl lived pretty well. Nice house. New furniture. Big SUV in the driveway, with three kids and a wife. Was the guy going to risk losing all that by murdering Jeff Zack for seven thousand dollars?

Carl's wife took the kids into another section of the

house while Carl sat down in the living room with
Whiddon and McFarland. They asked about Seth first.
"I've been working with him for about the past five
months," Carl said. He explained how he answered an
ad in the newspaper Seth had placed for an experienced floor tile person. "He asked me about working
insurance claim jobs. He wanted me to move to Florida
with him to continue the same type of work. We went
down there in March for spring break. We looked for a
house and checked out the school system. I grew up
in Florida. So did my wife. We went out to dinner a few
times. When we left, my wife said she didn't want to
move down there because she didn't trust Seth."

After Carl described how he moved away from Seth
weeks ago, after he found out he was "cheating customers out of money," Whiddon brought up Jeff Zack.

Carl said he met Jeff four years ago. "I helped coach
Jeff's son's youth football team."

Through that relationship, Carl and Jeff became
friends and started hanging out. It was clear that as he
began to talk about Jeff, Carl became, Whiddon wrote
in his report, "visibly upset" because of what he said was
a "close relationship" he had with Jeff and Ashton.

The seven thousand dollars in question was all Seth's
doing, Carl claimed. He was sick over it. Seth had even
managed to burn him out of the money he got from
Jeff's insurance company. "I tried to explain to Jeff that
I wasn't involved with it, but he didn't want to hear it.
He said he was turning the situation over to the insurance company's investigative unit and then going to
the police. I told him to get an attorney and sue Seth."
But Jeff didn't respond too well to the conversation,
saying, "Don't come over to my house anymore."

"What happened between Jeff and Seth?"

"He said he talked to Seth three times and threatened him verbally," Carl explained. "It got really heated. Jeff told Seth one day, 'I'm going to f— your wife and your family if you don't leave my family alone.' This happened about two weeks ago."

"What was your first reaction when you heard about Jeff's death?"

"I was in the shower. My wife came in and told me she saw it in the newspaper. My first thought was that Seth had something to do with it. I feel terrible. I introduced Seth to Jeff. Seth was always talking about *The Sopranos* and 'burning all of his bridges' here in Ohio before moving to Florida."

After checking out the alibi Carl had given Whiddon and McFarland, the CAPU felt confident there was no way Carl could have been involved in Jeff's murder.

32

Late Thursday afternoon, CAPU detective Vince Felber called the Silver Lake Police Department, (SLPD) in Silver Lake, Ohio, a little town about ten miles north of Akron, regarding an anonymous tip a Silver Lake police officer had received earlier that day. "The caller said," the officer told Felber, "the motorcycle you guys are looking for was in the Myrtle-Curtis part of Cuyahoga Falls."

"Any idea who the caller is?" Felber asked.

"I recognized his voice—he's a local cabbie."

After the Silver Lake Police Department gave Felber the name of the cab company, he made a call and found out the cabbie was out on the road. "Let him know I'm on my way over there to speak with him."

The drive took about forty minutes. For Felber, investigating Jeff Zack's murder was different from his normal work. For the most part, Felber spent his days (and sometimes nights) working burglary detail. Homicide wasn't his thing. He had gotten involved in the Zack case by the sheer process of elimination. He was working the weekend that the Zack murder took place.

Ed Moriarty had brought Felber in because he knew Felber had, at one time, worked as a bartender at Ed George's Tangier. Felber knew some of the people who worked at the restaurant. His knowledge of Ed George alone, Moriarty knew, would help the case immensely.

Felber met the cabbie in the parking lot. "He was very eager to talk to me," Felber wrote in his report.

The cabbie said he heard "two men" discussing Jeff Zack's murder. One of the men, the cabbie claimed, was driving a green-and-black Ninja motorcycle.

Felber said, "Tell me what happened."

"I was taking a nap on a small dock that sits on the river by a tackle shop where I work part-time. It was last Sunday afternoon, about eleven in the morning." While taking a nap on the dock, he said, he was awoken by the sound of an aluminum boat trolling by. "There were two men inside, they looked Lebanese or Greek. They were talking about 'whacking' some guy, blowing him away. They mentioned road rage and laughed about it."

It all seemed to fit.

"Can you identify these men?" Felber asked. It seemed too convenient. Too good to be true. But what the hell, what else did the CAPU have at this point?

"Sure. They were talking about heading down to the store to get a six-pack of beer."

"What about the bike? You said you saw a motor-cycle?"

"That was the next day. I was down at the same store where those guys said they were heading. I was Dumpster diving. I saw a white-green-and-black motorcycle parked near the store. I think the bike belonged to one of the guys in the boat."

Felber asked the cabbie if he would mind taking a

drive. He wanted to check it out for himself—see the dock, the store, take a look around. Maybe the cabbie was a crackpot? During any high-profile homicide investigation, there is no shortage of people who want desperately to be part of solving the crime. Since the advent of crime television and Court TV's wide variety of forensic shows, armchair detectives come out of the woodwork. Beyond that, the Silver Lake cop Felber had spoken to warned Felber about the guy, telling him that he was a local big mouth, a guy who liked to "be involved" in police work, but someone whose information rarely checked out.

After a short drive, Felber verified there was a dock positioned where the cabbie had claimed. But when it came to pointing out the house near the store where he said he saw the motorcycle, the guy had trouble recalling exactly where it was.

As they drove around, Felber noticed the guy was "overly eager to please" him, often rambling on and on, saying how much he liked to help the police. Felber had a keen sense; he knew how to read witnesses. He had worked the streets of Akron for years, using confidential informant (CI) sources as a means to solve burglaries. When Felber first joined the APD, he was a greenhorn kid working in the private sector for a marketing firm. Marketing and journalism were his majors in college. He grew up in what he described as a "lower-middle-class" section of the city and, before hitting the streets in a blue uniform, had never even been to the hardscrabble sections of the city he later patrolled.

In any event, it was not a good sign that this particular witness was overly enthusiastic about helping him. The guy didn't even seem nervous, which was another indication that his information was likely overexaggerated or entirely bogus.

Dropping him off back at the cab company, Felber said, "Listen, if you think of anything else, call me."

"I will. I will. Thank you, sir. Good luck to you."

It was worth following up. So Felber drove immediately back to the store and started asking questions. A young kid who was working that day told Felber he didn't know of anyone in the neighborhood who owned a green-and-black Ninja motorcycle. But he did know of "one Middle Eastern man with a Caucasian wife" who lived in the area and stopped at the store once in a while.

Cindy and Ed George?

The owner of the store said basically the same thing, adding, "I lived next door to Jeff Zack for about three months. But I didn't get to know Jeff too well. I wasn't there long enough. A friend of mine did know Jeff pretty well and was also his neighbor."

Felber left the store, shaking his head, wondering if the case could get any more complicated. If the CAPU had uncovered in just a week's time a dozen or more people Jeff Zack had infuriated throughout his life, how many more were out there they didn't know about?

The following day, Felber got in touch with a man he had arrested a year prior for stealing upward of forty thousand dollars from his then-employer, who happened to be Ed George's brother. He asked the guy about the business of vending machines in general. There was still a lingering notion that Jeff Zack had gotten into an altercation over a long-running dispute with someone messing with his vending machines.

The guy said the vending business was on the "up and up" these days. Fifty years ago, people in the business got their legs broken regularly, he added, for violating the mafia's control of the industry. But it wasn't like that anymore. "Problems today are fixed by the court system."

"Do you know any of the Georges?" Felber asked.

"I don't know much about Ed or his brother's personal life, only what I've been told."

"From whom?"

"This guy Red, who worked security for Ed George at the Tangier for almost twenty years."

"What'd you hear?"

"He said Cindy, Ed's wife, was involved in a number of affairs and that Ed knew about them all. Cindy runs that household. Ed is a doting father who has a very low opinion of just about everyone."

"Tell me about Cindy, specifically."

The guy seemed restless, like he was willing to talk, but unwilling to give details he had heard from someone else.

Because he had worked at the Tangier, Felber knew Ed and Cynthia George when they were first married. Cynthia was an airline employee when she met Ed. Many saw her as a hot-looking blonde with cheerleader legs, dolledup, shiny *Charlie's Angels* hair, with the perfect mixture of eyeliner and cherry red lipstick, serving up cocktails and little finger foods, while wearing a miniskirt, inside a major airline's Gold Club at the airport.

Throughout the time they sat and talked inside the guy's apartment, Felber felt the guy was "guarded," holding things back. He seemed antsy and nervous. When Felber asked him about Ed and Cynthia's children, he reluctantly said, "I know one of them is adopted . . . and one is, well . . . I don't know."

As Felber was leaving, he couldn't help but notice

how close the guy's apartment was to the store near
Silver Lake where the cabbie had said he saw the Ninja
motorcycle and heard two guys talking about whacking
someone.

   Coincidence?

33

Whiddon and McFarland weren't satisfied with what they heard about Seth and Carl; it was hard to scratch both men off the list. Seth was in Florida. If a break in the case, pointing detectives in another direction entirely, didn't come soon, a detective was going to have to fly down to the Sunshine State and question Seth. But still, Ashton Zack, Jeff's son, had mentioned Seth and Carl in his original interview with Bertina King. The boy was sure one of them had had something to do with his father's death—as much as he was sure it was Ed George. That threat Ashton had heard Seth scream at his dad: "I'll rip your throat out with a hot butter knife."

Strong words. Explosive. Violent. Intimidating.

Although the boy would grieve for the rest of his life, and was in no way over the initial impact of losing his father, McFarland and Whiddon felt Ashton could be helpful, and decided to reinterview him.

Regardless of the type of person Jeff Zack had become over the course of his life, most agreed he loved his child and treated him with the ultimate amount of respect, often devoting most of his free time to the boy. Jeff had been there, supporting Ashton's endeavors, whatever they were, regardless how many mistresses he had or what he and Bonnie were going through. It didn't make Jeff "Father of the Year," but it said something about his devotion to his son.

Bonnie answered the door after Whiddon and McFarland knocked. She said she knew they were coming. Someone from the CAPU had called. "Come in, please," Bonnie said pleasantly.

"Thanks, Bonnie," said Whiddon. "How are things?"

She didn't say much about how she felt, but was eager to have the investigators talk to Ashton, who was up in his room. "Go upstairs. Talk to him privately. I don't mind."

The sadness weighing on the boy was evident in the way he carried himself. His youth had been blindsided by tragedy, disrupting, perhaps, everything else that may have seemed important a few weeks ago. Still, he wanted to help catch his dad's killer.

"We need to go over a few things," Whiddon said caringly.

Ashton shrugged in agreement.

"Tell us about Carl and Seth, Ashton."

"Seth is short and fat, with a raspy and distinctive voice. Carl coached my football team for two years."

Essentially, Ashton couldn't offer anything new. He reiterated what he had told the CAPU the day his father was murdered, repeating that same threatening line from Seth.

About a half hour into the conversation, Whiddon asked Ashton if there was a feeling he had about his dad's murder.

"I think my dad knew he was going to die."

Whiddon and McFarland looked at each other. Whiddon asked, "What makes you say that?"

"After he died, I came across a box of old photos of my dad. My dad kept the box hidden. He didn't like people going through his stuff. I found it because it was out in the open. My dad was obviously going through it himself."

"What type of photos?"

"His whole life."

Ashton was a smart, articulate kid. Whiddon and McFarland appreciated how direct he was with his theories. Near the end of the conversation, Ashton described his dad's trip to Arizona during the Mother's Day holiday: "He wanted to make up with them, because he felt that something was going to happen to him."

34

Motive was the number one concern on Ed Moriarty's mind as the investigation seemed to grow colder during the early days of the second week. The CAPU had conducted upward of fifty interviews with the likes of ex-girlfriends and mistresses, former coworkers and acquaintances, relatives, siblings, Bonnie Zack, Cynthia and Ed George, Ashton and several people who had called in tips. "Motive," Moriarty recalled. "*What* would cause someone to be involved in Jeff Zack's murder? We had harassment on the table, and, well, harassment to me didn't feel like enough to kill someone. Not in this situation."

A question kept popping up as Moriarty studied the case: *How did the shooter know Jeff Zack was going to be at BJ's that morning?* It was possible—and the APD had a report—that the motorcyclist followed Jeff into the parking lot. But still, no one had reported a Ninja motorcycle hanging around Jeff's neighborhood. "So we started to look into Jeff's phone records," Moriarty said. "And that's when certain things fell into place."

Yes, Jeff Zack had spent time in Israel in the Israeli

Army, that much was confirmed. Yes, Jeff was pro-Israel and had gotten into several heated arguments with Arabs who were pro-Palestine. But did any of that have an impact on who murdered him? After studying the reports and interviews, Moriarty didn't feel Jeff's connections to Israel had anything whatsoever to do with his demise. "It just didn't fit. We checked it all out, but time and again came up with nothing."

When Moriarty found out that Jeff Zack had possibly fathered one of Cynthia's children, well, a motive for murder seemed to fit warmly into the context of the crime. Once that suspicion grew into a need to know, Moriarty felt compelled to take it a step further, setting out to first prove the allegation. If true, and Ed George knew about it, the possibility that he had Jeff murdered to fend off embarrassment would make sense. Everything else—and there was plenty, Moriarty knew—didn't fit together in a uniform fashion. There were other theories, sure, but there had always been one key element missing from each. Jeff fathering a child and Ed not finding out about it until just recently worked better than most.

With a need to know the truth, Moriarty said, "I got us a subpoena for a blood draw—a buccal swab from the child's mouth to compare for parental DNA."

That one simple test would answer a lot of questions. One simple scraping of flesh with a cotton swab from Ruby George's cheek would clear the entire matter up—and either bury a finger deeper into Ed George's chest, or begin to phase him out of the equation. Jeff Zack had lied so much—who could say the kid was his or not? Moriarty and other detectives had looked at photographs of the George family and seen the resemblance between one of the children and Jeff Zack. But a hunch certainly wasn't evidence.

DNA would clear it all up.

St. Thomas Hospital is a redbrick building in downtown Akron on Main Street. Inside the hospital is the CAPU's rape crisis intervention unit. Moriarty was able to get a court order that, by law, authorized him to have Cynthia and Ed George bring Ruby down to the hospital for a buccal swab of her right cheek.

Cynthia and Ed were livid, of course. More Cynthia than Ed.

Moriarty was waiting at the hospital for Ed and Cynthia to arrive with Ruby. It was going to take all of five seconds to swab the inside of the child's cheek and release her. "Cindy George was pissed," Moriarty said. "She did not want us to do the test."

Ruby was screaming as Cynthia and Ed walked into the hospital with the child. Cynthia confronted Moriarty, face-to-face, and yelled, "I cannot believe you're making her do this."

"Calm down," Moriarty said.

"This is going to hurt you, Ruby," Moriarty heard Cynthia say to the child, trying to put fear into her to make the test that much more difficult for the CAPU to complete. "They are going to hurt you, baby."

Ed George was just standing there, shaking his head. He couldn't believe it had come down to this: Here was his daughter being brought in like a common criminal to take a DNA test. Was this actually happening?

After a few minutes of yelling back and forth, Moriarty doing his best to calm everyone down, Ed put his daughter on his lap, while Moriarty managed to get Cynthia over to the door heading out of the room.

The nurse got the swab kit ready. While she did that,

Moriarty recalled, "I shoved Cindy out the door and closed the door behind us."

And that's when Cynthia went ballistic. "You motherf- - - er," Moriarty claimed she yelled at him. "Get out of my way. You son of a bitch. How could you do this? Get the f- - - out of my way. I want to see my daughter."

"Relax, Cindy," Moriarty said. "This is going to happen whether you agree to it or not. Don't make it tougher than it is. Ruby will be fine."

The child, likely confused and scared, began bawling. But it took only a few seconds to grab the oral swab of her cheek and send Ed and the child on their way.

Moriarty sent the swab to the lab with a request to have the results back as soon as possible.

It would take two weeks, he was told.

35

Detective Mike Shaeffer tracked down Rabbi Sasonkin, in whom Jeff Zack had confided over the years. At
first, the rabbi was a bit apprehensive regarding talking
to the police, not too thrilled about dishing on his private conversations with synagogue members. But after
Shaeffer explained that the rabbi could provide potential information that could possibly help catch Jeff's
killer, he agreed.

According to the rabbi, Jeff showed up at the synagogue in 1996 after he was arrested for "sexual harassment." Jeff's boss at the time had suggested he go see
the rabbi. Jeff was terrified of going to jail for the
charge. "I'm possibly facing some prison time," Jeff explained to Rabbi Sasonkin during their first face-to-face
encounter. "I cannot do time in jail. I'd rather commit
suicide."

The rabbi gave Jeff the name of a high-powered local
attorney. Through that relationship, Jeff was able to get
probation without having to serve any jail time. The
rabbi, however, believed Jeff was suicidal and encouraged

him to seek shelter from his demons by attending service and talking things out privately.

"How did Jeff get into the situation that led him to being charged?" Shaeffer wondered.

"Jeff," said the rabbi, "liked to talk to females." The rabbi wouldn't go any further than that; but was comfortable insinuating that Jeff had a hard time staying away from women and keeping his mouth shut when he was around them.

Going to court on sexual harassment charges changed Jeff. After it was over, he connected with the synagogue and started to attend service quite regularly. He even brought Ashton to "religion school," Rabbi Sasonkin said. "But it didn't last long," the rabbi added. "He started coming maybe every two weeks. Then, in the last two years, he stopped coming altogether."

Jeff was conflicted, the rabbi insisted. "The Jewish religion looks down on marrying non-Jews." That was what drew Jeff away from the synagogue, in the rabbi's opinion, more than anything else. "It is believed that your religion is passed through your mother. So in the Jewish religion, Jeff's son was not considered Jewish, since his mother wasn't Jewish. But he could become Jewish through conversion."

"Jeff ever talk about his time in the Israeli Army?" Shaeffer asked. As they spoke, the rabbi and Shaeffer walked through the synagogue. It was dark and eerie, as any empty house of worship would be under the same set of circumstances. The rabbi, though, seemed comfortable talking about Jeff after his initial uneasiness passed.

"Jeff never talked about it," the rabbi stated in a noticeable Yiddish accent. "But I can say that it is standard for all Israelis to go into the army for"—he held up two fingers—"two years."

As they sat down in a pew, Shaeffer asked, "Jeff ever mention anything about the Mossad?"

"No, sir. We didn't talk about his years in the army. . . . But I'll say that if one is in the Mossad, one would not talk about it or tell people. If one was going around saying he or she is in the Mossad, it is likely he or she is *not* in the Mossad."

Further along, the rabbi described Jeff in the same way many others had, saying he had a "big mouth," seemed "confrontational," used "rough language and was very aggressive." Jeff could be intimidating to people, especially because of his size, the rabbi insisted. "But he did have a soft side to him, which usually came out when he was in trouble. He always seemed to be on edge and never happy. He wanted more."

"That's helpful, Rabbi, I appreciate it," Shaeffer said.

While the rabbi walked the detective out, Shaeffer asked about a possible Israeli mob connection, and if perhaps the rabbi thought it played a role in Jeff's murder. Rabbi Sasonkin insisted there wasn't a strong "Israeli mob" presence in the Akron-Cleveland area, and didn't suspect Jeff was tied to the Israeli underworld in any way. "It's hard to find someone that is shot in America for their Israeli connections. I don't believe Jeff was shot for being Jewish or Israeli. If that was the situation, the Jewish community would have been alerted and they would have tightened up security."

It made perfect sense.

"If you need help translating any information," the rabbi said as he walked the detective to his car, "or conversations, call me and I'd be glad to help."

"We appreciate that, Rabbi."

36

Jeff Zack's old business acquaintance, Carl, agreed to take a polygraph on June 27. Although the test wasn't going to prove beyond a reasonable doubt, one way or another, Carl's involvement in Jeff's murder, it was a starting point. The test would tell CAPU detectives how much they should trust the guy.

"Do you know for sure who killed Jeff Zack?"

"No."

"Did you kill Jeff Zack?"

"No."

"Did you conspire with anyone to kill Jeff Zack?"

"No."

"Were you involved in an insurance scam with Jeff Zack and Carl?"

"No."

After a "careful review of the polygrams," Sergeant Terry Hudnall reported afterward, he believed that the "physiological change indicative of truthfulness occurred on all the relevant questions." According to Hudnall, Carl was telling the truth.

* * *

When the test results came back, the lab confirmed Ed Moriarty's suspicion that Jeff Zack was the father of Cynthia George's youngest child, Ruby.

This revelation changed some things for the CAPU. Realizing the investigation had taken a stunning turn, Ed Moriarty thought back to that threat he heard Jeff had made to Bonnie regarding taking Ashton and running away to Israel. "Knowing that," Moriarty recalled later, "I had to consider, *Did Jeff threaten Cindy with the same thing?* It seemed possible. . . . Now, speaking of motive, let's say Cindy wants to get rid of Jeff. She wants to end the affair. He doesn't want to end it. Threatening, on its face, didn't seem like a motive in this case. But you threaten to take a person's child and the entire scope of that threat changes."

All of a sudden, Cynthia was now a suspect. In fact, when the CAPU looked at all the pieces of the puzzle they had collected thus far, it seemed a hired hit had been sanctioned—which put Ed George back on the radar. Jeff Zack had been murdered in broad daylight on a Saturday afternoon inside the parking lot of a very popular and busy warehouse store outlet. Only a professional, it seemed, could have pulled it off. By all accounts, Jeff's murder had been a clean strike; definitely not the work—or so everyone thought early on—of an inexperienced killer. And now, with Jeff Zack tied to Cynthia in the way of a child, the thought that Ed George had found out and decided to clean up a mess his wife had created took center stage.

On Thursday, June 28, Moriarty spoke to fifty-seven-year-old Richard "Red" Stanick, who worked for the City of Akron, Police and Fire Communications. But it wasn't Red's current job, or the fact that he was an Akron police officer during the late 1960s and early

1970s, that Moriarty was interested in. Before becoming a city employee, Red had spent nearly twenty years working for Ed George as a security guard. If there was anyone who knew the ebb and flow of the Tangier, and could explain how Ed and Cynthia interacted on a day-to-day basis, Red was the guy. He had spent more time at the Tangier than anyone the CAPU had spoken to. Red knew something. Moriarty was sure of it.

Moriarty and Red knew each other because at one time they walked the beat as cops under the same badge. It was thought that Red had left the job because of a savage beating he once endured. The CAPU had talked to Red quite a bit throughout the years regarding other crimes, only because he knew many of the people coming and going at the Tangier.

Moriarty first asked Red about Jeff Zack.

He said he knew him. He had read about Jeff's murder in the newspaper the day after it happened. Putting the newspaper down that morning, Red explained, he immediately telephoned a friend, a woman who still worked at the Tangier. "We both had the feeling," Red told Moriarty, "that Ed George probably made the call that resulted in Zack's death."

"Did Jeff and Ed have a business relationship?" Moriarty wondered.

The CAPU had heard from several different sources that Jeff had worked for Ed throughout the years. If they'd had a falling-out, coupled with Jeff sleeping with Ed George's wife and fathering one of her children, Ed had even more explaining to do.

Red clarified that business between Jeff and Ed was minimal. Jeff may have bought things from Ed—tools and the like—but beyond that, they had no real business relationship. On that note, however, Red made a point to say that it was hard to work for Ed. He had a "very volatile temper . . . and treats his employees very gruffly."

Moriarty had sensed this side of Ed from being around him. The guy just had that look of hardness to him. If he treated his employees like that, how would he treat a guy who screwed around with his wife and fathered one of her children?

"You ever see Cynthia and Jeff together?" Moriarty asked.

"Jeff was an overbearing son of a bitch. He came to the restaurant all the time. He liked to act like a big shot, you know, but didn't have the clout to back it up."

Red then explained how Jeff started coming to the restaurant eight years before his death and usually hung all over Cynthia right there in the bar or restaurant for everyone to see. This, mind you, while Bonnie was right there. Red estimated that Jeff brought Bonnie with him about 80 percent of the time. It was the talk of the restaurant for a while: how Jeff would bring in his wife to seemingly humiliate her in front of everyone. Nobody could believe the gall the man had.

"Jeff followed Cindy wherever she went. Everyone knew Jeff and Cindy had something going on."

"How was Ed with that?"

"I'm not sure he was aware of it, to be quite honest. You have to understand that anything that didn't make Ed money, well, he wasn't interested in it. He was oblivious."

Moriarty shook his head. "Wow, no kidding. You don't think he'd be interested in who his wife was sleeping with?"

"I'm not saying that."

Jeff never drank alcohol, Red continued—or, rather, Red never saw him drunk. Cynthia liked her cocktails, but she never overdid it.

Red gave Moriarty a few names he thought would help.

37

While detectives worked the Ed George angle, reaching out to former and current Tangier employees, continuing to build a profile of Ed, tips continued to pour in for the CAPU. Until a viable suspect was brought in for questioning, and tangible evidence to support a possible arrest was in hand, the CAPU couldn't give up talking to people and checking out new (and old) leads. "We couldn't let up," Moriarty said. "Even knowing Jeff had fathered one of Cindy's children, we still didn't have anything. [Seth and Carl] looked real good, still. When you looked them over, on paper, they seemed like practical suspects. We never took that for granted—even after the polygraph."

An interesting call came into the APD over the Fourth of July holiday weekend. A local lawyer made a telephone call to the CAPU on the afternoon of the Fourth, saying she "had information in reference to the shooting of Jeff Zack." Bertina King took the call and interviewed the woman, who was certain a client of the law firm she worked for had had something to do with Jeff's murder.

"I had a conversation with a client one day, two years ago," the woman explained. "We were standing in the hall. We were talking about his case." The guy had been arrested for breaking into a car. "I told him he needed to be truthful with me concerning his case. I didn't feel that he was."

When the lawyer brought up the idea that he might be lying, the guy became incensed. "The trouble I'm in right now," he said, "is nothing. I'm going to kill a guy that has been messing with a friend of mine. This weekend this guy is going down. You are going to read about what I did in the newspaper."

Detective King thought it was interesting, yet didn't fit. The comment was made two years ago.

"Listen," said the lawyer, "he has a motorcycle."

"Well, thanks for the information," King said.

She wrote it up and put it in the stack of reports.

Over the next week, that tip and about a dozen others were checked out thoroughly, but all led nowhere. It seemed the case, every time the CAPU thought that maybe it was heading in a different direction, always turned back to the same people.

Ed Moriarty caught up with *Janice Hagin*, a contact Red had given him. Janice was a good-looking forty-two-year-old former bartender at the Tangier. She had worked there for "several years." Janice was well aware of Jeff Zack's presence at the establishment and, like many, didn't like him. "He was cocky and arrogant. I only spoke to him when I had to take his order."

Cynthia George had introduced Janice to Jeff. Cynthia seemed proud to show Jeff off, as if he were some sort of prize. It was like a game for Cynthia: parading around the Tangier with her catch. Part of it was, probably, designed to make Ed George pay more attention to her, seeing that he was always wrapped up in his work.

Jeff was one of Tangier's regular customers who had a house account. He could walk in and put anything he wanted on a tab. His normal time was between 2:00 and 4:00 P.M., Janice explained. And Jeff shunned all alcohol, opting instead for diet soda.

Beyond the things Moriarty had heard already from several different sources, Janice, if nothing else, backed up what the CAPU knew. Most important, the fact that Cynthia and Jeff had no trouble displaying affection for each other inside the bar and cabaret—which, Janice said, Jeff never paid to get in—laughing, joking and hanging all over each other. "They were always together," said Janice. "Always! And Jeff had been over to the Georges' house."

Moriarty was also beginning to learn a bit more about Cynthia herself. According to Janice, when she first started working at the Tangier, she noticed Cynthia had "very little to do with the day-to-day operations of the restaurant." But more recently, Cynthia became a fixture in the place, taking on the responsibility of what was an enormous remodeling effort. This caused problems, she said, between Ed George and his mother, who believed Cynthia should be at home with the kids.

38

In June 2001, Ed and Cynthia George celebrated their seventeenth wedding anniversary. When they married in 1984, amid some five hundred guests at St. Joseph Catholic Church in downtown Akron, Cynthia was a twenty-nine-year-old woman still living at home; Ed, a forty-four-year-old bachelor, was living at home as well. A self-proclaimed "country girl," she was born Cynthia Mae Rohr, into what published reports have described as a "strict Catholic family." One of four Rohr children, Cynthia grew up in North Canton, a town of mostly German immigrants, about twenty miles south of Akron. She went to North Canton's Hoover High School. At a young age, Cynthia seemed to embody the spirit of a woman unhappy with the life she had been born into, and when she spoke to a psychologist many years later, having lived for so long by then in the quintessence of luxury and leisure with Ed George, she admitted that one of her biggest fears was returning to a life of poverty. She couldn't imagine having to fall back into that lifestyle all over again, not after living like a queen in Ed George's castle.

Several neighbors of Cynthia's viewed her childhood slightly differently. "She had a loving family, they were close," said one neighbor. "I never saw Cindy unhappy as a child," said another. "She seemed to have anything she ever wanted. Her parents were great people. Loving. Caring. Always there for her. Her siblings were the same."

In high school, Cynthia excelled, as any beautiful blond cheerleader might, involving herself in the homecoming and pep club aspect of extracurricular activities, championing Hoover's sports stars, keeping herself busy by jumping into any popular group that would accept her.

If Cynthia later saw her childhood as underprivileged, the reality of it was quite common for the times. The house the Rohrs lived in off Main Street was a modest, one-story ranch, built during the war years, the late 1940s, early 1950s. The Canton region was booming then; Akron was known as the "Rubber Capital of the World," BFGoodrich having set up shop there in the early 1900s. Alcoholics Anonymous founder Bill Wilson began his crusade in Akron for alcoholics all over the world. Houses were built at an astounding rate, two times more than any year before or since; the rubber boom and coal mines offering jobs for the undereducated, blue-collar sect. In fact, Mr. Rohr was a hardworking, dedicated father, who spent many backbreaking years in the Ohio coal mines. Like most families during the 1950s and 1960s money was tight for the Rohrs, but they had a roof over their heads, food and clothing for their children.

As many pretty young girls do, possibly born from playing with dolls and acting out runway fantasies with girlfriends, Cynthia had always talked about winning the Miss America pageant one day, and had a hard time letting go of that dream as she settled into adulthood, setting her sights on art and design school after graduation.

But money kept Cynthia from fulfilling either goal. It wasn't looks; she had that in the bag, often fighting men off with a stick anywhere she went. Instead of college, she ended up as an optician at an optical company, which was not a bad gig considering her background. Then she went into the airline industry, at first working for US Airway's VIP club in Pittsburgh, before meeting Ed George.

On Saturday, July 14, 2001, Detective Vince Felber contacted Helen Rohr, Cynthia's eighty-six-year-old mother. Helen was a bit hostile and standoffish right off the bat. It was obvious to Felber that, despite her age, the woman was sharp and unwilling to give out any information without being asked.

Felber told Rohr that he was investigating the murder of Jeff Zack. He wanted to talk to her for a moment about the case. Would she mind?

"Why?" Mrs. Rohr asked.

"I want to talk about Cindy," Felber said.

"I hardly knew Jeff Zack and can't tell you anything."

"I understand, ma'am . . . but I'd still like to talk to you and your daughter (Cynthia's sister)."

"I'll see," Mrs. Rohr said. Felber could sense the resentment in her voice. "Let me call her and see if she's free. I'll call you back in thirty minutes."

Felber waited, but Mrs. Rohr never called. After forty minutes, Felber telephoned her again.

"I couldn't get hold of [Cynthia's sister]. *What* do you want?"

The persistent detective wanted to pinpoint Mrs.

Rohr down to a day and time to meet. He wanted Cynthia's sister there, too. Could she agree to that?

"I don't know. I'm busy. She's busy. I don't know when."

"There's no time in the next few days, ma'am?" Felber expressed how important it was that they talk.

"I have a birthday party on Sunday. I'll call you Monday to set something up. I have to go now."

"Can you give me [Cynthia's sister's] number?"

"It's unlisted."

"I'm a police officer, ma'am. I'm investigating a homicide. It's OK to give me the number."

Mrs. Rohr spouted off a number. Felber would find out soon enough that she made it up on the spot. That Monday, Felber called Mrs. Rohr back and asked her again about setting up a meeting. Why was she being so evasive? Didn't she want to help the investigation move forward?

"Look, my attorney, Bob Meeker (Ed and Cynthia's lawyer), told me not to talk to you."

"Why, ma'am?" Felber was a bit peeved. He hadn't accused anyone of anything. He was only doing his job, looking into a homicide. The CAPU knew Cynthia George had connections to the victim.

"Well, Detective Felber, I have a heart condition. This is making me nervous."

What about Cynthia's sister? Felber wanted to know if Mrs. Rohr had spoken to her daughter on his behalf.

"Mr. Meeker is also her attorney and he told her not to talk to you. Now, sir, I have to go."

39

Cops know when witnesses are being elusive and cantankerous; when they are either scared to say the wrong thing, or hiding something important. It doesn't necessarily mean they have crucial knowledge of a crime or are guilty of anything; but red flags pop up and cops become hungrier than ever to find out what those witnesses are so desperate to conceal.

Vince Felber had worked at the Tangier before becoming a cop. He knew some of the people who had worked there. After talking to Red Stanick a second time in late July, Felber got a name from the former Tangier security guard, someone he knew who could possibly provide information. Red was a bit hesitant; he didn't want to be known as a snitch. But when Felber said he knew the guy, Red opened up and suggested the detective track him down and talk to him. He might know something.

The Diamond Deli, on South Main Street, in downtown Akron, over by Canal Park and the University of Akron, seemed like the perfect place to meet. It was always busy, full of college students focused on themselves, oblivious to what was going on around them. If the CI was frightened of someone in town seeing him with Felber, the Diamond Deli could help curb that anxiety.

Aaron Brown was a forty-five-year-old former employee of Ed George's who hadn't worked at the Tangier in two years. The guy appeared hard and weathered, a cigarette hanging from his mouth, squinted eyes, an air of mystery about him. Since leaving the Tangier, Brown had been hired by a local brewing company as a sales associate and had been doing pretty well for himself. His major concern was that he and Ed were still friends. They had spoken a few days ago, but, Brown said, "there wasn't any mention of Jeff Zack's murder, nor has there ever been."

Ed George had always treated Brown as a friend, and Brown believed that if he ever asked Ed for anything, he would oblige without question.

A waitress brought Felber and Brown coffee. They were quiet until she walked away.

Felber asked Brown about Jeff Zack specifically: his comings and goings around the Tangier, how he acted inside the restaurant and bar. "Jeff would come in a lot during some time periods and then stop for a while," Brown said. "He was friends with Ed and Cindy. Jeff and Ed would sit down and talk like they were friends, sometimes in Ed's office. Jeff and Cindy were also friends, but I never had any reason to believe they were having an affair. I don't think they were."

If Ed George seemed like the CAPU's prime suspect on paper, the alternative question was: what would stop Ed from killing Jeff Zack? If there were reasons why he could have killed Jeff Zack, there were reasons why he wouldn't.

"I never heard Ed say anything bad about Jeff," Brown claimed. "I don't think he had anything to do with his murder."

"What makes you say that?" asked Felber.

"He had too much to lose."

That made sense. Would Ed George, sitting on millions of dollars in real estate and a successful restaurant, bar and cabaret, which had been in the family for decades, risk losing it all for a guy like Jeff Zack? It was the only broken spoke in the wheel.

Brown went on to say that, as far as he knew, everyone that hung around the Tangier was "on the straight and narrow. . . . There aren't any 'shady' characters that are regulars at the Tangier."

Detective Felber asked Brown a series of questions about Ed George's brothers and the various businesses the family was involved in. As Felber got deeper into Ed George's life, he noticed Brown had become more nervous and fidgety. He had a tough time maintaining eye contact with the detective. Not to mention the inflection in his voice became wary, almost reticent. His body language, Felber wrote later in his report of the clandestine meeting, was strange: he looked around the restaurant at times, searching the place for a familiar face maybe, moving and shifting in his chair. This worried Felber. He felt Brown was holding back. "His answers to my questions seemed guarded, short," said Felber's report. "He didn't divulge much that I didn't specifically ask about."

Moreover, when Felber asked, Brown agreed to talk to "other detectives" working on the case, but said he would only do it if Felber was present.

Near the end of the conversation, Felber brought up the fact that Brown's girlfriend was at the scene of Jeff

Zack's murder; there at BJ's that Saturday afternoon. Was it a coincidence? Felber wanted to know how Brown had heard about Jeff's death. Brown had mentioned earlier in the conversation that he read about it in the newspaper. Did he want to rethink that answer?

"She was out getting something to eat, or visiting her mother," Brown answered, keeping his remarks brief. "I . . . I . . . was shocked when she told me about the murder."

But Felber was curious—Brown had said he first read about the murder in the newspaper. Which was it? Hadn't his girlfriend, witnessing such a spectacle, mentioned it to him that day when they later saw each other?

"Well," said Brown, again acting jumpy, "she did tell me about it, but we didn't realize it was Jeff Zack until we saw his name in the newspaper. We'd been having problems," Brown added, "and Jeff Zack's murder didn't help."

40

Near the end of July, several CAPU detectives set out to canvass the Temple Trail neighborhood, where Jeff, Bonnie and Ashton lived. Ed Moriarty and Lieutenant Dave Whiddon had their suspicions about Ed George, and were still following the baby Zack lead. But they insisted on digging deeper. Don't ever stop, they maintained. After all, no shooter had been found, nor had the CAPU connected a Ninja motorcycle to Ed George or anyone else. In fact, that motorcycle was still out there. It was going be a major part of any prosecutorial case later on—it needed to be found. Maybe looking in the garages of Jeff Zack's neighbors might turn up something.

The most interesting story detectives found while canvassing the neighborhood turned out to be about the victim himself. Felber spoke to a former neighbor of Jeff Zack's, a rather good-looking thirty-six-year-old woman who had lived in the neighborhood for quite a while. She liked to sunbathe poolside, in the privacy of her backyard. On occasion, Jeff would wander across the street and stare at her. Several times, he had even walked into her yard to "make comments," she said. The woman's husband, fed up with Jeff's behavior, waited one afternoon and confronted him. When that didn't work, the husband squirted Jeff in the face with a hose. When that did little to stop him, the guy grabbed Jeff by the shirt and scuffled with him.

Finally the husband called a neighborhood meeting about Jeff. He had gotten hold of several police reports about Jeff's felonious behavior and distributed copies to everyone. One guy later said that his daughter used to babysit for the Zacks—that is, until Jeff greeted the girl one day at the door in a towel.

"I didn't know Jeff Zack's son or wife," the woman told Felber. "But I did hear her yell occasionally. One time, I recall hearing her scream, 'I'm not going to let you hurt me anymore.' But I never saw any physical abuse."

Several neighbors had interesting stories to add to Jeff's diminishing character profile, but the CAPU felt no one in the neighborhood would have gone so far as to murder Jeff Zack.

The following day, another neighbor confirmed what the CAPU had heard from someone else: Jeff Zack had stopped at a yard sale on the Saturday morning of his murder before heading straight to BJ's. On top of that, another neighbor complained of Jeff walking into her yard during the summer months to gawk at her while she sunbathed. Her husband had also squirted Jeff with a hose.

On the last day of July, Detective Felber telephoned Tangier banquet manager *Barbara Smith*, who had been a loyal Ed George employee for sixteen years. The forty-one-year-old was a hard worker, often spending ten to twelve hours per shift at the restaurant. Barbara knew Jeff Zack, she said, but only because she saw him regularly at the restaurant. They would say hello to each other on occasion, but that was the extent of the relationship. Still, she knew Jeff's voice because he had called the bar and restaurant so many times throughout the years. He'd never asked for Ed, she said; it was always Cynthia. And if Cynthia wasn't there, he'd make a point to say he'd call her on her cell phone. Cynthia had spent a considerable amount of time at the restaurant, Barbara added, making no secret of her leadership role in remodeling the place, but that ended abruptly about a month before Jeff's murder. Watercooler talk was that Cynthia had spent too much of Ed's money and was told to stay out.

The affair between Jeff and Cynthia, Barbara claimed, was no secret around the restaurant. It wasn't openly discussed, but "everyone knew about it." Barbara also had a story about Aaron Brown, relaying to Felber that Brown had been seen around the restaurant talking to Ed since Jeff's murder. However, she believed his visit was more for sales than anything else. At one time, Brown was being groomed to be Ed's replacement after his retirement, until he was fired one day when Ed brought in another protégé. This riled Brown, who felt torn over it.

Other than tying up a few loose ends, Barbara offered few new details. There was a time when Cynthia, she said, used to drop the kids off at the restaurant and take off for the day, leaving them with Ed. But that changed over the past few months.

Felber wondered why.

"They hired nannies."

Barbara gave Felber the names of two women specifically.

There was one more thing, she added, before Felber thanked her and cut her loose.

"I know that Ed changed the family's phone number a few months ago, I just don't know why."

Many people changed their telephone number. What was so important about Ed doing it?

Barbara felt it was odd because Ed hadn't told anyone at the restaurant. Shouldn't Ed's employees have the telephone number?

41

Lieutenant Dave Whiddon was sitting at his desk on August 15, around 2:30 P.M., when Bonnie's father, Bob Boucher, called. The man was frantic and out of breath. He seemed overly excited about something pertinent to the investigation into his son-in-law's murder.

"What is it?" Whiddon asked.

"I got a call from an old friend who gave me some information about who is responsible for Jeff's murder. It confirmed my suspicions."

Whiddon went through his mental Rolodex: *Suspicions?* There were several people from Jeff's side of the family who had theories. Carl and Seth were still suspects. Ed George was on the top of the family's list.

Whiddon told Mr. Boucher to slow down and relax. Take his time.

"I need to see a detective *right* now," the senior Boucher insisted. "I do *not* want to discuss this over the telephone."

Whiddon checked his watch. "I can meet you at about four-thirty."

"Hurry."

Walking into Mr. Boucher's apartment at 4:20 P.M.,

Whiddon asked the seventy-year-old about the telephone call. What was so darn important that he couldn't talk about it over the telephone? "Sit down," Mr. Boucher said.

They sat in the living room.

"I have a good friend who used to date Bonnie," the senior Boucher began. "He called me. He said he was talking to a woman. . . . She said she knew Jeff." As Bonnie's father spoke, Whiddon considered how unpredictable third-party information was—this woman had spoken to Bob Boucher's friend, who then relayed the information to Mr. Boucher. It had to be taken with complete skepticism, yet it could possibly lead to something important.

Listen to it. Check it out. Move on.

Whiddon was an experienced investigator, however; he knew one conversation could lead to another, and perhaps Mr. Boucher, without realizing it, had credible information to share.

The woman had a close friend who worked at the Tangier. That friend, Whiddon learned, had supposedly overheard a conversation between Ed George and someone else. Apparently, Ed had mentioned learning of the affair between Cynthia and Jeff and vowed to "take care of it."

Groundbreaking, no. Informative, maybe. Since he had Mr. Boucher's attention, Whiddon asked him what else he could share about the affair. Had he himself known about it, too?

"For the past five or six years," Boucher admitted. "It wasn't hard to figure out. Whenever Cindy called Jeff at home, he would stop whatever he was doing and jump up to the phone. Jeff and Cindy went bike riding together."

More of the same. The CAPU had indisputable proof that Jeff Zack and Cynthia George were an item. Hell, they had DNA evidence that Jeff had fathered one of Cyn-

thia's children. But what else was there? None of it
pointed to murder.

Bonnie knew about the relationship, too, her father explained. But she wanted to work on the marriage and
had put up with the affair because, being divorced once
already, she wanted to provide a stable environment for
Ashton. "I had contacted a police officer friend in Arizona when Bonnie first met Jeff," Mr. Boucher told
Whiddon. "He told me, after checking Jeff out, to tell
Bonnie to 'pass this one up.' But Bonnie wouldn't listen."

Perhaps without realizing it, Mr. Boucher was setting
in place a motive for his daughter to kill her husband
by providing Whiddon with a reason. During their conversation, Whiddon asked Bonnie's dad if he had ever
spoken to Bonnie about Jeff's relationship with Cynthia. To that, Mr. Boucher said, "Bonnie told me once
that one time when she and Jeff were arguing about
the affair, Jeff screamed at her, 'You know Cindy's
youngest daughter is mine.' But after the argument
ended, Jeff told her he was only kidding."

Jeff's father-in-law placed Cynthia at Jeff's house on
several occasions, which was something the CAPU
hadn't heard. Then he gave Whiddon a breakdown of
the George family businesses, adding that they were
"connected" and could easily "get things done."

"Jeff would not give Cindy up," Mr. Boucher said,
"even when Ed found out about the relationship."
Then, "It's odd to me that after Jeff's death, Bonnie received over forty sympathy cards, but none were from
the Georges and they never called."

To say the least, Whiddon left the elder Boucher's
home confused. He didn't know what to think of the
new information.

42

Ed Moriarty and Dave Whiddon felt they needed to clarify several pieces of information with Bonnie Zack. By August 21, enough time had elapsed where they could sit down with Bonnie and hash it all out. Although they considered Bonnie a suspect, they weren't too sold on the idea that she was behind her husband's murder. Bonnie Zack had been the "other woman" for ten years. She knew darn well her husband had fathered his mistress's child—she didn't need a DNA test to prove it. Still, could she have managed to finance and stage what was a perfect murder plot?

Moriarty and Whiddon didn't think so, but they had to consider the possibility. Moriarty had built a comfortable rapport with Bonnie over the course of the summer. He believed she was at ease with him asking tough questions. So he began the latest interview by asking Bonnie if she knew what people Jeff was involved with during some of the "troubles" with law enforcement he'd had back in Arizona. Could she give them any names?

Bonnie mentioned a man's name. Then, "Jeff told

me that [this guy] and his girlfriend ran [a prostitution] operation. All Jeff did was drive them around. He claimed he got caught in the wrong place at the wrong time."

During the conversation, Bonnie would stop and think about her answers, then continue. "Well," she said at one point, talking about the Arizona case, "I think Jeff went to the police when he knew there was going to be trouble." She paused, shaking her head. "I'm not sure if Jeff was telling me the truth, or just what I wanted to hear."

For the next half hour, they discussed the prospect that Jeff's death could have been the result of any number of the problems Jeff had gotten himself into with the brokerage company in San Diego that he had worked for, or a credit card company that he had tried to start in 1999. Cynthia had even worked for Jeff, Bonnie said, in the office of the credit card company, but the business never took off. Bonnie said a few disgruntled clients had called the house from time to time, but none of the calls were threatening in nature. Jeff had burned some people.

The reason Jeff and Bonnie had moved to Ohio, Bonnie explained, was because her mother had gotten sick. When they first arrived in town, Bonnie said, they rented a house. Jeff was able to find a "good job." Bonnie thought "everything was fine." They were beginning their lives together, but Jeff always wanted more. "He complained a lot and was having a hard time adjusting." San Diego and Akron were two different worlds then. Jeff lived for the fast lane, on the edge. Ohio was boring to him. That was why, when he and Bonnie started hanging out at the Tangier, Jeff felt like he was back in his element.

When Jeff and Cynthia met, Ed and Cynthia were in the process of building the enormous mansion they had lived in ever since. While the house was being constructed, Bonnie and Jeff had gone out there on several occasions, checking the progress. By then, Jeff and Cynthia had become "friends." Each time Jeff brought Bonnie out to the mansion, she said, Cynthia was there. She never thought anything of it then. But, of course, now it made sense. "She was, like, the contractor . . . ," Bonnie said. It seemed like building the house was Cynthia's full-time job.

Many times, however, Jeff took off to the house by himself to "help Cindy" with various jobs. "When the Georges' house was completed," Bonnie added, "Jeff moved them in."

Moriarty brought up Ed and Cynthia's children. Bonnie admitted Jeff had said angrily one day that Ruby was his, but pulled back from it afterward, adding, "I just wanted to see what your reaction would be."

"You ever confront Cindy," Moriarty asked, "about she and Jeff?" It was a fair question. Had Bonnie simply placated them, acted naïve about the relationship and played the happy wife role, as if nothing were going on? Or had she just accepted the strange fact that she had to share her husband with another woman if she wanted to keep him?

"Yes, once."

"When was that?"

"It was after I found a pair of her panties hidden in Jeff's dresser. Cindy was in Florida," Bonnie said, obviously distressed over having to recall the memory, "and she called Jeff. I had Jeff's cell phone with me and answered the call." Realizing who it was, Bonnie said, "I found something."

Cynthia answered, "Huh?"

Bonnie didn't tell her what she found.

"Bonnie," Cynthia said, "you don't know how much I am helping Jeffrey."

Moriarty wanted to know if Cynthia had said anything else during that confrontation over the telephone. This was pivotal. What Cynthia said could explain a lot.

Bonnie didn't answer. She shook her head, as if to suggest no.

Jeff had gone to Bonnie one day in 1998 and asked her if she wanted to have lunch with him and Cynthia so they could "work this out." Bonnie was offended, as any wife might be, and flat-out refused. What was there to work out?

A month before Jeff's murder, Bonnie said, he told her the relationship with Cynthia was over—but she had been under the impression that Jeff had ended it two years before. As she began going back, remembering that conversation, Moriarty noticed that Bonnie "started to digress, almost talking to herself about why Jeff told her it was over." It was strange, Moriarty said later. "She acted odd, but I knew her well enough by then to know that it was just in her nature to act this way when talking about Jeff."

As Bonnie drifted away in thought, Whiddon and Moriarty realized it was time to conclude the interview. "Thanks for everything, Bonnie," Moriarty said. "We appreciate all the help you've been. If we have anything else, we'll be in touch, OK?"

Bonnie nodded and saw the two investigators out the door.

As Moriarty and Whiddon drove back to the station house, Moriarty looked at his understudy and said, "It's time."

"I know," Whiddon agreed. "We'll get on it right away."

PART TWO

43

If the 1960s were a time of great social change and political unrest, the 1970s ushered in an era in American pop culture that seemed to curb any collected anxiety that had accumulated up until then. Optimism ruled. As did bell-bottoms, love and peace. Investigative reporters Carl Bernstein and Bob Woodward blew the roof off political corruption, exposing the Watergate break-in, proving how inadequate our elected public officials could be with power at their fingertips. The smiley face emerged. So did Rubik's Cube, the mood ring, the lava lamp and platform shoes. It was a time when you could "clap on" and "clap off" your lights; when families piled into station wagons and RVs and argued their way across country. In Manhattan, Studio 54 fueled the rise of disco. John Travolta tore up the screen in *Saturday Night Fever,* heightening the popularity of sexual promiscuity, the blow-dryer and snorting cocaine into the wee hours of the morning. America had changed. She had emerged from war, protest, cynicism and the psychedelic era a more edgy, open, free republic.

By the late 1970s, Akron, Ohio, had grown into a city of 275,000, with public housing and contemporary office-space infrastructure rising on just about every major street corner. This population figure was down from the 1960s, when Akron's populace hit its peak at three hundred thousand. Crime had always been a problem, of course, same as it was in any major American city. But Akron saw an unusually large number of methamphetamine labs pop up amid downtown and its surrounding suburbs; and cops knew that where that type of homemade drug exsisted, death was not too far behind.

According to sources of mine who knew Ed George personally, Ed was never an outgoing, "let's watch the sunrise type" of barhopper or partier. Just because he grew up in that generation, and had spent his life (since he was fifteen years old) in a restaurant and bar, it didn't mean he had to conform to the shameful habits of its patrons. Ed was a working man. His father had opened the Tangier in 1948, and built the operation into an Akron staple for entertainment and authentic Mediterranean cuisine. The décor of the place allowed patrons to feel as if they'd walked onto the set of a period film. Yul Brynner or *Ben-Hur* came to mind upon entry. People loved the authenticity and feel of the place. It was different from anything else in Akron. Ed learned from his father rather quickly that there was no substitution for hard work—and the restaurant-going public benefited from the Georges' hard-nosed European work ethic.

In 1976, the elder George passed away. Ed, then thirty-six years old, having gone to one of Akron's most elite private schools, St. Vincent, and then to Michigan State and John Carroll University (studying what else,

business administration), took total control of the
Tangier's day-to-day operations, and continued to turn
his father's vision into his own dream. Two years after
he took the reins, with business booming, Ed was walking one night from the kitchen to the bar when he was
stopped dead in his tracks by the sight of a gorgeous
blonde tearing up the dance floor. There she was:
showy, thin, attractive, radiant. People were obviously
drawn to her; she controlled the room. Without her, it
would have been just another night at the Tangier, but
Cynthia brought a brilliance to the place and turned
the night into something more festive and flamboyant.
She was twenty-three then, full of life, working for an
airline, ready to take on Akron.

Ed and Cynthia talked. And quickly hit it off. Ed fell
in love. Soon Cynthia was a fixture inside the restaurant. People were shocked. Ed had lived a solitary life
of work for so long, he seemed destined to die alone
(probably inside the restaurant). He had been a bachelor and proud of it. But Cynthia had managed to work
her way into that world and change his mind.

During the late 1970s and early 1980s, the Tangier
took off. Ed was a smart—though sometimes crude—
businessman, and people respected him. By 1984, Ed
and Cynthia, dating now for nearly six years, decided
to make it official.

At St. Joseph Catholic Church, near Cynthia's home-
town in Canton, the happy couple exchanged vows in
front of not only five hundred friends and relatives, but
a sixty-piece choir, which included Cynthia's mother,
Helen Rohr, belting out a reported two solos during
the ceremony.

An Akron power couple was born.

With a wedding ceremony of such immense size, it

seemed only fitting that the reception following the
service should be fit for a king and queen. Always
thinking business, Ed and Cynthia decided to marry
on a Monday so the reception wouldn't affect any
weekend business at the Tangier. They departed the
church, according to some who were on hand for the
ceremony and published reports, in a limousine
dressed with tin cans dangling from the bumper; from
there, the fairy tale continued as they sat in a horse-
drawn white carriage, pulled by a white horse.

In 1988, in one of the many articles written about Ed
and the Tangier, the *Akron Beacon Journal* asked Ed about
his life, noting that he and Cynthia, who had lived in a
condominium since tying the knot, built a large farm on
a 126-acre lot of farmland Ed owned. "I don't know what
the hell is going on," Ed told *Beacon Journal* reporter Abe
Zaidan. "My wife says she needed room to breathe.
We're going to have a lot of room to breathe now." Later
in that same article, Ed added, "I used to be a male chau-
vinist. Now I have three women (a wife and two daughters) at home, and whatever they tell me to do, that's
what I do. I married a woman that doesn't let you get
away with anything. I change diapers and dress the kids.
Sometimes I make mistakes and put their clothes on
backward or inside out. But I'm learning . . . I'm now
doing all of the things that I used to criticize other
people for doing."

Ed embodied the change; he loved being a father
and husband. He and Cynthia had the perfect life:
healthy kids, booming business, big house and more
money than they needed.

But business slowed into the 1990s and Ed felt the
restaurant needed a major makeover. By 2000, he was
in the middle of a reported $750,000 reconstruction

project, which Cynthia was overseeing on just about every level. "We're going to go back to the past," Ed told *Akron Beacon Journal*'s business writer Shana Yates at the time, "to remind people of how we were and how important we are to the community."

As time moved forward, and Cynthia George continued to give birth to Ed's growing little army of children, she was obviously unhappy on some level. Several friends and former Tangier employees later said that Cynthia was always flirting with men and being overly friendly, which, many assumed, led to several affairs throughout the years. Cynthia never seemed content. She always wanted more. Maybe even thought she deserved it.

Maybe because he was so busy trying to save a sinking ship, or focusing any free time he had on raising a large family and keeping his material wife happy, Ed either knew about Cynthia's affairs and looked the other way, or was simply blinded by, as Cynthia later said in court documents, his "workaholic" ways.

In either case, the CAPU had many questions for Ed that attorney Bob Meeker was keeping him from answering. Ed Moriarty would pop into the Tangier from time to time and corner Ed, but he knew what to say. Moriarty felt Ed wanted to talk—like he had something he was always ready to spill—but he could never get him to open up.

44

On September 6, Detective Russ McFarland and a colleague flew down to Florida to interview Seth. Carl had been scratched off the CAPU's list of suspects. He had an alibi and had done fairly well on a polygraph. If Seth wasn't willing to take a polygraph himself, there was going to be a problem. The ongoing dispute Seth had with Jeff Zack at the time of Jeff's murder was enough for the CAPU to drag the contractor in.

Much to McFarland's surprise, Seth was "cooperative" and eagerly agreed to take a polygraph, signing a release the moment it was placed in front of him. According to Seth, Jeff's family and others had the story all wrong. Indeed, he and Jeff had been involved in a bad business deal regarding some work on Jeff's house Seth had proposed, but they had dealt with it, up until the end, fairly civilly. Their talks had never gotten heated or personal—that is, Seth said, "until Jeff called me on."

"What happened?" asked McFarland.

"Jeff made a remark about my wife. He said, 'I f---ed her in the ass.'"

"Leave my family out of it," Seth shot back, seething, "you motherless f---."

Jeff had never taken an insult himself without responding. That much the CAPU knew.

"I know people," Jeff said next, according to Seth, "that can slit your throat."

"I became enraged," Seth explained to McFarland. "I told him, 'Don't you ever threaten me, because you may be looking over your back the rest of your life.'"

McFarland took out the tape of the threatening voice mail Jeff had received shortly before he was murdered. "I want you to listen to this," he told Seth.

"Play it."

"Was that you?" McFarland asked after they listened to the tape.

"No. It's not me, and I have no idea who it is. I had *nothing* to do with Jeff Zack's murder. Nothing whatsoever."

During his polygraph, Seth was asked, "Do you know for sure who killed Jeff Zack? Did you conspire with anyone to kill Jeff Zack? Do you know for sure why Jeff Zack was killed? On June 13, 2001, did you make the telephone call to Jeff Zack that we just played for you?"

Seth answered no to the four questions. Polygraphist Sean Methany, who had made the trip with McFarland, later calculated that "based on analysis of the polygrams generated by [Seth], it is my opinion that physiological change indicative of truthfulness occurred on all four relevant questions."

"I spoke with [Seth] twice on the telephone before going to Florida," McFarland said later. "He admitted to having heated exchanges with Jeff Zack and even admitted to threatening to kill him. He also said Zack threatened to kill him. But he adamantly denied acting

on his threat. When Methany gave [Seth] his polygraph, he passed on all questions. He was then eliminated as a suspect."

On the morning of September 11, 2001, McFarland
and Methany packed their bags, left Sarasota and traveled to Fort Myers, where McFarland had some unfin-
ished business regarding another homicide. It had been
a productive trip; Seth could be scratched off the
CAPU's short list of suspects. At least for the time being.

When McFarland and Methany left Fort Myers and
started traveling on I-75 north, heading toward the airport in Tampa, passing through Sarasota, news that a
plane had hit one of the Twin Towers in New York City
came over the radio and startled them. "Our first impression was that it was a small plane. A short time later,
news came over the radio that a second plane hit the
other Tower. Then things became clearer."

As they continued toward the airport, *Marine One*
flew overhead at a high rate of speed. By the time they
reached the outskirts of Tampa, news that all of the air-
ports in the country were closing came over the radio.
Within a few minutes, they learned that the worst ter-
rorist attack on American soil had just taken place.
There was no way they could fly out of Florida, back to
Ohio. "We turned in our rental car," McFarland recalled, "and had to walk two blocks to another rental
agency that did out-of-state, point-to-point rentals. We
got the last rental car out of Tampa. We had to settle
for what was available, so we rode to Pittsburgh in a
Lincoln Town Car. We picked up a [CAPU] car there
and drove back to Akron."

45

Back in Ohio, as McFarland and Methany headed home in a rental car, the morning of September 11 began in a panic. But not for the events unfolding in New York, Washington and Pennsylvania—or because of something having gone wrong in the Jeff Zack investigation.

Dave Whiddon and other members of the CAPU were preparing to serve a search warrant on a house where the CAPU believed a career criminal named Daniel Laniesky, who had gone by the alias of Daniel Hopkins, lived. The CAPU had been investigating a home invasion in which two suspects broke into a home in one of Akron's more affluent neighborhoods and tied up the owners. Over the past few weeks, Whiddon and his team had tracked credit cards stolen from the couple and found out they were being used at a Super Kmart in Montrose, just outside of Akron. Whiddon had gotten his hands on video surveillance from the store and saw Laniesky and another guy going through the store on a shopping spree. While this information was coming in, the CAPU found out Laniesky had several federal warrants already out for his arrest. On the morning of September 11, Whiddon got a search warrant for a house where he believed both suspects were holed up. So he assembled a SWAT team. But during a briefing that morning about the case, someone walked into the room and interrupted, saying terrorists had attacked New York. "We canceled the warrant," Whiddon said later, "because everyone was now watching CNN. The mayor also called and wanted all available personnel on the street."

In the meantime, a call came in about a shooting—the CAPU had another homicide on their hands. Whiddon sent most of his detectives to the shooting.

When "things," as Whiddon later put it, quieted down toward the afternoon, the detective working the home invasion case wondered if it was a good time to serve the search warrant. "We hit the house, but Laniesky and [his partner]," Whiddon recalled, "were not there. We did find out from one of their girlfriends that they were at the Red Roof in Montrose."

And that's where the situation took a frantic turn.

Whiddon and Ed Moriarty drove out to the hotel and met with the SWAT commanders (one of whom was Terry Hudnall, who had also become part of the Jeff Zack investigation) in the parking lot of the Cracker Barrel Restaurant, located in back of the Red Roof Inn.

For the next four to five hours, there was a standoff between law enforcement and Laniesky, who had barricaded himself in his room and, speaking by phone with a negotiator, said he wasn't coming out alive.

For Whiddon, the day had been a series of traumatic events. He remembered the day well because September 11 is also his birthday. His wife, on that day, had called him repeatedly to wish him a happy birthday. Whiddon's kids had baked him a cake. His wife wanted to know when he was going to be home to blow out the candles and open presents. Regardless of what had happened in New York, Whiddon and his wife—God bless them—wanted their children to have as normal a day as possible.

After hours of negotiations going nowhere, a decision was made to flush the guy out of his room with tear gas. Whiddon was standing next to a detective when he heard the explosion of the gas go through the window. "We ran out of the lobby, and just as I was coming around the corner, Laniesky came out. . . ."

Outside the hotel now, Laniesky had an arsenal of firepower and started to unleash a barrage of bullets on anything in his way.

Within seconds, however, the SWAT team responded and, returning fire, dropped Laniesky with several rounds to his head and chest.

As that happened, Whiddon's cell phone rang.

"Yeah," he said excitedly, out of breath.

"When are you coming home?" his wife wanted to know.

"Not for a while."

In the volley of bullets going back and forth, Terry Hudnall got shot in the foot.

Finally, around three o'clock the next morning, Whiddon walked through the door of his home. Sitting on the couch with his wife, just trying to catch his breath and take in all that had happened, he realized he hadn't eaten anything all day long. So he shoved down a piece of birthday cake and called it a day. "[My wife and I] just sat there talking in disbelief about all that went on that day," Whiddon recalled, "both in New York and Akron. September 11, 2001, was the longest day of my police career—but absolutely nothing compared to what the NYPD and NYFD had gone through."

46

When the CAPU contacted Bonnie Zack after the dust of September 11 cleared, and life had gotten back to as normal as it would ever be, she agreed to take a polygraph. Bonnie wanted to clear her name and help the CAPU keep its focus on, she and many of her family members were certain, Jeff's real killer, Ed George. Anything she could do to further facilitate the investigation, she assured Ed Moriarty, she'd be happy to help. Strap that armband on, set those dials, start asking questions.

"I'm ready."

Overall, "I'm pretty upset," Bonnie told polygraph examiner Sean Methany, over "my husband's death." It hadn't been as easy as people might have thought. Despite Jeff's infidelity and loathsome behavior, she had loved the man. Bonnie explained that she tried keeping herself busy around the house, hoping to lessen the pain, but some days were harder than others. The day before the polygraph, she explained, she had spent building a rock garden in her yard. She was exhausted.

Before the test started, Bonnie was questioned about her potential role in Jeff's murder, but she "denied any

The Akron, Ohio, BJ's Wholesale Club fuel station where
44-year-old Jeff Zack was murdered on June 16, 2001.

44-year-old Jeff Zack.
(Courtesy of Elayne Zack)

Retired Detective Sergeant Ed Moriarty, a seasoned cop
who initiated the investigation into the Jeff Zack homicide.
(Courtesy of Heather White)

Jeff and Bonnie Zack.
(Courtesy of Elayne Zack)

Jeff and Bonnie Zack, along with their teenage son, lived in this Stow, Ohio, home, just outside Akron.

This grainy surveillance video tape image shows Jeff Zack's killer *(arrow pointing to motorcycle)* leaving BJ's after perfectly placing one fatal shot in the back of Zack's head. *(Courtesy of the Akron Police Department)*

This view of the concrete wall near BJ's fuel station shows where the bullet exiting Jeff Zack's head hit the wall and fell to the ground.

Several witnesses described this "Ninja-style" motorcycle leaving the scene of BJ's at high speed. *(Courtesy of the Akron Police Department)*

Ed and Cynthia George lived in this multimillion-dollar, 8,100-square-foot estate just outside Akron.

A second view of the Georges' mansion shows how secluded Cynthia George's life had become.

The Tangier restaurant/banquet hall/nightclub, where Jeff Zack met Cynthia George, has been in the George family for over five decades.

Attached to the banquet hall is the popular bistro restaurant, which is routinely under renovation.

Cynthia George and her seven children were devout members of
St. Vincent Church, the oldest Catholic church in Akron, a few
blocks north of the Tangier on Market Street.

As the investigation focused on Cynthia George, Akron Police Department (A.P.D.) Detective Dave Whiddon, the department's youngest lieutenant, took over for a retiring Ed Moriarty.

The Harold K. Stubbs Justice Center, in downtown Akron, where the A.P.D. is located.

The A.P.D.'s Crimes Against Persons Unit is located on the sixth floor of the Harold K. Stubbs Justice Center.

A.P.D. Detective Russ McFarland.

A.P.D. Detective
Terry Hudnall.

A.P.D. Detective
Mike Shaeffer.

For four years, Summit County
Chief Assistant Prosecutor Mike
Carroll determinedly pursued
justice for Jeff Zack's murder.

When Christine Todaro, pictured with her son, Tony, came forward and agreed to record conversations with her ex-husband, the investigation into Jeff Zack's murder turned up a surprising new suspect.

Christine Todaro's ex-husband, John Zaffino, became the A.P.D.'s main focus as Christine risked her life to expose Jeff Zack's true killer. *(Courtesy of Christine Todaro)*

John Zaffino. *(Courtesy of the Akron Police Department)*

John Zaffino moved out of this apartment complex shortly before
Jeff Zack was murdered.

DRIVER'S LICENSE #	STATE	VEHICLE MAKE / MODEL	YEAR	VEHICLE LICENSE #

CHECKING ACCT. NO. _____ BRANCH _____ SAVINGS ACCT. NO. _____ BRANCH _____

EMERGENCY CONTACT NAME	RELATIONSHIP	PHONE
CINDY ROHR	FRIEND	
ADDRESS	CITY	STATE	ZIP
MA	MEDINA	OH.	N/A

dditional sources of income? If yes, explain: _____ NO

ave you ever been sued, evicted, wages garnished, or filed for bankruptcy? If yes, explain: BANKRUPTCY

Applicant authorizes the Landlord or its representatives to use the services of a credit reporting agency and to contact any of the above named ferences, employers, and landlords to obtain credit history and other background information on the applicant and to use such information in deciding whether not to accept or reject this application. Information requested on this form is for credit purposes only and will be held in strict confidence.
Applicant acknowledges that this application is a contractual agreement to rent the above-stated suite from Landlord. Applicant agrees as follows: If proved by Landlord, the applicant will be required to sign a lease and take occupancy of the suite for the period of time indicated on this application. plicant's deposit will be applied as shown above and shall not bear interest. If applicant does not sign a lease and take occupancy of the suite, the full deposit l be retained by the Landlord as liquidated damages suffered by reason of applicant's refusal to abide by this Agreement. Applicant may cancel this eement by the end of the first business day following the date of application. If Landlord rejects this application, or if applicant cancels this agreement within specified time, that portion of the deposit applied towards the rent security deposit will be returned to applicant within thirty (30) days of the application date; wever, that portion applied as an administrative fee, in the sum of twenty-five and 00/100 dollars ($25.00), shall be non-refundable and shall be used by ndlord to cover (a) verification of residency, (b) verification of employment, (c) credit checks, and (d) other administrative expenses.
ALL APPLICANTS ARE SUBJECT TO THE OWNER'S APPROVAL. IT IS THE POLICY OF THE LANDLORD TO ACCEPT, PROCESS, AND LECT APPLICATIONS WITHOUT REGARD TO RACE, COLOR, SEX, RELIGION, HANDICAP, FAMILIAL STATUS, OR NATURAL ORIGIN.

Applicant agrees to transfer both electric and gas services into their name no later than the initial date of occupancy. Additionally, Applicant agrees t they will be responsible for water/sewage as billed to them by the Landlord.

r ' of Applicant _____ Date: 8-5-00

ndlord Signature _____ Date: 8/5/00

PLICATION APPROVED ☐ ____ APPLICATION DECLINED ☐ ____ APPLICATION CANCELLED ☐

On Zaffino's rental agreement, he clearly links himself to Cynthia
George by naming her as an "emergency contact."
(Courtesy of the Akron Police Department)

The A.P.D. believes John Zaffino and Cynthia George wanted to kill Jeff Zack on this bicycle path in Cuyahoga Falls, Ohio—but Zack failed to show up for the meeting.

This is the same bicycle path where Jeff Zack and Cynthia George used to meet and ride bicycles together; a loaded handgun was later found across the street from this parking lot.

John Zaffino was finally arrested for the murder of Jeff Zack more than a year after he committed the crime. *(Courtesy of the Akron Police Department)*

A year after John Zaffino was convicted, former Mrs. Ohio America third runner-up Cynthia George was arrested in connection with the homicide of Jeff Zack. *(Courtesy of the Akron Police Department)*

Oddly enough, after Cynthia George was convicted in late 2005, she smiled for this booking photograph.
(Courtesy of the Akron Police Department)

JEFF ZACK
BELOVED SON, FATHER, AND HUSBAND
JANUARY 20, 1957
JUNE 16, 2001

Jeff Zack is buried in this traditional Jewish cemetery outside Stow, Ohio.

involvement," Methany wrote in his report, "in the death of her husband . . . [adding that she] strongly believed Ed George was behind her husband's murder because of a long-term affair Jeff was having with Ed George's wife, Cindy." After that, Bonnie said, "Jeff told me that he fathered Cindy's youngest child, [Ruby]. My son, [Ashton], told me that Jeff told him that 'if anything ever happened to him, tell the police to go after Ed George.'"

Whiddon and Moriarty questioned Bonnie during the polygraph. She felt most comfortable with them.

"Do you know for sure why Jeff Zack was killed?"

"No."

"Do you know for sure who killed Jeff Zack?"

"No."

"Take it easy, Bonnie," Moriarty suggested at one point. She was yawning and moving around. She seemed entirely uncomfortable, agitated, tired. It wasn't the test, Moriarty knew, but more the idea of having to do it.

"Did you conspire with anyone to have Jeff Zack killed?"

"No."

After a careful review of the polygrams, Methany concluded, Bonnie's answers were "inconclusive." Yet Methany wrote the results off as being due to Bonnie's exhaustion on that day and suggested Moriarty and Whiddon wait awhile and polygraph her again.

Near the end of September, Bonnie showed up at the APD for a second test. She put her initials by the waiver she had signed previously while Whiddon reread Bonnie her Miranda rights. She seemed more relaxed than the previous time.

Bonnie answered the questions in the same manner.

When the test was over, Methany called Moriarty and
Whiddon into another room and went through the results. "It is my opinion," Methany said, "that there's deception on three of the four questions."

Whiddon and Moriarty were surprised. Moriarty
dropped his head. *Could this investigation get any more
puzzling?* Suppose Bonnie had had something to do
with Jeff's murder: where would they start? It didn't fit.
They had checked out her entire background thoroughly. Her family. Her bank accounts. Where would
she get the money? How could she have hired someone
without anyone else knowing about it? It was as if just
when their investigation was gathering steam again,
suspects being crossed off, new suspects being questioned, old theories quashed, here comes this anomaly.

Nevertheless, Moriarty and Whiddon headed into the
room where Bonnie was waiting. Beforehand, they had
decided to confront her with the allegations the lie detector suggested. There was more, however. Russ McFarland had just returned from interviewing an inmate at a
local jail, a lowlife who was making some pretty shocking
accusations against Jeff. Another deviation had been
thrown into the mix, seemingly making Bonnie appear
as though she had some things to hide. When Whiddon
and Moriarty finished talking to McFarland, they were
more determined than ever to get to the bottom of
Bonnie's possible involvement.

"You think she could have done it, Ed?" Whiddon
asked.

Moriarty shrugged. "Shit, I guess at this point anything's possible."

47

Jonas Little had known Jeff Zack for a few years. They had worked together for a temp agency. Jonas, who said he knew Bonnie well, was a forty-two-year-old hard-looking drifter, with salt-and-pepper hair, a scruffy mustache, bulgy eyes, pronounced chin and the wrinkly face of a guy who had done his share of time in the clinker. Right off, he admitted some of the rotten things he had done in the past. But Jeff Zack, he insisted, was no damn better.

Little claimed to have reached out to a cop friend after he heard Jeff had been murdered, and told him he believed Jeff was murdered by an "Iranian businessman" who worked at one of the malls where Jeff had several vending machines. McFarland, who picked Little up at the jail and drove him to the APD, was curious, of course, as to a motive. Why Iranians? How did *they* fit in? Little was claiming Jeff's vending machine business was a façade for something else—something entirely illegal.

"Its main purpose was a front for gunrunning," Little told the CAPU. "Jeff sold guns to [various people]."

Not one or two pistols he bought at a Wal-Mart or off

the street, Little insisted. But crates of automatic weapons. Jeff Zack, Little said, was a major gun trafficker in Akron.

If true, here was another layer of Jeff Zack's character the CAPU had no idea existed. Could the guy's past be any more complex?

Little was scared of talking to the CAPU, but, McFarland reported, he opened up mighty quick once he knew the stakes. Little said he had been with Jeff on several occasions when Jeff delivered the guns. "Whenever Jeff would make a [vending machine] delivery," Little told McFarland, "he would pull into a receiving area behind these stores. He would enter the rear of [one] store first. The back door was always unlocked." Little was shaky, speaking with a hurried distress, yet sounded sure of himself. "Once inside the back of the store, he would go down a long and narrow hallway to get into the business area of the store." He drew a map. Sketched out the entire area of the mall he said Jeff had routinely visited.

Right there was the door. He drew an X. There, that Dumpster, that's where Little said he saw the motorcycle parked.

Motorcycle?

Entering the mall from the back, Little said, allowed Jeff to go from store to store and deliver the guns to several customers he had in the same section of the mall.

McFarland was confused. How could a guy have walked through the back of a mall with all these guns and no one noticed?

"The longer weapons, such as rifles and AK-47s," said Little, "would be brought in green-and-black fiberglass cases. The handguns, such as 9 millimeters, .357s, and .44s—never anything smaller than a .38—would be brought . . . inside twelve-pack soda pop cartons."

At first, Little's details impressed McFarland. It made his story sound credible—however over the top it may have seemed. "Whenever Jeff dealt with the Iranians, he would speak with them in a foreign language, like Arabic. I never knew what they were talking about. The gun transactions were usually once every two weeks—but there were times when he made two deliveries in one week."

Little said he had been over to Jeff's house about fifteen times. He told McFarland exactly where Jeff stored most of his automatic weapons. "Under the steps to his basement and behind his furnace."

Gun-trafficking allegations obviously opened up a new door into the investigation. If Jeff was a gunrunner, there was a chance someone from that crowd could have put a hit out on him to silence him for some reason. Maybe Jeff had gotten into a jam he couldn't get out of? If, for example, Jeff mouthed off to one of those gun buyers, threatening to expose him, it wasn't hard to believe the guy paid for a hit.

Little said Jeff usually carried ten grand inside his SUV; he kept it in a gray plastic box. He remembered this precisely because he was shocked by the "carelessness" Jeff displayed by keeping so much money lying around his SUV.

McFarland wanted names and addresses, so Little gave him several, along with a few of the stores to which Jeff had sold guns. The Iranians, Little added, had asked Jeff at one time to "find men that would do arranged marriages for two Iranian girls in their twenties so they could get their green cards." Little said he offered himself up, but the Iranians took one look at him, laughed and shot him down, saying he was "too old, had a criminal record, and wasn't suitable."

At this point, Little began to shed tears. He was a

wreck, totally overwhelmed and ashamed of himself. But then he relayed a bit of information that seemed, well, too good to be true, fitting too perfectly into the context of the case. "In the receiving area [of that one store]," Little said, "where Jeff always parked when doing business . . . there was a motorcycle often parked next to the Dumpster."

"What kind of motorcycle?" McFarland asked.

"One of those crotch rocket types," Little insisted. "It was green, white and black in color. I'm certain of it. The rear end of the bike was black."

"Why do you think Jeff was murdered?"

"Blackmail. A white employee [at this one store] had gotten married during this time when Jeff was gunrunning and Jeff had gone to the wedding. A short time later, the guy's wife had a baby." Was Little saying Jeff Zack had fathered the child? McFarland was curious.

McFarland dropped Little back off at the jail and drove away shaking his head at this new twist in the case. It was incredible. If Jeff was dealing guns and going back to his old habits, anything was possible.

McFarland, along with a colleague, set out to check into the information Little had given the CAPU. It all had to be corroborated to make any difference in the investigation. If there was one common theme running through the entire investigation, it was that everyone who knew Jeff Zack had a story to tell that smacked down his credibility, if not morality. Jeff had been involved in so many illegal activities, according to many of the people who knew him, it seemed that any one of them—even a pack of Iranians snuffing him out over a bad gun deal—could have had him murdered. The problem the CAPU faced, however, was separating fact from fiction.

48

Armed with the information Russ McFarland had gotten out of Jonas Little, Ed Moriarty and Dave Whiddon confronted Bonnie Zack. They felt she had not been all that forthcoming with them. Now, with the results of the polygraph indicative of "deception," they needed Bonnie to open up. For example, if Jeff was selling weapons, and hiding those weapons in the house, there wasn't a chance Bonnie didn't know about it.

Bonnie laughed at Little's accusations. "That's funny," she said, rolling her eyes. "*Really* funny." She knew Little was nothing more than a convict lowlife looking to make himself look good in front of the cops, probably trying to get himself a deal on any charges he was facing.

"Funny?" Moriarty asked condescendingly. "You think this is *funny*?"

Bonnie smiled, then denied having anything to do with Jeff's murder. It didn't matter what the polygraph results reported, or what Little had said. "No," she kept repeating when Moriarty and Whiddon questioned her about Jeff's murder. "No. I didn't have anything to do with it. Nothing." ("She was evasive and non-committal in her responses," a report of the interview noted.)

"I don't think it meant that Bonnie had anything to do with her husband's murder," Ed Moriarty told me later. "But I think in her heart, Bonnie believed she knew who had killed Jeff. That's why the answers she gave during the polygraph came back positive."

49

The role of the investigator can sometimes be side-tracked by the most tedious tasks, thus setting a fast-paced investigation back a few steps. The information Jonas Little had injected into the mix, along with Bonnie's failed polygraph, only made CAPU investigators work harder to corroborate the information or write it off. This took time, however. A lot of legwork, coupled with knocking on new doors and working old sources. Russ McFarland had zeroed in on the possible owner of a black-white-and-green motorcycle Little had claimed he saw parked in back of the mall where, he seemed certain, Jeff was not only delivering soda pop, but guns.

On Tuesday, October 16, the CAPU held a morning meeting to discuss these new developments, if they could be called such. Most of the talk focused on Little's accusations and how much of what he said could be considered credible. What gave Jonas Little's allegations a bit more weight among the CAPU was that it was first-hand information. Little had said he was there with Jeff, in his truck, alongside him during the alleged gun buys.

What reason would he have to lie about such an allegation? He said he didn't want anything. He even said he'd wear a wire and make a gun buy himself if the CAPU didn't believe him.

McFarland found out that one of the stores Little had remembered as being a major gun buyer had not even existed during the period in which Little had claimed Jeff laundered guns through it. So the guy's memory, right away, had to be taken into consideration. One guy, *Burt Lance,* who, Little said he was certain, drove a Ninja motorcycle and parked it in back of the mall near the Dumpster, seemed to be a suspect the CAPU needed to speak with quickly. For the CAPU, Little's description of the bike was particularly informative, seeing that the color scheme—green, white, black—was almost an exact description witnesses at BJ's had given, especially Little's mention of the rear end of the bike: "all black." Other witnesses later described a black-green-and-white bike, a black bike with green stripes and various other combinations of the same three colors. But Little hit it spot on.

A coincidence? Luck? Whatever it was, the CAPU was obligated to check it out thoroughly. "[Jonas Little]," McFarland explained to his colleagues during the meeting, "was only the second person in the investigation to put those colors in that exact pattern." Furthermore, a Kawasaki dealership in the Akron area said that if the killer's bike had those exact colors in that specific pattern, the paint job must have been customized. The factory didn't ship those types of bikes with the same pattern.

After the meeting, McFarland and a colleague drove to the mall and started asking questions. They needed to find that bike and question Burt Lance.

McFarland found one of Lance's old partners. Lance ran a telephone store in the mall, which Little had claimed Jeff sifted guns through. Lance's partner, however, said he never, in all the years he knew Lance, had heard that Lance owned a motorcycle. The guy drove an SUV. McFarland steered clear from the gun issue, saving it, he wrote later in his report, "for a follow-up interview."

After showing a photograph of Little to the managers of all the stores with entrances from the back of the mall, not one person recognized Jonas Little. Even more telling, not one person could say that he or she ever saw a motorcycle parked by the Dumpster.

Another high-five opportunity deflated.

50

Jonas Little's allegations proved to be a waste of investigatory time for the CAPU. As it turned out, the man knew nothing. Moreover, Bonnie Zack had no more killed her husband than Mickey Mouse. From a CAPU management position, the investigation into Jeff Zack's murder took on a different feel after the new year dawned: Ed Moriarty, who had been intricately involved moments after Jeff was shot, was slated to retire in April. Moriarty promised to work on the case as a consultant, but he wouldn't be involved day to day. The man now leading the investigation in lieu of Moriarty's departure was Lieutenant Dave Whiddon, one of the youngest lieutenants to ever wear a blue uniform in Akron.

Whiddon had learned from one of the best, he said later. As April approached, Moriarty, who had brought Whiddon along on most everything he had done in the Zack investigation, knowing he was going to be passing the case over to him one day, knew he had left the investigation in good hands. Moriarty had essentially broken Whiddon in. Some worried about how well

Whiddon was going to perform. He had eight years in the department, and here he was taking over one of the APD's most high-profile murder investigations. "Dave studied very hard for promotions," said a former colleague, "made lieutenant and was put in charge of the CAPU very early in his career."

Moriarty had always been known as an "opinionated" guy, and some would later call him a pain in the ass who had butted heads with a lot of cops in the department, behavior that placed a host of white collars after him. When Moriarty believed in something, however, everybody knew it. There was a tenuous feeling about the office that Whiddon and Moriarty were going to clash. Some wondered when Moriarty was going to explode and give Whiddon a good lashing, yelling and screaming about how he thought Whiddon had risen up through the ranks on his name alone. But it never happened. Instead, Moriarty gave Whiddon the respect his hard work had earned him. "Dave came in," Moriarty said later, "and he wanted to learn the job. He wanted to do everything he could. He's just that kind of guy." Dedicated to the core. A career man. Willing to do anything he needed in order to get the job done. Moriarty would call Whiddon at two in the morning, "It's time to come in. Get up and let's move." Whiddon would be there.

With Whiddon running the investigation, however, nothing had essentially changed. First it seemed as though Bonnie could have had something to do with her husband's death; then Seth or Carl came into view; Ed George, of course, had always been thought to be a likely suspect. But there was no corroborating evidence. Nothing to back up a theory. A failed lie detector test meant, in the scope of things, nothing. For detectives, it told them the answer was still out there—if only they could keep banging on doors and talking to people. Having a new leader wouldn't change any of that.

Back in November 2001, one witness came forward and claimed it was possible Bonnie's father had "put a hit out" on his son-in-law. That seemed ridiculous on its face. The Iranian connection, devoid of any gun-trafficking accusations, was made yet again. The assumption of the Russian mafia routinely surfaced, likely because Jeff had spoken the language. Then the Mossad. Who knew if Jeff had even been an operative? The Israeli government wasn't talking. Jeff's past as a stockbroker came up again. Had he burned one too many investors? Had one of his many mistresses grown tired of Jeff's womanizing?

Circles. Investigators felt like they were running on a treadmill. Every promising lead turned out to be a dud, once it was followed through. *Where do we go from here?* became the mantra. As the 2001 holiday season fell upon Akron, investigators were no closer to solving the murder of Jeff Zack than they were on day one. Prosecutors demanded evidence. The CAPU hadn't even served a search warrant by the time Christmas rolled around. They had theories, speculation from sources, but none had amounted to material evidence.

But then something happened shortly after the new year dawned. Never in their collective one hundred or so years of law enforcement experience had CAPU detectives working the case seen the actual perpetrator coming. It was a name no one had heard thus far—no one, in fact, save for one person.

51

In April 2002, Lieutenant Dave Whiddon and Detective Vince Felber contacted a CI they had run into—and used—from time to time. Inside the guy's attorney's office, they questioned him regarding "hearing something" about Jeff's murder. The CI said he was at a local restaurant one night two weeks after Jeff's murder. He was sitting at the bar talking with a friend he had known for thirty-five years when Jeff's name came up. "You hear anything about that Zack murder?" the CI's friend asked him.

"I read about it in the newspaper."

"Jeff Zack was playing around with Ed George's wife. You hear that?"

"No, I hadn't."

"Well, Ed George reached out to me," claimed the CI's friend. "I contacted someone I know from Pittsburgh to come down here in a rented truck with a motorcycle in back of it. After the murder, the truck, with the motorcycle, went back to Pittsburgh."

The CI shook his head. "No kidding."

Detective Felber was curious, to say the least. "Did he go into detail about the murder at all?" he asked.

The CI explained the remainder of the conversation. His friend had told him that another guy, a friend of his, had "helped . . . carry out the plan. He's well connected in Pittsburgh. We used to be in the bond business together. He knows Ed . . . because he was involved in [a business with him]."

The CI didn't see his friend for quite some time after they shared that drink and spoke of Jeff's murder. "But I met with him recently," he explained further to Felber and Whiddon. "I was trying to set up a trip to Las Vegas. He sells stolen jewelry out of his trunk. He told me he meets with the Georges at the Akron Women's City Club. The actual meeting about the hit took place, he said . . . across the street from the Tangier."

Whiddon asked how the "actual hit" was carried out. Details. How'd it go down? You can't just throw this accusation out there without tying it together with some facts.

"They knew that Zack always went to the BJ's Wholesale Club and they knew Zack's habits. They had been following Zack around. They had the truck with the motorcycle in the back ready to go. As soon as the hit was carried out, the motorcycle went back into the truck and back to Pittsburgh."

Was it worth getting excited about? After all, most of what the CI said was public information. Anyone could have learned those details from reading the newspapers, following the case. Was it possible the CI was in trouble? Perhaps he was setting up an information swap. Maybe he wanted a reward?

A few weeks later, on May 13, Felber and Whiddon paid a visit to Helen Rohr, Cynthia's mother. They'd had no luck the previous year when they reached out to Helen via telephone. For the most part, they had stayed away from Helen and Cynthia's sister ever since. But why not give it another try?

Whiddon and Felber drove up to Canton this time. It was a raw day, 45 degrees. Raining. When they pulled into the driveway, they noticed two cars, one of which was Cynthia's sister's.

Great, they're both here. Lucky break.

Helen answered the door and looked disgusted to see them.

"Can we talk to you a minute about Jeff Zack, Mrs. Rohr?" Whiddon asked.

"I never really knew him. He was a friend of Cindy's and was at one of the kids' baptisms. But that's all I can tell you."

"Was that Ruby's baptism?"

Whiddon and Felber were waiting to be asked inside the house. They were standing on the porch in the rain. It seemed awkward that Helen wasn't inviting them in.

"No."

Cynthia's sister then came from around the back of Helen and presented herself at the door next to her mother. She, too, had a look on her face that implied, *You again!*

"We'd like to ask you both about Jeff Zack," Felber said, breaking what was an uncomfortable silence.

"Look," snapped Cynthia's sister, "we don't know *anything* about him . . . and you're really upsetting my mother." According to Whiddon and Felber's report, she was livid. Seething. Obviously disturbed by the surprise visit and equally appalled by the questions.

"Listen," Felber said, "the last thing we want to do is

upset your mother. Is there somewhere private we can talk for a little bit?"

Helen spoke up. "Stay there on the porch," she said.

"Mom, it's raining," Cynthia's sister said. Felber and Whiddon looked on. *Hello, it's pouring on us here. How 'bout a little hospitality?*

"Go over to the screened-in porch on the side of the house," suggested Helen, pointing.

Whiddon and Felber walked into the slanted rain, onto the lawn and around the side of the house before stepping into a porch area. Now, at least, they were out of the rain. Helen met them by walking through the house. She stayed inside, behind the screen door.

Cynthia's sister spoke first. She was standing by her mother's side again. "I talk to my sister regularly," she said. "We're close."

Whiddon asked about Cynthia and Jeff's relationship. "[Cynthia's sister] feigned ignorance," Felber wrote later in his report of the conversation. She acted as though she knew nothing about it. Like it was a shock to them.

So Whiddon came out with it: "Did you and your mother know that Cindy and Jeff were having an affair?"

Both Helen and Cynthia's sister said they didn't.

"Did you know that one of Cindy's children was fathered by Jeff Zack?" Felber asked, directing his question toward Cynthia's sister.

Helen spoke, offering, "She looks like her grandfather." Meaning Cynthia's dad.

Cynthia's sister said, "We didn't know that."

Neither Helen nor Cynthia's sister, however, looked all that surprised by the disclosure, Felber reported later. It was apparent they knew. And that grandfather remark; where'd it come from? Helen seemed proud of the resemblance.

"How did Helen know which child I was talking about?" Felber asked. He had never mentioned which of Cynthia's seven children was Zack's. Helen acted as if she knew.

Cynthia's sister responded, "You said the affair was seven years long." She implied that, while standing there, they had calculated the simple math. Ruby was the only child young enough to fit the criteria.

Both Cynthia's sister and Helen asked how they knew "for sure" Ruby was Jeff's. Neither detective said the CAPU had done a paternity test; instead, they ignored the question.

"Is my daughter a suspect?" Helen demanded to know.

"No," Felber said. "But we have no idea why she won't speak to us."

"It's Bob Meeker. He won't let her."

Felber threw up his hands. "It's Cindy's decision, not Bob's. If a friend of mine had been murdered, I'd want to do anything possible to help. We don't get it."

"I agree with you," Helen said.

"Cindy never told me that she was having an affair with Jeff," Cynthia's sister added, "or that one of the kids was fathered by him. She never said she had a fight with Jeff."

Felber asked about the affair, the child and if Cynthia had ever mentioned Jeff's murder.

Cynthia's sister said no.

"Cindy and Ed have a wonderful marriage," Helen added. "They never fight."

As the wind picked up behind the two investigators, Cynthia's sister chimed in and said, "I'm going to my

attorney and telling him about this interview." She
became hostile. Then appeared as if she was going to
cry, adding, "I have *nothing* more to add," putting her
hand over her mouth and walking away.

Whiddon and Felber left.

Felber was determined to break the case. He knew
from experience it was a matter of talking to people.
Beating them down, in a fragile way, and getting them
to open up. Helen and Cynthia's sister weren't going to
crack—and there was some question about how much
they knew, anyway. As far as the Rohr family was concerned, Cynthia and Ed had a great marriage, which
the detectives knew was a stretch.

At nearly the same time Felber and Whiddon were
driving back from Helen's, another CAPU detective
made contact with a CI by the name of *Tim Gardner,*
who the detective had heard might have some information about Jeff's murder. When he ran into Felber later
that afternoon, the detective gave him Gardner's name
and telephone number, saying, "Call this guy."

Felber looked at the name. "Thanks."

On May 15, 2002, Felber made contact with Gardner.
"I'm a detective with the persons unit," he said over the
phone. "I need to speak with you immediately."

"I can't talk right now," Gardner said. He sounded
anxious. It was clear he was uncomfortable talking to
a cop on the telephone. "I'll call you back."

Felber waited, but Gardner never called.

It would be five days before Felber tracked Gardner
down, but Felber's dogged determination to locate
Gardner would pay a huge dividend. Almost a year after
Jeff Zack was murdered, a break was in the works—all
generated by a routine telephone call to a confidential informant.

52

Felber kept calling Gardner. And kept getting no answer. But on May 20, Gardner finally picked up the telephone. "What do *you* want?"

Felber was quick: "Listen, I'm interested in a motor-cycle you told [one of our detectives] about."

Gardner had originally explained that a guy had given him a Ninja motorcycle as a payment for drugs. A well-known local dealer, Gardner didn't want to in-criminate himself by freely giving the information to Felber. Admitting to taking personal property for drugs was a mistake; if the motorcycle had been stolen, it would fall on Gardner's shoulders, not to mention the drug sale. Plus, there were people, Gardner claimed, that if they knew he was talking to the cops, weren't going to be happy about it. He was scared.

Felber was more concerned about where Gardner got the bike than why he had it. "I thought you wanted me for something else," Gardner said. "If I knew it was about the bike, I would have called you back sooner."

"That's OK," said Felber. "Tell me about that bike."

"This guy who owed me money gave me a clean

black-green-and-purple-Ninja-style motorcycle instead of the money. There wasn't any plate on the bike. It was last year, June sixteenth."

The date of Jeff's murder.

And although the color purple didn't match with the descriptions they had, investigators couldn't be sure if the bike was purple or black—the colors were interchangeable, and they could be one and the same as a blur driving by.

"How do you know it was that date?" asked Felber.

"I heard about the Jeff Zack murder . . . you know, and here's this bike in my possession. So I broke it down into parts and had them crushed and scrapped inside of some junk cars."

Son of a gun.

As Felber began to sulk, Gardner came back with some good news. "Listen," he added, "I kept the engine block with the VIN number on it. I can get that for you."

A few days later, a CAPU detective picked up Gardner and one of his friends, *Fred Abers,* and brought them down to the CAPU to meet with Whiddon and Felber. The CAPU was onto something, for sure. Whiddon and Felber could feel it. There was a certain authenticity to the information. It made sense. Gardner and Abers were scared, sincerely reluctant about meeting at the APD, which told them something about how credible the information could possibly be.

Felber and Whiddon wanted the name of the guy who had given Gardner the bike.

"We're afraid," Gardner said as they sat down in a CAPU interview room. Gardner was looking around timidly, fidgeting with his hands. "This ain't no shit, man, we'll be seriously hurt if anyone knows we're here. You have to do everything possible to keep our names *out* of this."

Felber promised he would.

Gardner began by telling the same story: the bike in exchange for the drugs, the VIN number on the engine block. This guy, he added, who had given him the bike, he was sure the guy couldn't ride a motorcycle. He knew it was stolen. "His name's [*Marcus Dooby*]." Felber and Whiddon had heard the name a few days before. They had been to Dooby's house already, but his brother and sister said he was running scared and thought they were going to arrest him. Dooby's sister promised she'd try to talk him into coming forward. Continuing, Gardner said, "Dooby told me to get rid of the bike a few days after giving it to me. He didn't know anything about Jeff Zack's murder, but once he found out a bike like the one he gave me was used in the murder, he told me to get rid of it."

The story seemed plausible. The two guys were incriminating themselves. Beyond them believing that a reward for twenty-five thousand dollars existed (which was untrue), what purpose was there, what motive existed, for them to lie at this point?

Sitting, listening to his friend talk, Fred Abers was sitting on—whether he realized it—the break the CAPU had been waiting on for nearly a year. Speaking up, Abers told Whiddon and Felber he knew something about Jeff Zack's murder. He had been holding out.

Whiddon and Felber asked what it was he knew.

He gave them two names: Christine Todaro and John Zaffino. Todaro lived in Cuyahoga Falls. Zaffino had two addresses, one in Akron and another in a little town called Rittman. "Zaffino," said Abers, "was married to Todaro for about a year and a half. He hit her and, on one occasion, I heard he broke her arm. They've been divorced for over a year, but Zaffino still calls her."

"How does this fit into the Zack murder?" Felber wondered.

"Todaro told me that Zaffino was crazy. He bragged to her one night about two people he killed—one in Pennsylvania and the other was"—he paused, stared at the two detectives—"well, the other was Jeff Zack."

This was the first time the CAPU had someone admitting to the murder, actually saying he or she had done the job. But Abers wasn't finished. He had more.

"What else did she say to you?"

Abers made a point to explain that he wasn't saying any of the information was true; he was simply repeating what he had been told, adding, "She (Todaro) said Zaffino told her that he used a motorcycle to kill Zack. He had researched Zack on his computer and later threw away his hard drive in order to cover it up. He was following Zack around until an opportunity came up to kill him."

Although quite groundbreaking on the surface, it proved nothing. During the interview, neither Felber nor Whiddon ever brought up Ed George.

"She told me," explained Abers, meaning Todaro, "that Zaffino told her that an 'Ed' had hired him to kill Zack. Zaffino said he had beaten up Zack before, but then 'Ed' decided he wanted him dead."

"We're curious," asked Felber, "why you were talking to"—he stopped for a moment and looked down at his notes—"Christine Todaro about . . . John Zaffino?"

"Zaffino kept calling her, sometimes while I was there at her apartment. Listen, this Zaffino drives a truck or owns a trucking company. . . . I'll talk to Todaro and get you guys some more information."

Within the next few days, the VIN number from the stolen bike came back and Felber found its owner. There was no way the bike could have been used in the homicide, the owner said, because it was in his garage during the murder. It was stolen two weeks later, near the end of June.

Still, Felber needed to track down John Zaffino and Christine Todaro. Having been fingered in a murder-for-hire scheme, it was clear that both had some explaining to do.

53

Forty-year-old Christine Todaro had grown up on a farm and lived in and around Akron her entire life. It was back in the mid-1990s when Christine worked as a receptionist for North Canton (Ohio) Transfer, a fuel and oil tanker company. She was beautiful and outgoing, and had been married once, but it hadn't worked out. Through that marriage, however, Christine had two children, a boy, Tony, and a girl, whom she loved and adored more than anything. "They are my life," Christine told me later.

One day, while shuffling paperwork at North Canton Transfer, in walked John Zaffino. Christine saw a spark. He was quite good-looking. He had a rough edge about him, but she liked that. Zaffino drove his own truck and did subcontract work for NCT. He would stop in the office at certain times and pick up and drop off paperwork. For a year, Christine said, Zaffino tried to get her to go out with him, but she brushed off his advances. Finally, after Zaffino kept persisting, she agreed, which was, she knew, against her better judgment. "I knew he was unstable, but I said, what the hell."

What Zaffino saw in Christine is rather obvious: a sweet, phone-sex-type voice, sexy lips and a streetwise pulse about her that spoke of a sociable, "not afraid to tell you how she feels" woman. Christine was tough. Her own person. Zaffino fit the protector role; he wasn't afraid of anyone, that much was rather obvious to Christine right away. He loved her long, flowing, curly blond hair and perfect model figure. She was a catch, for sure, especially for a brute like Zaffino.

They dated for eighteen months before settling on marriage. During that time, Christine saw a different man emerge. Zaffino could turn violent, she claimed, with the drop of a hairpin. One of those guys who, even if you thought you were saying the right thing, would twist it into something that offended him. Their marriage, from its earliest days, was filled with violent outbursts by Zaffino, generally brought on by an overwhelming, uncontrollable jealousy he couldn't shake, mixed with a large appetite for, Christine said, booze.

Lots of alcohol.

The marriage ended, for the most part, one night when Christine saw Zaffino knock her son down and bloody the boy's mouth. As she told it, Christine and her son were eating with Zaffino and his parents one afternoon. "John and his father had a very violent relationship," she insisted. "It's like a love-hate type of thing, but that doesn't even begin to describe it well enough."

Christine's son, Tony, was thirteen at the time. A good kid. Well behaved. Adored his mother and considered himself her protector. At the time, Tony was around the age where he was starting to worry about his appearance. Before they left for the restaurant, Tony decided to wear a hat. He didn't feel like comb-

ing his hair or tidying up. He wanted to roll out of bed
and go to lunch. Typical teenager. As they sat down at
the restaurant, however, Zaffino's father told the boy,
"Take that hat off." He thought it disrespectful for the
kid to be wearing a hat at the dinner table, especially
out in public.

Christine rolled her eyes. She knew the family. *Here
we go*.

Tony didn't want to remove the ball cap. "My hair's
all screwed up, Ma. I don't want to do it." The kid had
worn his hat at the dinner table plenty of times around
Zaffino and Christine. All of a sudden, because Zaffino's father was present, it turned into what Christine
later described as some sort of "big issue."

"John had this thing about his father. . . . He was
always trying to impress him and seemed to act different around him."

Because she knew Zaffino could go from "zero to
Mach ten in seconds and was likely to blow a gasket,"
Christine encouraged the boy to take the hat off. "For
me," she said softly to Tony as they sat waiting for their
lunch. "Come on."

Albeit begrudgingly, Tony obliged when Christine
snatched the hat from his head and put it on her knee.

Although Tony acquiesced, the incident ignited a set
of circumstances that would have grave consequences
for Christine as the night wore on.

Zaffino looked at Tony after he took the hat off and
said, "Nancy boy." Teasing him. Taunting. *Nancy boy*. It
had always been a joke between them. Zaffino had said
it before and nothing ever came of it. On this night,
however, the boy didn't want to hear it.

"Shut up," Tony said.

When they got back to the house, Zaffino's mother

used the downstairs bathroom while Christine went upstairs. This, of course, left Zaffino, his dad and Tony alone in the kitchen.

When Christine returned, Tony was on the floor, his mouth, she said, "full of blood." Zaffino had whacked him good. The boy was moaning, calling out.

"What the *f- - -* happened?" she screamed, getting nose to nose with her husband. "What did you do?" When her child's welfare was at stake, Christine said, she didn't care how big Zaffino was, or what he could do to her. "I was going to defend my child no matter what."

What shocked Christine more than anything else was that Zaffino's father stood by and not only watched his son strike the boy, but even egged Zaffino on. "You gonna let your wife talk to you like that, boy?"

Christine told Tony to clean himself up and get in the car. "We're leaving."

That same night, Christine found an apartment and moved in, but she had nothing. No clothes. Blankets. Furniture. She needed to get back into her house and get some things so she and Tony could begin a new life. She was finished being pushed around, hit and, at one time, "strangled by Zaffino," she said, so hard that she "saw stars and couldn't talk or swallow for a week."

It was over. Enough was enough.

So Christine let the situation settle for a few weeks, living off things her friends and family had given her. But there came a time when she needed to go back to her house and pick up all the personal belongings she could. Zaffino was calling the entire time, obsessively telling her he was sorry, it wouldn't happen again, just come home and everything would be all right.

She had heard it all before. It was over.

Christine showed up and Zaffino was waiting. Greeting her at the door, he seemed calm. "Come on in."

She walked across the threshold and entered without a problem. But when she got farther into the house, Zaffino closed the door, twisted the lock and dead bolt in place, then leaned against the back of it.

Shoot, she thought. *I'm in big trouble.*

"I want your e-mail address," Zaffino said.

Christine looked at him strangely. "What?"

"I want your account password so I can look at it."

Zaffino had been accusing Christine of cheating on him with a man she knew (her boss). He believed they'd communicated through e-mail, simply because she had locked him out of her account and wouldn't give him the password. It became more suspect to Zaffino after she moved out of the house, and he was, in his blatant insecurity, convinced she had been carrying on an affair. His jealousy was so profound that Christine said she had quit jobs in the past just to "protect my bosses, because I knew John would do something to them."

"I f- - -ing knew it," he said. "You bitch." He was still blocking the door.

"I am not giving you the e-mail address, John. I just want to get some things and I'm out of here."

Zaffino was composed. He had a sort of bashful smirk on his face that told Christine he believed he was in control of the situation. And that's what it came down to: control. Zaffino wanted to and tried, according to Christine, to control every aspect of her life, same as any wife beater.

"You're not leaving," he said, "until I get that e-mail account."

Christine took a look around. She saw several shotguns in the corner of the kitchen—one of which was a double-barrel and sawed-off. Zaffino was a gun freak. Loved to embrace the cold chill of the wooden grips, admire the long channel of steel. "An expert shot—he liked to shoot things," Christine recalled. She said she was with him once at a shooting range on a piece of her father's property; being the braggart he was, Zaffino put a nickel on the top of a target and walked about seventy-five feet away. "Watch this s- - -," he said. *Pow!* He hit that nickel square in the center. No problem.

The guns, insisted Christine, were a means of intimidation for John Zaffino. He picked one up one day and "threatened to shoot one of my old boyfriends because he *thought* we were *talking.*"

Now she was standing in her former home, staring at several guns, scared shitless that her husband wasn't going to allow her to leave, thinking, *He's going to kill me.*

"OK," she finally said. "I'll give it to you. Let's go sign on."

They walked over to the computer.

Zaffino then looked at her. "What is it?"

After signing on and checking Christine's e-mail inbox, Zaffino realized there was no mail. He had been proven wrong, which was not a good thing. One of Zaffino's sayings, Christine later said, had always been, "I'll always"—never, ever forget this—"be proven right, no matter what."

Christine went for the door. She wanted to leave. Now.

"No," he said, getting up from the computer and blocking the door.

"Come on, John," she pleaded.

He grabbed her, then put her arm behind her back,

much like a cop might do when subduing a suspect. He held her there by the door. She couldn't move.

"You're gonna break my arm," she said. *"You're gonna break my arm."* Each word rose in pitch as Zaffino pushed her arm up her back toward her head, tighter, and tighter, as she could feel that her arm wasn't going to bend any farther.

Zaffino then placed one of his hands on Christine's elbow and the other on her wrist and began pushing them in opposite directions until he heard a sharp snap.

Christine not only heard her arm break like a piece of peanut brittle, she felt the shock of it, electric, shoot up her arm into her shoulder. "Ow, John, you broke my arm," she cried.

With that, he stopped and let her go.

Standing, contemplating the situation, Christine thought, *I'm dead. . . . What does he have to lose now . . . he's going to kill me.*

As she sat in a chair at the dining table, Zaffino, now the caring, worried husband, ran into the kitchen and got her some ice to put on her swelling arm, saying, "You cannot tell anyone about this. You can't tell anyone I did this." He looked outside. It was snowing. There was plenty of ice on the ground. "Just tell people you fell on the ice."

"OK, John. I will." She wanted to leave.

"You can't tell Tony. I don't want him to know."

"Yes. I know."

Zaffino allowed her to leave at that point. She had been there about two hours. Christine drove home. In the meantime, Zaffino called Tony and explained that his mother had fallen on an ice patch and twisted her arm pretty badly.

When Christine got out of her car, Tony was waiting. He was crying. "What happened? Did you fall on
the ice?"

"No . . . John broke my arm."

From there, Christine tried driving to the emergency
room. Along the way, she pulled into a Hardee's restaurant, thinking it was the hospital entrance. She was
going into shock. "You're going to have to drive," she
told Tony. "Can you do it?"

He jumped in the driver's seat and got her to the
hospital. Scared, she told hospital officials she slipped
and fell on the ice outside her apartment. Back home
later that night, Christine called her father. She was terrified Zaffino was on the move, on his way over to her
apartment.

He's coming to kill me.

54

While talking to her father, Christine Todaro, in a cast, nursing what doctors diagnosed as a "major fracture" to her elbow, explained what had happened. Christine's father, rather fed up with his abusive son-in-law's aggressive outbursts, drove his daughter to the sheriff's office the following day and she filed a complaint against Zaffino, who was ultimately charged with felonious assault, aggravated kidnapping and domestic violence.

That was the end of Christine's marriage to John Zaffino. But filing divorce papers, which Zaffino refused to sign for upward of a year, failed to get rid of him. He continued to bother Christine, calling at a ridiculous rate, following her, dropping by her apartment unannounced. Perhaps in the same manner Jeff Zack had treated Cynthia George, he was unable to take rejection. Christine had to quit one job she had at the time because Zaffino would show up and threaten people. He sat in the parking lot and waited for her. The company even changed the locks, giving everyone a special "key card" to get in. They had security personnel keep an eye on him. But when all that failed, Christine thought it better she move on to other employment, instead of constantly worrying what her soon-to-be ex would do to an innocent coworker who might haphazardly end up in his way.

At the time she met John Zaffino, Christine had been dating a guy named Frank Roppolo. She noticed early into her marriage that Zaffino would become incredibly jealous of Roppolo, because Christine and Roppolo had remained somewhat close friends after she got married to Zaffino. Inside that circle—Tim Gardner, Fred Abers, Marcus Dooby and Roppolo—it became known that Christine had possible information about the Jeff Zack murder, which ultimately got the ball rolling for the CAPU. According to Christine, however, Tim Gardner's true motivation in coming forward wasn't that he was a concerned citizen in pursuit of justice. Gardner, Christine later claimed, "thought there was a reward being offered. He wasn't giving up the information for any honorable motivation—it was *all* about money. . . ."

As Zaffino and Christine went about their lives as a married couple, she began to notice Zaffino's penchant for blowing up at the slightest whim over, well, just about anything. Where Frank Roppolo was concerned, Zaffino held a particular bloodthirstiness for the guy. He yearned to *hurt* Roppolo. Months into their marriage, Zaffino told his new wife he wanted to buy a shotgun so he could do some target shooting. There was just one little problem, however. "You know I'm not from Ohio, Christine." Zaffino had grown up in Pennsylvania. By law, an interloper to the state couldn't purchase a gun legally. "Can you buy the gun for me?"

Christine bought him the gun, thinking, *What harm could it do?* He wanted to target shoot with her dad, who had acreage in the country. *Maybe it'll keep the guy busy and help him burn some of that negative energy.* She admitted later that she really didn't know Zaffino well enough at that time to consider the gun would make him even more dangerous than he was already. It was a mistake, she said. But she did it—and eventually had to live with it.

Within a few weeks after Christine bought Zaffino the gun, he decided he'd heard enough from her ex-boyfriend Frank Roppolo. "He just told me one day that he wanted to beat the hell out of him," Christine recalled. "I guess it would have made him feel good. I don't know. He's nuts. But I didn't know that then. John was a major fighter. He fought everybody. Any reason he could find to fight, he fought."

Zaffino was thirty-six years old then and just a hair under five feet five inches. Somewhat jokingly and somewhat seriously, Christine said later that she believed he, like some short people, "suffered from Napoleon syndrome." Zaffino had a complex about being short and tried to compensate for it by being a bruiser, always looking to defend his honor. Add that to his insatiable appetite for booze—"He once," she added, "drank a thirty-pack of beer in front of me and it didn't affect him"—and a recipe for a madman percolated inside him, Christine believed as the first months of her marriage blossomed. "He put fear into people—especially me," Christine said.

On the other hand, Christine said, Frank Roppolo wasn't in any position to defend himself against Zaffino, a relentless fighter who would keep coming at you until he succeeded. Roppolo, she said, wasn't the toughest guy around. If Zaffino had set his mind on giving Roppolo a good beating, it would happen. Zaffino would squash him like an irritating fly.

Zaffino and Christine were sitting at the dinner table

one night. "I think," Zaffino said, lifting a fork filled with food into his mouth, "Frank wants to f- - - you."

"Oh, John, you're nuts." Christine wanted nothing to do with her ex-boyfriend. She was married. "There's a reason," she remarked later, "that Frank's an ex-boyfriend."

"What do you think?" Zaffino asked.

"John, I don't think so. He's not like that."

Before she realized what was going on, Christine recalled, Zaffino had given her a quick backhand to the face and knocked her off her chair. "I never even saw him swing. It happened that fast. I guess I gave him the wrong answer."

Roppolo, though, did want Christine back. And he had been trying to get her to leave Zaffino, whom he believed to be abusive and verbally insulting.

After Zaffino struck Christine, he said, "Give me Frank's phone number."

It's going to look real bad, she thought, collecting herself, rubbing her red face, *if I don't give him the number.*

"Call him," Zaffino ordered. He was, by this point, "really drunk." Slurring his words. Getting that drunken look about him she had seen many times before. When John Zaffino made up his mind to do something, no one was going to stop him from doing it. "Call him right now," Zaffino said again. He raised his hand. By then, he had taken one of his shotguns and placed it on the counter in the kitchen, chest level with Christine, as she sat by the telephone and debated in her head what to do.

With a shotgun basically pointed at her, Christine dialed the number. With Roppolo on the line, Christine told him that Zaffino wanted to meet him. Roppolo started talking loudly, calling Zaffino out, she remembered later.

This was a bad idea.

As Christine talked, Zaffino swung the barrel end of
the gun around and pointed it—although it was still on
the counter—at her face. He was staring at her, she felt,
thinking . . . *Don't say the wrong thing.* Mocking her.
Acting like the tough guy he thought he was pointing
a shotgun at a female's head.

Zaffino then got on the telephone with Roppolo and
set up a meeting between them, acting as if he wanted
to be his friend.

Later that night, as Zaffino got drunker, he opened up
to Christine. She admitted later that she had no idea if
he was telling the truth, he could just have been telling
a story to improve on his tough-guy image. But at some
point that night, he asked her, "If I tell you something
bad about me, will you think different of me?"

"No, John, of course not. What is it?"

Zaffino, in a drunken slur Christine had become all too
familiar with, said he had killed two men in Florida a few
years before they were married. He was working for a fence
company, he explained, and two guys had ripped his boss
off over a botched drug deal. So he went and shot the guys.

Christine didn't know what to say. She changed the
subject.

As the sun was about to rise on a new day, Zaffino left
the house to get more beer. As soon as he left, Christine
called Frank Roppolo. "What are you doing?" she said
huffily. "Don't meet with him. He's not your friend. He's
got a f----ing shotgun here. What the hell is wrong with
you? Don't talk to him anymore. Don't meet him." She
was hysterical. "His intentions are to hurt you."

Frank Roppolo said, "OK, Christine, I get it."

55

On the morning of June 12, 2002, Bertina King and Vince Felber, with an FBI agent tagging along, drove to Christine Todaro's apartment. After they knocked on the door, she invited them into the kitchen. The FBI had become part of the investigation because several witnesses had made an "organized crime" implication. If there was a mafia element to the murder, the FBI could help.

"Go downstairs," Christine told Tony. (Her daughter, by then, had gone to live with her ex-husband.)

They sat down at the dining table. Christine explained that she had been married to Zaffino, but they had been divorced—"finally"—for some time. "I left him after . . . he punched my son and knocked him to the ground. After we left the house, I went back to get my belongings [later] and John held me in the house for two hours."

"Like kidnapped, against your will?" King wondered.

"Yeah. He broke my arm." Christine couldn't believe law enforcement was finally standing in her apartment. It was a relief, actually, with all she knew about the murder of Jeff Zack and Zaffino's possible involvement. "What took you so long?" she asked in jest, shaking her head. Although she was glad to see law enforcement, she was fearful of Zaffino, who was still a major presence in her life. Because of that, she wasn't about to tell Felber and King anything at this point. She felt Zaffino was somehow setting her up to take the fall for the murder. She worried greatly that she had, without realizing it, become involved.

King and Felber looked at each other after hearing Christine reiterate her feeling of what had taken them so long to track her down. It was good news. They sensed the CAPU would be getting somewhere.

As Christine explained it to King and Felber, Zaffino had been arrested a few times for hitting her, and possibly other violent episodes that had nothing to do with her. Then, "He may be dating a girl from Medina."

Cynthia George lived in Medina.

In truth, Zaffino was a street thug, a tough guy. Short and stocky, medium-cut black hair, he sported a goatee sometimes. Some later described him as the type of guy to stop at a local dive for a few beers after a day's work and fight his way through the night. Anything, others said, would set the guy off: an awkward look from a stranger, an unsuspecting comment, someone beeping the horn at him on the road. He was a time bomb, ready to go off on some violent rampage the moment he felt the least bit threatened.

King and Felber wanted to know more. They were investigating a murder. Christine was married to the guy at one time. She knew him better than most. A possible girlfriend in Medina was a good start, but what else?

"He's been taking medication for an anger management problem, Effexor, or something like that. He sold his trucking business, which he had for eleven years. I think he's doing electroplating now."

"Does he have a motorcycle?"

Important question. Could clear up a lot of unanswered questions and get things really rolling.

"As far as I know, he's never had a motorcycle, except for when he was a kid. That's what he told me. He owns two long-barrel shotguns, though, I know that." She gave them Zaffino's cell phone number. She told them where his mother and father lived and gave them their numbers as well. "He has a sister—"

Interrupting, Felber came out with it. "Do you have any idea why we're here asking these questions?"

"No." She seemed nervous now. Quick with her answers. Trembling. Scared.

"Do you know if John's involved in anything illegal?"

"No."

It was a lie in some respects; his entire life could be classified as illegal.

"We think John might have been involved in a homicide."

Christine reacted "shocked and alarmed," Felber wrote in his report of the conversation. "Oh, my goodness," she said.

"Has John ever talked about anything like that?"

"No."

Good investigators are patient. They know how to plant a seed, walk away and allow that information to germinate in the mind of a potential source. In a way, a source, like Christine Todaro, was a veiled adversary, only to be trusted to a point until she proved herself. Keeping her walking on eggshells, wondering, waiting, was going to be an asset to the investigation. It was clear she knew more, but they didn't want to push her right now.

Felber took out his card and handed it to Christine. "If you think of anything else, can you call me?"

"Sure."

When they left, Christine sat down at the table and wondered why she hadn't just come out with it. By contrast, she was scared to death of John Zaffino. If he found out she was talking to the police, without even thinking twice about it, he would "stomp the s - - -" out of her, or, worse, she believed, "put a bullet in my head. He had already killed one person," Christine said later. "I *know* he wouldn't have thought twice about killing me to cover up the entire thing."

With the CAPU gone, Christine, now filled with emotion and fear, decided the best thing to do was to call her ex-husband. *Contact John and see what he knows.* Christine knew the guy, his moods, how he thought. If he knew the CAPU had been to her house, she'd be able to hear it in his voice.

She dialed his number, thinking, *What if he drove by my house while they were here?*

Christine was now very much concerned about her role in helping Zaffino throughout the past year. Had she committed a crime herself? Zaffino was acting as if he had something over her. She had always questioned whether he had committed the murder—he had never come out and told her, yes, it was me—but she knew in her heart, not to mention several comments he had made, that he could have done it.

Zaffino had recently given his telephone number to Christine's father, telling him to let her know to call him. Now was as good a time as any.

"John," she said after he answered, "the cops were

just here." Playing dumb, she asked, "What is going on?" Then, "I'm not going to jail for anybody . . . if it comes down to me or you, it's going to be *you*." Christine said later that she had used that line on her ex-husband just about every time they spoke, repeatedly reminding him, regardless of the consequences, that she wasn't "going down" on his behalf.

"F- - - those cops. Don't tell them anything," he said.

"They were *here*, John. In my house." She felt like he didn't believe her, which offered a bit of comfort. At least she now knew he hadn't driven by or heard it from someone it on the street.

"F- - - them." He was chuckling a bit. "Tell them to f- - - off. Don't answer any of their questions."

"I have their business cards."

"I want them."

"The cards?"

"Yes . . . I'm on my way over."

56

Christine Todaro was fully aware of the consequences she faced once John Zaffino found out she was talking to the CAPU. She needed protection as much as she needed to finally tell police all she knew about the murder of Jeff Zack, which was a lot more than anyone thought. Felber and King showing up at her apartment to talk to her was one thing—but the FBI's presence terrified Christine. Things had turned serious—and she knew it. She handed off the business cards to Zaffino and managed to find sleep after he said a few nasty words about the cops and took off. But this was it. She couldn't hide what she knew any longer.

First thing the next morning, June 13, Christine decided to drive to the APD and explain everything. "I realized," Christine recalled, "I just couldn't go through my life with all that I knew about this—not to mention John had threatened to kill me on a daily basis. But it wasn't so much just me. It really bothered me when John started threatening my dad and Tony."

Once inside the confines of the CAPU's sixth-floor office, Christine sat down in the conference room with

Detective Vince Felber, Captain Beth Daugherty and
FBI special agent Roger Charnesky.

She talked about how, where and when she met
Zaffino. Daugherty did most of the questioning while
Charnesky and Felber watched Christine's body move-
ments and studied how she answered questions. Then
Christine gave Daugherty a complete rundown of
Zaffino's family, before Daugherty asked, "Can you tell
us about your marriage to John?"

Christine, of course, sighed, bowed her head and felt
a sharp pain in her gut. "Horrible," she said. "Absolutely horrible."

"What happened?"

"He was very abusive. *Very* abusive. You know, he
almost strangled me to death once in front of my kids."

After a brief description of how violent Zaffino had
been throughout their marriage, Christine talked
about how she realized her ex-husband was involved in
Jeff Zack's murder. It started when Zaffino told her one
night "to watch out for [herself]." What he meant was,
there were a few guys after him, he claimed, and they
would be after her as well. All because, Christine told
Daugherty, Zaffino had "beat the shit out of this Jeff
Zack guy, but he didn't use [Zack's] name."

Felber said, "OK?" Implying, *How do we know it was
Jeff Zack he was talking about?*

"I knew who he meant."

"How did you know?" Daugherty wondered.

"Because he talked about this white-haired . . . guy—
that's what he called him."

"Oh?"

"OK, and he said it's 'Zack Something,' OK?" Christine said.

"OK."

The murder—and Zaffino's involvement—all started to make sense to Christine, she recalled, when the *Akron Beacon Journal* ran its first story about the Zack murder during the early morning hours of June 17, 2001. Before she saw the article, she was quick to say, she believed Zaffino's role in Zack's murder to be another tall tale he was telling, trying to act like the tough guy he had always wanted to be. She had gone out with friends that night and picked up an early edition of the newspaper on her way home. As soon as she looked at the headline, the thought hit her: *He did it. John did it. Son of a gun. He really killed that guy.*

What had given Christine cause for alarm? The events that led up to that day, she said. Zaffino showed up at her house, before the murder, asking if he could "talk." He sat down. "I want to tell you that someone is looking for me," he said with a serious effect. Christine wondered who. Why? What was going on? It was around the first of the year, 2001. "I was a bit pissed off," she recalled later, that he was in her apartment to begin with. Their marriage was over. According to her version, Zaffino was a wife beater. She wanted nothing to do with him. But he wasn't the type of guy she could just brush off. Ever since the split, she had moved from town to town trying to avoid him. But he always tracked her down. She knew he had met someone else, which was good. "A blonde," he described the woman to Christine, "with money. Her name is Cindy." But that was it. He went no further.

Zaffino continued talking. "The guy [that's after me] is a white-haired Israeli. He's looking for me because I beat the shit out of him in front of his posse. He knows who you are, too." Then he said that "Ed George has something to do with this, so I want you to stay out of the Tangier."

Christine figured out rather quickly that the woman her ex-husband was talking about had to be Cynthia George. But at that time, Christine believed Cynthia was Ed's daughter—and thought for sure that the "white-haired" guy was also dating "Cindy."

To Christine, Zaffino had always been a braggart; he liked to tell "stories" about himself. She never knew what to believe. But if the Israeli, as Zaffino put it, was out and about looking for him and also knew where she lived . . . "What the hell are you doing here?" Christine asked Zaffino in a panic. She didn't want the guy after her, too.

"Get out of here," Christine finally said as Zaffino carried on about the guy and how he had been going back and forth with him.

Zaffino ultimately left. Christine was glad to see him go. It was the first time she had heard about a white-haired Israeli who Zaffino claimed was causing problems for him.

Sometime later, she explained to Felber, Daugherty and the FBI, Zaffino showed up again. "Anyone looking for me?" he asked. "Anybody been around?" They were standing outside her apartment by Zaffino's car.

"John, I'm through with this shit. Get out of here." As she spoke, Christine noticed there was a gun holster on the seat of his car. "What's that?" she asked, pointing to it. "Is that for me?" she wondered out loud. More intimidation. Scare tactics. She thought Zaffino had brought the gun along to frighten her, same as he had in the past.

"No, no, no. That's not for you," Zaffino said, kind of laughing at the suggestion. Then he opened the car door, grabbed the gun and began waving it in front of her face. It was a handgun. A .38 caliber. Christine knew guns. She had grown up around them. Her father was an avid collector. She had target shot her entire life. She wasn't some naïve female who had never seen or handled a handgun before and jumped back like a mouse was in the room at the sight of one. "I've been raised around guns," she added.

After showing off his gun, Zaffino left.

Then the telephone calls started.

Reassessing the balance of power, Christine decided that she needed to move again. Zaffino had a handgun. He was a hot button and could snap, she believed, at any moment. She had to get away from him.

Not long after she moved, Zaffino found her. But not only did she believe Zaffino was "following her," but it seemed everywhere she went—to clubs, bars—with her girlfriends, "the same two guys would appear." One time, she confronted one of the guys inside a bar. "Don't you think it's strange that wherever I go," she said in jest, "you guys are always in the same place?"

The guy shrugged.

"Aren't you friends with Ed George?" Christine asked.

"I can't stand Ed George," the guy said.

Christine had put the Ed and Cynthia George connection together after being at Zaffino's apartment one day picking up some of her belongings. The telephone rang while she was there. She glanced over at the caller ID while Zaffino was out of the room, and noticed the name "Cynthia George" on the little screen. By then, she had figured out that Cynthia was Ed's wife. She had even written down Cynthia's cell phone number (and later handed it to the CAPU).

As they sat and listened to Christine tell her story,

Felber and Daugherty were interested. But part of Christine's story seemed too perfect. Captain Daugherty was pessimistic. She had been a cop for twenty years. She had made captain in 2000, had been a lieutenant for five years prior to that, a sergeant for three years leading up to making lieutenant. She was skeptical about Christine Todaro. *Maybe she was involved in the entire plot,* Daugherty wondered. *Perhaps she had come in to score the best deal because the heat had been turned up.* "But," Daugherty told me later, "we had Christine tell her story from beginning to end. Then we asked her to tell it backward. Then from the middle. And every time she told her story, it never wavered. It stayed the same, every detail. We knew then that she was telling the truth."

Christine said later, "At first, I thought that maybe Ed George had chosen John and brought Cindy in and it was his plan to have John be the fall guy. But as I got to know the story better, I realized that it didn't appear that Ed [George] knew John at all."

57

As Christine Todaro told her story to the CAPU, it was clear that, over the course of the past year, John Zaffino had waged a careful campaign to get her involved in the murder of Jeff Zack. Some sort of "If I go down, so do you" scenario. Zaffino, she said, had taken all of his guns and ammunition and given them to her, asking her to hold on to them. What was she supposed to do? The guns were in her name. Of course she had to take them. As time went on after the murder, Christine became bolder and carried on like a detective, trying to figure out how and why Zaffino had murdered Zack. But not so she could run to the police—more so she could protect her own interests. "I was *not* going to go to jail for that guy."

So when Christine saw the newspaper on the night of Zack's murder and stared at a photograph of Jeff Zack accompanying the article, everything Zaffino had said began to make sense. "I didn't even have to read the article," she recalled. "I went through it all in my mind. I knew that John had told me that [someone] had bought him a motorcycle. I recalled the 'white-haired Israeli' comment John had made to me . . . the fact that this guy was bothering John and John said he had beaten the shit out of him 'in front of his posse.' I had seen John with that handgun. I knew what the guy looked like."

It all added up to murder. She felt Zaffino wasn't bragging this time; he had actually killed someone.

On top of it all, there was another comment Zaffino had made to Christine later on that further confirmed her theory. While talking to Zaffino one night on the telephone, asking him about the guy who was suppos- edly bothering him, Zaffino, in his condescending, coldhearted voice, told her not to worry about it any- more. There was no need to be on edge about the guy.

"Why not?" Christine asked.

"He is going to have a hard time parting his hair from now on," Zaffino said coldly.

When she heard those words come out of Zaffino's mouth, Christine took it as a yes, she told Beth Daugh- erty and Vince Felber. "To me, that was a yes."

Detectives from the CAPU wondered what had stopped Christine from coming forward sooner? When they looked at it on paper, it seemed convenient that in walked the answers to a murder case that had baffled the CAPU for a year. It was hard for some members of the unit to get around why Christine had waited so long. "Fear," she said. "[John] has been threatening me the whole entire time."

"Have you ever [seen] John on a motorcycle?"

"I never saw the motorcycle or him on it," she said later. "Like I had said, he used the motorcycle as a weapon." In other words, he was a soon-to-be ex- husband. "He was bragging [to me] about all the things that his 'new girlfriend' was doing for him." Then another key statement: "New clothes, money, motorcycle, cell phones, new residence." According to Christine, which she later testified to in court, John Zaffino's girlfriend, Cynthia George, had bought him a motorcycle and he bragged to her about it.

The CAPU had its most interesting—if not compelling—witness thus far. It had taken upward of a year, but it seemed the case had just taken a major turn.

"Are you willing to work with us?" Dave Whiddon asked Christine at some point. "Maybe wear a wire and record conversations with John Zaffino?"

Christine thought about it. What else could she do? She was in up to her neck at this point. "Yes," she said, "I think I can do that."

58

The CAPU had some serious work ahead of them. Before dragging John Zaffino in, detectives needed to learn as much as they could about him. Christine Todaro was going to help. But setting her up with a wire and recording device for her telephone was going to take time. It had to be done in the normal course of Christine's relationship with Zaffino. She couldn't go running to him now asking questions about the white-haired Israeli if she and Zaffino hadn't talked about it in some time. It would seem too suspicious.

Once the CAPU had some information about Zaffino, be it from Christine or other sources, questioning him would be more productive—maybe they could even gather enough evidence to make an arrest. It wasn't hard to get a rap sheet on Zaffino. Lieutenant Whiddon and Vince Felber asked Carrie Stoll, the CAPU's true ambassador of the most tiresome jobs in the office, to come up with a complete printout on Zaffino, while they continued working on setting Christine up with the recording devices she needed, as well as briefing her on what to do.

Meanwhile, on June 13, 2002, Summit County investigator Dan Kovein, who worked for the Summit County Prosecutor's Office, called the CAPU and explained to Vince Felber that one of the two addresses Summit County had for John Zaffino must be wrong. Felber had heard that Kovein's daughter had lived at one of the addresses, so he put in a call to the investigator to ask him about it. Kovein said his daughter had lived there the previous year. But they came to find out, she had lived in apartment number 1603. Zaffino lived next door in 1602. After talking to his daughter, Kovein said she remembered Zaffino fairly well.

He had a "sporty" motorcycle. "She saw him frequently," Kovein told Felber, "with a blond—very skinny—girlfriend."

The following day, Felber drove out to South Akron, the last known address of John Zaffino. Along the way, Felber couldn't help but notice Zaffino's apartment was a straight shot down Route 8 from the Home Avenue BJ's. On a good day, without any traffic, it was maybe a ten-minute drive. Certainly a lot quicker on a Ninja motorcycle.

Felber stopped at the manager's office and found out Zaffino had been living at the address in June 2001 and had signed a rental agreement for the place back in August 2000. He listed one employer—himself—on the agreement. Zaffino had a son, twelve years old then, who had stayed with him on weekends from time to time, the office manager told him.

"What can you tell us about Mr. Zaffino?" Felber asked, looking down at Zaffino's application.

"Aggressive," she said. "Annoying. Yeah." She shook her head.

"You ever see him with anyone, or riding a motor-cycle?" Felber asked.

"No, I don't recall."

What was interesting, Felber noticed, was that on the rental agreement, where it asked a potential renter to supply what person the management office should contact in case of an emergency, Zaffino had written "Cindy Rohr." He also gave a telephone number where Cynthia could be reached, but failed to put her address or any other personal information.

Interesting development. Here was evidence that John Zaffino and Cynthia George knew each other.

From the office, Felber drove out to the address to see if any of Zaffino's neighbors remembered him. The apartment was quite nice. It looked like a condo from the outside and the landscaping on the property had been kept up: pricey shrubs, delicate golf course–like grass, a gorgeous common pool area, new asphalt drive-way. Tidy and moneyed. Looking at the place, knowing a bit about Zaffino's background, Felber found it hard to place him there. His reputation didn't fit with the style and resident list—a bar-brawling truck driver, he seemed out of his element.

One neighbor had trouble recalling Zaffino, but after some time to reflect, remembered him having "two motorcycles" and hanging out with a "female who drove a dark pickup." The daughter of another neigh-bor remembered Zaffino as a "well-built guy who owned a motorcycle . . . had a blond female visitor who had long hair, but then cut it short. . . ." A woman down a few units remembered Zaffino well. "He owned a mo-torcycle," she said. "He spent a lot of time with a female friend who spent a lot of time talking on a cell phone. She was sickly thin, blond, close to [fifty] years old but looked a lot younger. She drove a dark gray Suburban with a bike rack."

"How can you be sure it was a Suburban?" Felber asked. The woman seemed so certain about the vehicle. Felber knew the Georges owned the same type of vehicle.

"I'm familiar with those types of SUVs," she said. "The blond woman never stayed overnight. She would show up and then they would leave together."

"She ever have kids with her?"

"No, I never saw any—and I never said hi or anything like that."

The neighbor had been friendly with Zaffino; she said she believed he worked at an electroplating company. "I remember when he moved out. I spoke to him. He said he was moving in with the blonde . . . a house with a *lot* of land."

"You think you'd recognize the woman and the Suburban from a photo?"

"Certainly."

When Felber returned to the CAPU, that same neighbor called him. She had spoken to another neighbor she knew fairly well and they had come up with a description of the motorcycle they believed Zaffino drove. "Light green and dark purple or black."

"Thanks," Felber said. "If you recall anything else, call me back."

Felber gave the information to Captain Beth Daugherty. "That's good," she said. Bertina King was standing in Daugherty's office with Felber. Looking up at them from her desk, Daugherty said, "You and Bertina get over there as soon as you can and reinterview that neighbor. Get her on tape."

Felber and King drove back out to the woman's

apartment. They had six photographs, one of which was Cynthia George. Felber brought a new digital recorder with him, but had trouble getting it to work. Regardless, it didn't change what the woman had to say, at least according to Felber's report and a second recording he made with the woman a few days later.

When Felber asked her to describe Zaffino, she said, "He wore a motorcycle helmet which was full-faced and had a very dark face shield. I remember this because he used to wave to me while pulling in on his bike . . . and I didn't realize it was him until [after he took it off]."

After going through the photograph lineup, the woman eliminated five of the photos rather quickly, stopping at Cynthia's, saying, "This *could* be her. I'm not positive, you know, because this woman has a pony-tail and I never saw that woman he was with, with a ponytail. This woman in the photograph here looks heavier, too. But I *think* it's her."

She recalled the woman with Zaffino as being so skinny that she could have "worn kids clothes . . . maybe eighty pounds, she weighed." But a detail that couldn't be overlooked was that Zaffino's blond girl-friend, the neighbor remembered, had a Starbucks coffee mug in a holder in her Suburban.

How could she recall such an odd detail?

She used to park next to the SUV and, while walking by, had seen it.

"I saw John kiss her on the mouth once, a good-bye kiss or something."

"Tell me about Zaffino," Bertina King asked.

"He was egotistical and conceited, annoying. He wouldn't shut up. He told me this story once about accidentally sucking his pet bird up into a shop vac."

"You have any idea where he went?"

"Him and his son packed everything up one day into his pickup truck and just left. Haven't seen him since."

Detective John Bell located the address of forty-year-old Frank Roppolo, Christine Todaro's ex-boyfriend. The CAPU had heard Roppolo was connected to Christine and wanted to talk to him. Some within the unit felt Christine was a tricky character. There was a feeling maybe she had information she still wasn't sharing. If so, how well could she be trusted? Detective Mike Shaeffer had his misgivings about Christine from the get-go. "I never trust a snitch," he said later. "Essentially, whether it helped us or not, she was snitching on someone."

Early on, the question of whether Christine was involved in hiding evidence and obstructing justice was still on the table. She hadn't proven herself yet. All she did was tell her side of the story.

Regardless, a circumstantial—if not rough—connection to Jeff Zack was being made: John Zaffino was looking more and more like the link between Ed George and Jeff Zack. Still, how did it all fit together? Had Cynthia broken it off with Jeff Zack to go out with John Zaffino? Apparently, from the evidence thus far, Cynthia was dating Zack and Zaffino at the same time, a fact that would be confirmed in court later. Had Zaffino and Cynthia actually been lovers? It was the only part of the puzzle that didn't quite make sense. Whereas Jeff Zack was a ladies' man—a good-looking, well-kempt man—John Zaffino, when investigators took a hard look at him, seemed like an unlikely candidate for Cynthia George's affection. Zaffino was a "thug," several detectives later said. A short, chubby, gangster wannabe. He wasn't the type of guy you'd expect to see on the arm of the adorable, lovely Cynthia George, wife of a very wealthy man, who had lived a life of distinction. It was no secret Cynthia liked her men rough around the edges, but John Zaffino?

"The question for us became," a detective working the case later remarked, "how did Cynthia George end up with John Zaffino? He wasn't her type by any means."

The CAPU, if it wanted to build a case against John Zaffino, was going to have to make that connection.

"Keep looking," Dave Whiddon told his unit. "The answers are out there somewhere."

On the one hand, the case seemed to be opening up. Christine Todaro was aboard. She was planning on recording Zaffino. On the other, it was almost as if the CAPU was back to square one again, chasing something that was probably never going to materialize into an arrest.

59

Detective John Bell and a colleague arrived at Frank Roppolo's house in downtown Akron one afternoon during the second week of June. Roppolo, a cabdriver, wasn't home, but his mother invited Bell and his partner into the house. Mrs. Roppolo said she was concerned for her son. Was he in trouble? Under arrest?

"No, ma'am," said Bell, "we're looking to talk to him about a police report he had filed [sometime ago]. How can we reach him?"

Roppolo had filed a report about Zaffino. It was during a period when Zaffino believed Roppolo and Christine were seeing each other (which they weren't). Even though Christine pleaded with Zaffino to believe her, Zaffino couldn't let it go. Roppolo had a truck parked in Christine's yard. Zaffino trashed it one afternoon, bashing the vehicle with rocks in an act of rage—trying to warn Roppolo to stay away from Christine. In the end, Roppolo had to total the vehicle with his insurance company. He was livid at Zaffino—but also quite unnerved by the entire episode, scared of what Zaffino was obviously capable of doing. "It got to the point," Roppolo told me later, "where I [was scared Zaffino would] kill me and my son. . . ."

Based on the police report Roppolo filed, Bell and his partner were elected by Captain Daugherty to find out exactly what happened, and also find out if Roppolo had heard from Zaffino lately. Was there still any animosity between them?

"Is this about the shooting?" Roppolo's mother asked.

Both detectives looked at each other. "Which shooting?" They hadn't mentioned anything about a shooting.

"The one at BJ's?" Mrs. Roppolo offered, according to Bell's report of the interview.

"Yes, we're interested in that incident, too."

The woman moved slowly. She was obviously in some pain and told the detectives that she had recently suffered a stroke. It was one of the reasons why she had a "tough time" remembering things, but she promised to do the best she could.

"That's OK, ma'am, take your time."

"I do remember the shooting at BJ's."

Bell asked if she knew Christine Todaro. "Sure. But she's *bad* news."

"How can we find Frank?" Bell asked.

"He'll be home around four-thirty," she said. "He's working. I'll call him."

While Mrs. Roppolo was dialing her son's cell phone number, the detectives heard a car pull up outside. It was Frank. Both detectives walked outside to greet him as he got out of his taxicab.

In the report Roppolo had filed with the police, he stated that he believed Zaffino and Christine Todaro were suspects in the murder of Jeff Zack.

They stood in the parking lot talking. Roppolo said, "He [Zaffino] threatens to beat me up all the time.

He's even threatened to kill me. I'm afraid of him. He said he'd come after me with a gun."

The detectives wanted to know how well Roppolo knew Christine. Why was Zaffino so interested in making his and Christine's lives so miserable? Had they all been friends at one time and hung out together? What was it that sparked the hatred Zaffino had for Roppolo?

Roppolo said he was Christine's boyfriend at one time, for many years before she met Zaffino; and after they broke up, they remained good friends. Once she met Zaffino, however, things changed.

"Tell us about Christine," Bell said.

"I'll tell you that she told me once John Zaffino admitted to her that he was the one who killed Jeff Zack. I told her I didn't want to know anything about it. I know the type of person John is. Christine and I are in danger if we talk about it." It was surely the reason why Christine, when the CAPU approached her, hadn't mentioned anything about Zaffino killing Jeff Zack, but then decided to go to the APD and tell them her entire story. "I believe her . . . simply because she's so deathly afraid of John."

Roppolo made a point to explain that if Christine had come forward and said *anything*, knowing that she would eventually have to talk to the cops, thereby putting her life at even more risk than it already was, it spoke of her integrity. Beyond revenge, what motive was there for Christine to lie about such a thing and then, when the cops finally asked her about it, not mention anything significant? If she wanted to sell out Zaffino, she had every opportunity to do so. That alone, at least in Roppolo's view, meant she was being truthful.

Roppolo went on to say Christine acted strange whenever he brought up the subject with her, like she didn't want it mentioned anymore. Adding, "John thinks he's above the law, as if the world revolves around him."

It wasn't smart standing there in the driveway talking. Someone in the neighborhood might see them and put two and two together. Heck, if Zaffino was after Roppolo, he might even drive by the house himself. The last thing Roppolo wanted was word to get back to Zaffino that he had spoken to the cops.

So they walked inside.

Standing, Roppolo continued to speak. "Christine told me that the shooting was a hit, a murder for hire. Zaffino, she said, has been doing 'things' for the Georges. . . . This is why she is so scared—from not only John, but the people that hired him."

By Roppolo's estimate, Zaffino was someone people on the street feared; a point man, a strong arm for more powerful players. "If you beat John up, he will keep coming after you. . . . He's definitely the type to just walk right up to somebody and shoot them. Listen, I don't want to get involved in this."

Bell looked at his partner. They were thinking the same thing. *It was too damn late for that now.*

"I'm still good friends with Christine," Roppolo continued, "and I'll protect her to the end. But I will say this—she's not telling you guys everything she knows. I'll try calling her later and get some more info for you. If I get anything, I'll call."

Roppolo tried calling Christine that night, but couldn't get hold of her. So he swung by her apartment. Her car was in the driveway. Once inside, Roppolo learned that Christine hadn't been answering her telephone because she was frightened it might be Zaffino and she didn't want to face him. She had a feeling he knew she had spoken to the police. Roppolo noticed she was pacing the room, fidgeting with things, chain-smoking cigarettes. He'd never seen her so nervous. Zaffino had gotten into her head. Under her skin. Changed her entire demeanor. The master intimidator. In many ways, Zaffino was still controlling her.

"It's OK," Roppolo promised. "It'll be all right." Even though they hadn't dated in some time, Roppolo still cared deeply for Christine.

"It's *not* all right," Christine raged. Just then, the telephone rang. "Shhh," she said, as if the person calling could hear them talking, "that's John. I know it is."

"You don't *know* that."

Christine was anxious, Roppolo later told police. She was mumbling. The telephone rang three different times while he was there. She believed it was Zaffino each time. (It wasn't, though. Detectives later told Roppolo they had been trying to contact her for another interview.)

As the telephone rang, Christine told Roppolo to be quiet. Then, "John cannot know you are here."

When Christine heard from Roppolo that detectives been over at his house to speak with him, she was furious. *How dare they put me in danger like that.* If Zaffino ever found out that cops were over there talking to Roppolo, he'd put it all together. She couldn't believe that after she had gone into the APD and told them all she knew, and agreed to wear a wire, that they would still send detectives over to Roppolo's house to talk to him. "They didn't know then if Frank and John were friends or not," Christine said later. "They could have been sending a message to John that I was talking to them."

Scared, Frank Roppolo left Christine's apartment and drove straight to the APD.

60

Christine Todaro knew Frank Roppolo was on his way down to the APD to speak with detectives. He had told her where he was going (and why) before he left her apartment. Ever since that night when the CAPU and the FBI had shown up at her house, Christine had been waiting for the ball to drop and Zaffino to show up unannounced in some sort of frenzied, angry rant, accusing her of turning on him. When she proved to Zaffino that the cops had been at her house by giving him their business cards, it only further heightened Zaffino's escalating anxieties that the cops were onto him. He started calling Christine more than he had in the past, asking if they had been back, and urging her to "tell them to f- - - off." This became one of Zaffino's trademark comments to Christine. "Don't tell them *anything*. They have *nothing* on me," he'd repeat.

Christine would kindly oblige her ex-husband by saying, "Of course." But as the vise tightened, Christine felt Zaffino was going to find out sooner or later what she was doing. And when he did, that was it. She'd have to go into exile, move away, running from the guy like she had so many other times in her life.

After Roppolo left her house, Christine was more scared than she had ever been, not to mention "pissed off that the cops had spoken to Frank," and, in her opinion, put her life in more danger. She decided to go down to the CAPU and give detectives a good old-fashioned reaming for showing up at Roppolo's house, knowing full well that the visit might alert Zaffino to what was going on.

Before leaving, Christine called Vince Felber and told him she was on her way. "I need to talk to all of you *right* now," she raged.

Coming out of the sixth-floor elevator inside the APD, Christine was on the prowl for the first detective she would run into. Once they realized she was there, Whiddon, Felber and Daugherty, along with several other detectives working the case, shuffled her into a conference room adjacent to the reception area. Frank Roppolo was in another part of the office already speaking with detectives.

"You might as well put a gun to my head and pull the trigger right now," Christine screamed. "What if, by chance, Frank and John were friends . . . you didn't *know* that when you sent those detectives over there to talk to him. You didn't know that he wouldn't go running to John to tell him what I was doing."

"Calm down," Whiddon said. "Relax, would you."

"Christine . . . ," Felber tried to say.

Roppolo had been at the CAPU for about an hour. He said later that from the room he was in down the hall, he could hear Christine screaming. He also said detectives were trying to play good cop/bad cop with him. "They were trying to say, 'You're involved and we know it. Tell us what you know.' But I didn't really know much of anything."

"Relax?" Christine said sneeringly. "What the f- - - is that . . . relax. How am I supposed to *relax*? If John finds out, I'm done. He'll kill me. Don't you *get* it?"

Things were getting too close for comfort. Christine had known, basically, for nearly a year that Zaffino was involved with Zack's murder; yet she had not come forward because she believed her life—and that of her son and father—was in danger. She was convinced Zaffino thought she was covering for him, even working on his side to make sure police didn't find out what she knew. She had to make him believe this because she feared him so much. On top of that, she had agreed to help the CAPU by wearing a wire and initiating contact with Zaffino. But if they were going pull these types of Keystone Cop maneuvers and jeopardize her safety, she was finished. "I won't help you. Arrest me. I don't care."

Whiddon tried comforting her. Finally, after allowing Christine to voice her concerns, she agreed to continue with the plan.

"What else could I do at that point?" she told me later. "They left me with *very* few options."

61

Early in the morning on June 16, Captain Beth Daugherty called Bertina King. Daugherty was at home. She had an idea. "Check with the LEADS operator to see what kind of vehicles John Zaffino had registered in his name—specifically, *motorcycles*."

No one had thought of it. If Zaffino had purchased a bike to use for the murder, there was going to be a record of it. Maybe they'd get lucky and come up with a match. Moreover, was John Zaffino that stupid to have registered a motorcycle similar to the one used in the murder, in his own name—if, in fact, he had bought a motorcycle for the sole purpose of killing Jeff Zack?

Some believed he was.

Daugherty arrived at work by about noon. She immediately got together with Vince Felber and Bertina King and went through the printout King had in her hand. There it was: a 1995 motorcycle registered to Zaffino, which was previously registered to Midwest Motors on Massillon Road in Uniontown, Ohio.

Things seemed to be coming together.

Daugherty called Midwest. She got hold of the man-

ager, Chris Hause, and explained that she was conducting an investigation and needed information
about a motorcycle Midwest had sold in the neighborhood of a year or more ago.

After Hause looked up the paperwork, he said, "Kris-
tine Petaya was the salesperson."

"Can you fax me a copy of the sales receipt?"

"Sure."

Daugherty had a look at the receipt and called
Hause back. "Can you describe the particular model of
motorcycle Mr. Zaffino purchased?"

"That's a Ninja-style bike . . . black, with a green or
yellow stripe. It's a CBR 1000."

Bull's-eye.

When Daugherty spoke to the actual salesperson
who had sold Zaffino the bike, she said she remembered he was "pushy" and "appeared to be in a hurry. I
felt as though he was in such a hurry that he had to
have the bike on *that* day."

The receipt indicated the bike was sold on May 23,
2001, about 3½ weeks before Jeff Zack was murdered.

"Was he with anyone when he bought the bike?"
Daugherty asked.

"A female. She was thin and white."

Daugherty made an appointment with the salesclerk
to meet at her apartment later that night. She wanted
to ask her a few more questions about the bike. As soon
as they hung up, Daugherty swiveled around in her
desk chair and logged on to the Internet. Then, using
a common search engine, she typed in 1995 Honda CBR
1000. She wanted to see if there was a bike for sale anywhere on the Internet. It was worth a shot, she believed. If Zaffino had sold the bike or given it away, that
person or dealer could have put it up for sale on the

Internet. The eBay craze had created a digital flea market–like stir on the Internet. Even though it left a cyber paper trail, if someone wanted to get rid of evidence, eBay provided a meeting place to dump a bike and hope the buyer was from out of state, or maybe even another country.

Daugherty found several models, but all were manufactured during different years.

Before leaving the office, Daugherty grabbed two photos, one of Christine Todaro and another of Cynthia George, then headed over to Petaya's apartment. It was around seven o'clock.

After asking several questions related to the sale of the bike, she showed the woman both photos, saying, "Recognize either of these women as having been with Zaffino on the day he bought that bike?"

Petaya shook her head. "No, sorry. But you may want to talk to Ken Colpo, our finance manager. I bet he'd remember the sale." Zaffino had paid cash for the bike. It was odd someone would lay out $5,200 and change *in cash* for a motorcycle.

Odd, sure, but not a crime.

Zaffino, Petaya mentioned next, had been into the store a few times in relation to the sale.

"Thanks. I was wondering," Daugherty asked, "would you have any brochures or catalogues with photos of the bike that I could have?"

"You can find the bike on the Internet," Petaya said.

Daugherty wanted to chuckle, albeit respectfully. She had already covered that angle. "I checked it out," she said. "I found nothing."

"Do you have a moment to wait while I go upstairs and do a quick Internet search?"

"Of course."

What Daugherty would soon learn was that when searching the Internet for information or a specific item, the most important factor of the search is *where* you look for the information. It can make all the difference.

Petaya's computer was in her bedroom on the second floor. "Come with me," she said to Daugherty.

They went upstairs. Within a few minutes, Petaya logged on to a specialty motorcycle trader site that Daugherty later described as being "similar to eBay, only that it was dedicated to [the sale of] motorcycles."

It was something Daugherty hadn't done.

As Daugherty stood in back of Petaya, the glare of the computer screen strobing in their faces like a flickering jack-o'-lantern, Petaya typed the make and model of Zaffino's bike into the site's search engine.

And there it was. Only one bike listed under that make and model. From the photo, Petaya was sure it was the same type of bike—maybe even the specific bike Zaffino had purchased.

She printed out the page.

When Daugherty got it into her hands, she realized that the bike had been put up for sale by a used-car lot in Pennsylvania. *Zaffino has an ex-wife in Pennsylvania . . . ?* she thought, standing there and reading the printout. But she couldn't think of the city just then.

"Can I use your computer?" Daugherty asked.

Petaya got up from her chair. "Sure," she said with a curious stare. She could tell Daugherty, in deep thought, was onto something.

Indeed, Daugherty logged onto MapQuest and typed in the name of the city Zaffino was from and found it to be within seventeen miles of Pittsburgh and about seventy miles outside Youngstown, Ohio. "I felt this was very close (in terms of mileage, distance) to where I knew Zaffino had ties," Daugherty later wrote in her report. "The bike on the Web site was the exact model and coloring of the one Zaffino had purchased."

The CAPU now had an enormous advantage on Zaffino; the circumstantial evidence pointing toward him was beyond reproach. At the least, he would have some explaining to do, even if he wasn't involved.

Daugherty and Petaya went back downstairs into the kitchen.

"Can you call the number listed on the Web site?" Daugherty asked. Together, they decided it would be best if Petaya depicted herself as a salesperson who had an interested buyer for the bike advertised on the site. Daugherty knew she couldn't pull off the call herself. She hardly knew anything about motorcycles. The seller might get nervous. And what if the seller was connected to Zaffino? Maybe he had taken the bike to cover up the crime for his friend? Without even trying, Daugherty could destroy a potential piece of evidence just by tipping the guy off that she was interested in the bike. On the other hand, the call was worth the risk: it would tell Daugherty rather quickly if there was anything to get excited about. For all she knew, the bike could have been sold weeks ago. Maybe the Internet ad was old.

Petaya dialed the number and spoke with a man by the name of Russell Forrest. He owned the used-car lot where the bike was being sold. "I got the bike from my fiancée's ex-husband as payment for back child support," Forrest said. He seemed willing to freely give out information. It was a good sign, Daugherty thought.

"Do you still have it?" Petaya asked.

"Yeah. It's in excellent condition."

"Have there been any repairs made to the bike?"

"We replaced one of the tires."

"Thank you for your time, Mr. Forrest. Let me get back to you if my buyer is still interested."

After she finished the conversation with Forrest, Petaya told Daugherty the bike she sold to John Zaffino had a tire replaced prior to the final sale. This was important. The CAPU had taken a rubber sample at the scene of the Zack murder. Now, there was no way they could match up the rubber samples. But at the same time, why was the tire replaced? The tire replacement alone could mean something.

Daugherty left Petaya's apartment around 8:00 P.M., letting her know she was going to call her the following morning. Once she got home, Daugherty called Vince Felber, who confirmed the name of the city where Zaffino's first ex-wife lived. It was a match. The ex-wife's name, he said, was Nancy Bonadio. Through an FBI office in Cleveland, Daugherty was then able to connect the VIN from the sale of the bike to Zaffino and criss-cross it with Forrest Motors, which was owned and operated by Russell Forrest, the man Petaya had spoken to on the telephone—who just happened to be engaged to Bonadio, Zaffino's ex-wife.

It was obvious to Daugherty that she had made the connection between Zaffino and the bike. It all fit. So she called her boss, Paul Callahan, and explained what was going on.

In a sense, Daugherty had broken a major part of the case. She had found the bike. After some heated discussion over what to do next, it was decided the CAPU was going to send two detectives to Pennsylvania as soon as possible. Daugherty called the Pennsylvania State Police (PSP) and discussed the prospect of sending detectives to Pennsylvania to interview Russell Forrest and Nancy

Bonadio. During the course of the trip, the CAPU would, with any luck, get their hands on Zaffino's motorcycle.

"Please don't interview, drive by or in any way have contact with Nancy or Russell until we can devise our strategy for picking up the bike, OK?" Daugherty said to the trooper.

"Sure. No problem."

Later that afternoon, Daugherty met with Petaya again, and got her hands on the original file connected to the sale of the bike. "I recall a few of the details of the sale," Petaya offered, after going through the file. "John Zaffino had been to the store on at least two occasions referencing the same motorcycle. The first time he came to the store he gave me his name as 'John Smith.'"

Petaya, of course, laughed at the name and knew it was fake.

During the time Zaffino had owned the bike, he had hardly put any miles on it. When it was sold, Petaya explained, the bike's odometer read 10,120 miles. The mileage on the bike for sale at Forrest Motors was listed as eleven thousand. Furthermore, there had been a customer promotion going on when Zaffino bought the bike. Whenever they sold a bike, the salesperson photographed the buyer standing next to his or her new purchase. They had a wall of photographs with smiling customers and their new bikes. But after a search, no one could locate a photograph of Zaffino and his purchase. Either he refused to be photographed, a salesperson said, or someone had taken the photo down. There were empty spots on the wall where it appeared photographs had been taken down.

And so it appeared as if the CAPU was finally going to get its hands on the motorcycle that had eluded the detectives for a little over a year. With that motorcycle and Christine Todaro's work with Zaffino getting ready to begin, it certainly seemed like they were narrowing their focus. An arrest, detectives were confident, was coming.

62

When John Zaffino's name became part of the investigation, along with the possibility that the CAPU was going to get its hands on the motorcycle he might have used to murder Jeff Zack, a year certainly had made all the difference in the search for Zack's killer. It seemed that whomever detectives spoke to regarding John Zaffino, each person further placed the former truck driver into a position that at least made him look guilty. Because of this, the CAPU calibrated its investigation and focused exclusively on Zaffino.

"By the time we learned about Zaffino in the spring of 2002," Dave Whiddon recalled later, looking back on the investigation, "we had cleared all of our other leads and really had nowhere to go. . . . When Ed Moriarty retired in April of 2002, the case was pretty much at a standstill. . . . When everything started pointing toward Zaffino, he quickly evolved into our main suspect. The more we found out about him, the more he started to emerge as the shooter."

The turning point, added Whiddon, came when he received a telephone call from a narcotics detective near the same time Captain Daugherty located the bike. It was something, Whiddon added, "I will never forget."

"Hey, Lieutenant," that detective said, "you know that motorcycle I was telling you about?"

"Yeah?"

"Forget about that. I've got something much better."

A few days later, Tim Gardner was sitting in a conference room inside the CAPU talking about Fred Abers, who was dating Christine Todaro at the time. From there, Zaffino's name became part of the investigation.

"It changed everything," Whiddon said. Then Christine decided she wanted to help—and the investigation was reignited.

Even more compelling, as the end of June neared, one of Zaffino's neighbors told detectives that Zaffino had gotten rid of his "neon yellow and black or blue Honda CBX or CBR" right before he moved out of his apartment, which was thought to be the last week of June or first week of July 2001.

The timing fit.

The CAPU soon got a court order to dig deeper into Zaffino's personal records at the management office of his former upscale residence. Those records could be helpful, especially when looking for more people to talk to about Zaffino. The thought was, he must have put down references on the application; personal information he couldn't lie about.

While detectives pored through Zaffino's electric bills, rental agreement and other paperwork connected to his onetime dwelling, the apartment manager, standing by watching, said she needed to say something she had thought about since the last time the CAPU interviewed her. It was about Zaffino's bills. She had no idea how he paid for his living expenses. He was always on time with the rent, but she never really knew him to work all that much.

At this point, detectives asked to speak to anyone that would have had access to Zaffino's apartment: maintenance men, cleaning people, utility workers.

One of the detectives pulled out a photograph of Cynthia. In the photo, she was standing next to Jeff Zack and his son, Ashton. One of the maintenance men, an old guy in his late sixties, pointed to Cynthia and said, "That's Zaffino's girlfriend, all right. And that boy"—Ashton— "has also been in his apartment hanging around with [Zaffino's] boy and a girl [who had to be one of Cynthia's kids] that was younger than the two kids."

According to one detective, the maintenance man was wrong about Ashton. There was no reason Ashton would have been at Zaffino's apartment. The guy was mistaken; he was more likely talking about Zaffino's son, who was around the same age as Ashton.

"Did John have a motorcycle?"

"Sure did," said the maintenance man, the keys hanging off his belt clanking like chimes every time he moved to look down at the photos.

"How do you know?"

"He parked it underneath the upstairs porch. I had to go tell him not to park it there because it was a fire hazard. He had no trouble moving it and never parked it there again."

Here was one of those seemingly insignificant pieces of information that spoke to the heart of the case: the motorcycle. *Find the motorcycle, find the killer.*

Detectives were getting close.

A fairly convincing sketch of Zaffino materialized from the scores of interviews the CAPU had conducted ever since Zaffino's name became part of the investigation. Alone, none of the information proved much of anything substantial; together, a plot of murder emerged.

During a CAPU morning meeting the day after Captain Daugherty found the bike on the Internet, another interesting development—quite a bit more significant—emerged. Daugherty explained to the unit that a woman by the name of Nancy Bonadio, who lived in Allegheny County, Pennsylvania, south of Pittsburgh, had received a Honda CBR 1000, a "black crotch rocket type of motorcycle," as payment for back child support from her ex-husband.

"Who is the ex-husband?" one of the detectives at the meeting asked.

"John Zaffino," said Captain Daugherty. "We're going out there today to take a look at that bike and interview Bonadio and her fiancé, Russell Forrest."

Daugherty then explained that she had been in contact with PSP trooper David Bova, who had recently faxed her a copy of the bike's registration. On the back of the bike's original title (generated from Ohio), John Zaffino had signed ownership of the bike over to Bonadio, who then transferred the bike into her fiancé's name so he could sell it.

Finally the motorcycle every CAPU detective working the case had been looking for seemed to be within arm's reach.

With that information, which pretty much solidified the CAPU's theory that Zaffino had owned a Ninja-style bike at the time of Jeff Zack's murder, Paul Callahan and Beth Daugherty pulled two detectives—Russ Mc-Farland and Mike Shaeffer—aside and told them to pack a bag and drive immediately to Pennsylvania to speak with Bonadio and Forrest. "With any luck, we can locate and seize the motorcycle," Daugherty said.

Shaeffer and McFarland put some things together and got ready for the trip. McFarland had to first set it up with a towing company the department used so that a truck could meet them in Pennsylvania. They had to have everything in order. One of the first rules of productive police work is, any investigator will agree, assume nothing, be ready for anything. "We wanted to go out there before," McFarland later wrote in his report, "[the motorcycle] ended up missing as a result of any renewed efforts on the part of the suspect."

The CAPU, Daugherty explained later, still didn't know then if Russell Forrest and Nancy Bonadio were in cahoots with Zaffino. In a way, they had to assume they were. The worry was that if Zaffino had gotten a sniff of what was going on, there was no doubt he was going to head out there himself, call ahead or do something to obstruct the investigation, whether he had anything to do with Jeff Zack's murder. That bike seemed to be the key right now; it was as good as the CAPU was going to get to a fingerprint left at the murder scene. If Zaffino found out what was going on behind the scenes, the CAPU was never going to see the bike. And without the bike, they knew they didn't have much of a case.

Then there was Christine Todaro: if Zaffino knew what was happening, there was a chance he was going to blame it on Christine, which would, in her view, put her, her son and her father in even greater danger.

"It was that important," recalled one detective.

"Go to that car lot," Captain Daugherty told McFarland and Shaeffer, "and get the bike. If you run into trouble, attempt to get it through a search warrant. The PSP will initiate a warrant while you guys are en route."

McFarland and Shaeffer were excited—the big break everyone had been waiting for. "Still, you never know," McFarland said later, "what can happen. The way the case was going, this could have been just another lead gone astray."

"I was thinking," Mike Shaeffer later told me, "it's going to be a long day. With the possibility of doing a search warrant and the process it takes to get one, and the interviews [with Bonadio and Forrest], plus the two-hour drive both ways, we were going to be gone for a while. I was excited to [possibly] get the motorcycle and to hear what Bonadio and Forrest had to say. I figured this would be a big break in the case and I was more than willing to put the time and effort in to assist."

McFarland added, "We were optimistic. The bike was a key piece of evidence."

Time would certainly tell.

63

Russ McFarland and Mike Shaeffer arrived at the PSP barracks Troop B Headquarters at about 3:00 P.M. They had talked during the drive, but not about the case. Instead, they caught up on family, friends, football. "You know," Shaeffer said later, "we aren't like TV cops, racing to a scene, talking about the case the whole way. We live it. So when we have some driving time, we catch up on family, knowing that once we get to the location, it's going to be *all* business."

Trooper Bova was waiting to greet them, along with two other troopers designated to help any way McFarland and Shaeffer needed. After briefing the PSP about Zaffino and his possible relation to the Zack homicide, filling them in on what had brought them to Pennsylvania, McFarland said, "We want this to be low-key."

It was something Captain Daugherty had encouraged from the moment she found the bike on the Internet. *Patience . . . we can't jump the gun on this.*

The PSP understood. It was agreed one trooper would hang back from the pack of unmarked vehicles heading out there. They would all dress plainclothes, so as not to cause too much of a commotion when they arrived. If word got back to Zaffino even at this late juncture, things might start happening: witnesses disappearing, evidence tampered with. Christine Todaro would be in big trouble. They couldn't chance any of it. They were too close.

By 3:30 P.M., they pulled into the driveway of a ranch-style home. There was a car lot carved out of the side yard, where a large portion of land had been cut like a divot from a steep embankment. Small, triangular-shaped red, blue and white flags hung like Christmas lights, flapping in the slight wind, around an assemblage of cars on display for sale. The sign out front read "Forrest Motors." It was a mom-and-pop place started, apparently, by someone who had lived in the house at one time. The living room and bedroom, McFarland and Shaeffer could see after pulling into the driveway, had been converted into office space. There were about twenty cars out front—no bike that either detective could see—and a spacious two-car garage in the back.

McFarland looked toward the garage as he turned off the car, saying, "That's where it is."

"I bet you're right."

When they got out of the car and walked up to the front door, a woman approached. She said her name was Nancy Bonadio. "Can I help you?"

It was odd that four men were walking up to the office door.

Bonadio seemed genuinely surprised—which was exactly what they wanted.

"I'm Trooper Bova, ma'am. Is Russell Forrest here?"

With a look of grave concern on her face, Bonadio

yelled into the back of the house for Russell, who quickly came out of his office, saying, "Yeah . . . what's up?"

"Mr. Forrest," Trooper Bova said, pointing to McFarland and Shaeffer, "these are two Akron, Ohio, detectives. They want to talk to you."

Forrest seemed fine with it. "Sure, sure . . . what can I do for you?" He invited them into his office.

Closing the door behind them, McFarland began the conversation. "We're investigating a homicide and have good reason to believe that a motorcycle you have"—McFarland pointed to the VIN of the bike on a "waiver" he had in his hand, showing it to Forrest—"was involved. We would like to seize the motorcycle for processing and possibly confirm its involvement [in the homicide]."

"You can have the bike," Forrest said right away, anxiously. "Where do I sign?"

While Forrest signed, McFarland said, "Sometimes a person in possession of a vehicle uses it in a crime and gets rid of it and the bike passes from hand to hand." McFarland offered the comment as comfort. He didn't want it to seem like they were focusing on one particular person, or suggesting anyone was a suspect. It was a tactical move. He and Shaeffer weren't prepared to offer up Zaffino's name.

After Forrest signed the waiver, he shook his head in agreement with McFarland's statement, as if to say, *You bet I'm not involved, but I have a feeling who is.*

Bonadio was standing nearby, not saying much of anything. But there was no doubt she knew by then that the target of the investigation was her ex-husband.

Forrest then spoke up. "I know it's John Zaffino you're looking at." He pointed at Bonadio. "She's my fiancée. She used to be married to him." Forrest had a look of utter contempt on his face; it was clear there was some history between Forrest and Zaffino.

Shaeffer changed the subject and asked Forrest where the motorcycle was being stored.

"In the garage out back," Forrest said, getting up and walking toward his office door. "Come on, I'll take you there."

64

When Christine Todaro decided to come clean with CAPU, in effect she made a decision to put her life on the line. She was fearful of John Zaffino and what he was going to do once he found out—and sooner or later, she knew, he would. Although Zaffino had been playing Christine for the past year, using her as a mark, she still believed he viewed her as an ally. Definitely not someone who was going to turn on him and begin a relationship with the police. "He thinks," Christine later said, "even right up to the day I walked into the Akron Police Department, that I am working for him. I wouldn't have wanted it any other way."

After the CAPU spent hours interviewing Christine and believed she was telling the truth, they hooked up a recording device to her telephone. Wearing a wire and meeting with Zaffino in person was the next step, but first they wanted to hear what Zaffino was telling Christine over the telephone.

As it were, John Zaffino was becoming increasingly paranoid. As each week passed, he had acted more strangely and out of character than the previous. No one had to tell Christine that a paranoid person was capable of anything if he or she felt threatened. And if there was one thing Zaffino had made clear to Christine throughout their relationship, it was that he didn't want to ever end up in prison. Faced with that option, Christine assumed, he was capable of anything. Even, she said, "another murder to cover up the first one."

As the day neared when Christine was going to have to engage her ex-husband in dialogue about Jeff Zack's murder, she grew unsure of herself and what she had agreed to do. But after a long discussion regarding how to handle Zaffino, the CAPU assured Christine that her safety would always come first. There was going to be plenty of "backup" there to support her anytime she went out to meet Zaffino.

It was then decided that the best way to draw Zaffino out was to put him on the defensive. "We go to the *Akron Beacon Journal*," Dave Whiddon explained to Christine, "and we ask them to do a one-year anniversary article about the case."

The article would serve two purposes: one, it would push the Zack case back into Zaffino's face and tell him the CAPU was not giving up; and two, show him that they were no closer to catching their killer than they were on day one.

The article was going to provoke Zaffino, yet also give him a sense of relief. Maybe even throw him off, which would allow Christine to wiggle her way into his embrace and, with any luck, get him to admit he had, in fact, killed Jeff Zack.

Near the end of June, the *Akron Beacon Journal* ran a fifteen-hundred-word article—a lot of space for a daily newspaper—under the headline WHODUNIT PERPLEXES DETECTIVES: ONE YEAR AFTER HIT MAN GUNNED HIM DOWN,

POLICE WONDER WHO WANTED JEFF ZACK DEAD. In the piece, written by *Journal* staff writer Stephanie Warsmith, the idea that the CAPU was at a standstill in its investigation was made clear: "A year ago Sunday . . . a motorcyclist pulled up behind [Jeff Zack], got off the bike and shot him in the head. . . . The identity of the shadowy figure remains a mystery. Police have not yet made an arrest, though they now believe a hit man was responsible. . . . Over the last year, detectives have focused on who might have hired a professional killer—and why."

Ed George was never mentioned in the article as a possible suspect in what the CAPU was saying could be a murder-for-hire plot. Road rage was publicly ruled out for the first time. The CAPU said its focus was now on several new suspects, but urged the public to come forward with any information. Elayne Zack had been interviewed. It was obvious that time had not lessened the pain of losing her son, regardless of what people were saying about him. "He did a lot of nutty things. But he didn't deserve what he got," Elayne told the *Journal.* She said she had spent the past year in counseling, dealing with the loss.

Although the article seemed to imply that Jeff Zack's murder was the result of an affair he was having with Cynthia George, Cynthia's name, like her husband's, was never mentioned.

As the article hit newsstands, Christine went about her daily routine of work and raising her children, waiting for the moment when she felt Zaffino had seen the article and, undoubtedly, wanted to speak to her about it. "The article was designed," Christine said later, "specifically so I could call him after it was published."

A few hours after the article ran, Christine called

Zaffino. He wasn't answering his telephone, so she left him a voice mail: "Hey, it's me. You need to call me right away."

A short while later, Zaffino returned the call.

"What are you doing?" Christine asked.

"Oh, just getting ready to go. I got to get a part for [my son's] four-wheeler."

"Did you see the paper today?"

"No."

"You need to read the paper, John."

"What'd it say?"

"It's in there about that guy—that guy you took out."

65

Late afternoon was upon western Pennsylvania. It was near 4:30 P.M. Nighttime in certain parts of the state can be as dark as a cavern, the sky a shadowy purple velvetlike blanket scattered with sparkling white specks. Not that cops worried about working in the dark, but it was much easier to move around a foreign location during the day. Getting the bike and having it shipped back to Ohio for processing was one of the most important reasons for the trip. Patience was an asset now. Forrest and Bonadio probably had a lot of information to offer, but the bike was the catch.

As they all walked toward Russell Forrest's office exit, en route to the garage, Mike Shaeffer asked Forrest if he, by chance, had any helmets Zaffino might have given him along with the bike.

"Yes, we do," he said. "They're in the closet. Let's go there first."

Inside the closet, Forrest took out two identical helmets: black-gray-and-white. Then he grabbed a saddlebag he said Zaffino had given him, along with the helmets and bike, saying, "When John rode up here from Ohio, he had these two helmets, the saddlebag and title."

"That's it?" Shaeffer asked.

"That's it. Right, honey?"

Nancy Bonadio nodded.

As they walked out to the garage, Forrest began talking about the problems he and his fiancée had been having with Zaffino over the past several months, and as far back as a year ago. McFarland and Shaeffer were of course eager to hear it all. "It was over the helmets," Forrest said. "Three weeks ago, John called my fiancée and said he wanted the helmets back. He apparently had a buyer for them. Nancy said she didn't want to give back anything, since the helmets would probably be sold with the bike."

"What did Zaffino say to that?"

"John threatened Nancy, saying she wouldn't get [their son] back." Zaffino had the boy for the weekend. If she wanted to see her son again, he said, he'd exchange the boy for the helmets. "When Nancy got off the telephone, she came to me and told me what happened."

Forrest called Zaffino. "You're not getting the helmets back," Forrest told Zaffino after a round of yelling and screaming obscenities at each other. "That's final, John," he added, hanging up on him.

Forrest told Nancy that if Zaffino called back, asking about the helmets, explain to him that they had sold them.

When they picked up the boy the next time, Zaffino came wandering out toward the car with a cocky look on his face.

"What do you want?" Forrest asked.

Zaffino smiled. "You don't want to mess with John

Zaffino," he said, talking about himself in the third person. "He's a *bad* dude. If you cross him"—Zaffino waved his finger in front of Forrest's face, back and forth—"he'll get even." He sounded intimidating, Forrest told them.

Forrest told Shaeffer and McFarland that they could take the helmets and saddlebag. "I'll help you guys any way possible." The detectives believed him. He came across sincere, eager to sink Zaffino, who obviously had been a pain in his ass ever since he knew him.

Next to a classic Jaguar—"Nice car," McFarland said—and an RV, which Forrest owned, there sat the motorcycle, kickstand down, standing erect. Both the PSP and Shaeffer took Polaroid photographs of the bike as it stood like the suspect it had become. They wanted to document how they found it. One of the PSP troopers called into the barracks for the tow truck McFarland had set up before he and Shaeffer left Ohio, so it could come in before dark and tow the bike away. Later, that same truck would return the bike to Akron.

Back at the PSP barracks, McFarland and Shaeffer separated Forrest and Bonadio and began asking questions about John Zaffino. It was an official recorded interview. Neither Forrest nor Bonadio had to concede to the interview, it was up to their own discretion. Both wanted to talk, though. They had nothing to hide. "Their body language and facial expressions," McFarland later wrote in his notes of the interviews, "were indicative of truthfulness. Their replies to our questions were immediate. They had no idea we were coming when we did and, therefore, could not be prepared for the interviews. . . ."

Forrest was quick to tell stories about Zaffino that painted him as the thug the CAPU thought he was.

There was one time just recently, Forrest explained, when he drove to a meeting point in Ohio, a restaurant, to meet Zaffino and pick up Bonadio's son. When he arrived, Zaffino was there waiting.

"Go into the restaurant," Forrest heard Zaffino tell his son, "and get yourself a soda." He handed the boy a few dollars.

After watching his son walk into the store, Zaffino addressed Forrest. "The cops are wanting to talk to me. They left business cards at my place."

"What's it about?"

"A homicide."

Bonadio was in California at the time, visiting a family member. Forrest called her when he got home and told her what Zaffino had said. "What?" Bonadio answered, surprised. "My God, Russell, I'm scared for [my son]."

"I know. I know."

They had no idea, according to Forrest, that the situation was connected to the motorcycle, or to Jeff Zack.

Sitting, talking to McFarland and Shaeffer, Bonadio was "terrified" and "nervous," she said. McFarland told her to relax. She wasn't in any trouble. They just wanted to find out a few things about Zaffino.

After she got comfortable and described parts of her life with Zaffino, Shaeffer asked Bonadio if she knew of any girlfriends Zaffino had. "Since I left him? Oh, boy, yes I do. I don't know her last name, but her first name is Cindy. That's what he tells me."

"Who's that?"

"He refers to her as 'Cindy,' and she owns a well-to-do club or restaurant kind of club . . . um . . . and I can't"—Bonadio paused, trying to recall the memory best she could—"I don't even know where, but it's in

Ohio, and he says she got a lot of money and she's probably about my age and he's been with her for . . . I would say, a year anyhow."

"What color hair?"

"Blond."

"How does she wear it?"

"I don't know."

Next they talked about the child Zaffino and Bonadio had together. Bonadio had been married to Zaffino from December 1989 until, she said, "I left him in March of 1995." There had been some sort of trigger that made Bonadio leave; she said she had run to her sister's house in Pittsburgh because she "didn't want John to find" her. The only reason she'd stayed in contact with him was because they had a child together.

Minus the child, it sounded an awful lot like the story Christine Todaro had been telling. Now the CAPU believed John Zaffino terrorized females. That much was clear from what two independent sources were saying.

McFarland wanted to know if Bonadio had ever met Zaffino's new girlfriend, "the blonde." Bonadio said she had. Then she said she knew "Cindy" was "married. . . . And I think her husband is ill, or he's an older gentleman and . . . whether it's her husband's money or the money that they, you know, made together, per se, in a business."

"Does she buy [John] things?"

Bonadio answered immediately: "Yes."

"Like what?"

"She—he actually told me that she bought him the bike." (Nancy Bonadio would later testify to this statement in court. Additionally, the CAPU recorded these interviews with Bonadio and Forrest.)

"Which bike?"

"This bike."

McFarland wanted to know how Bonadio knew.

"I was very upset when he told me that he had a bike," she explained, "because I wasn't getting child support. So I said, 'Well, how the heck can you afford a bike if you can't afford to pay me any child support?' And he said, 'Cindy bought it for me.' He's been out of work sporadically for the past couple of years and I know that she has given him—he tells me that she's given him money."

Not only did Bonadio say that Cynthia purchased the motorcycle for Zaffino, but that she had probably put him up in the well-heeled apartment he had lived in.

Further along into the conversation, McFarland brought up an important point, asking, "Now, when he up and gave you the bike and told you it was for [back child] support, how did you react? Was this out of character for John?"

"I kinda didn't give him a choice. He wanted to get rid of the bike."

"What was that? He wanted to get *rid* of the bike?"

"He told me that he *had* to get rid of the bike and he couldn't take it back to Ohio, and I said, 'Well, you know what then, I'll just keep the money.' I told him you need to get rid of the bike and I need my back child support, so let's just do a fair trade."

McFarland and Shaeffer interviewed Bonadio and Forrest for almost two hours, getting everything they could. McFarland had a way with talking to people, making them feel comfortable. Bonadio was crying during portions of her interview, thinking that she and her fiancé were in legal trouble for taking a bike that was, in her words, "used to hurt someone."

"We're not going to do that to a person who has

helped us," McFarland promised. He was building a
rapport with Bonadio and she began to trust him. "We
view our relationship right here as being nothing but
complete cooperation and help, OK?"

Shaeffer chimed in, adding, "The . . . the only way
you could be, where you had done something wrong,
is if he (Zaffino) would have said, 'Hey, I robbed a bank
and I used this bike.' OK. Then you know a crime
happened."

"When we part today," McFarland added, "we want to
part in peace and confidence that you did the right
thing. Please don't turn anything inward and fault
yourself. You have made no mistakes. Nancy, please believe me on this. You have done nothing wrong."

"All right."

As Bonadio and Forrest were about to leave the PSP
barracks, Bonadio mentioned how afraid she was that
Zaffino would find out she gave the motorcycle to the
police. She feared what he'd do once he realized it was
gone and the police now had it.

"My son—" she started to say through tears.

McFarland promised they would protect the boy at
all costs. Bonadio wasn't too worried Zaffino would
hurt the child, but felt he might take off with him and
run if he found out what was going on.

"We'll do what we can," Shaeffer added. "It's important that you keep us informed as to what is going on
at all times."

Bonadio promised she would.

66

When John Zaffino heard his former wife Christine Todaro say, ". . . that guy you took out," he became defiant and angry. As Christine later described it, he "blew a gasket. That's when you could really see his true personality—when you pissed him off. His true self would emerge."

In a way, Christine felt she was betraying her ex-husband—that sneaking around, and working, essentially, for the CAPU as a CI was a form of deception on her part. Between June 14 and June 21, Christine recorded five telephone calls with Zaffino. "I felt bad, because there was the potential that John could go to jail forever. But, at the same time, I felt worse for Jeff Zack and his family. I loved John when I married him. I never expected my life to end up the way it did with him."

During those early weeks leading up to the first recorded conversations, Christine felt "psychotic," she remembered. "It was weird." The past year had consumed her, physically and mentally. She had lost at least twenty-five pounds: a frail, anxiety-ridden caricature of herself. She had trouble keeping a job because she couldn't focus on what she was doing and rarely got a full night's sleep.

"Chris," Zaffino said after she mentioned the newspaper article and "that guy you took out"—getting louder with each word—"how *dare* you say that."

"Well, there's . . . there's cards on my door from the cops."

"Chris—"

"John," she said jarringly, right back.

"Were you—"

"Well, what am I supposed to say to Tony?"

"What's the card say?"

"They're . . . they're business cards."

"Well, what was in—what'd the paper say?"

"There was a story in there about him," Christine said, and then explained the story.

"OK, well?"

"What am I supposed to tell Tony? They keep showing up here."

"I'd appreciate it if you didn't talk on the phone about stuff, please. OK?"

"Yeah."

"Cause, you know . . . you know they listen."

For Dave Whiddon, as he listened to the telephone call later on that day, Zaffino's reaction was significant. "It was John's reaction when Christine said 'that guy you took out.' John didn't laugh it off and say, 'I didn't do anything.' He told her not to talk about it over the phone." Why wouldn't he say, "You're crazy. I didn't kill anyone"?

Zaffino continued advising Christine not to talk over the telephone about anything having to do with the murder of Jeff Zack. He was adamant. Concerned. Worried that she was saying too much. As they spoke, he became more annoyed with each response Christine offered. At one point, Zaffino said, "Listen to me. When you start panicking, then you start saying stuff that you don't even know what you're saying and get it all screwed up. But see, the thing you got to remember is, they only want to talk to me, that's what they told you, right?"

"Right," Christine said, rolling her eyes.

"So what's, what's the big deal? They only want to talk to me and they don't know where I'm at and they think they do."

"Well, why don't you go talk to them then? If you're not worried about it. You know, so they'll get off me."

"They'll get off you. They'll get off ya. I know they will, and even if they don't, all you gotta do is say, 'Hey, f- - - you. Get the f- - - outta here'."

"I'm not gonna say that."

"That's all you gotta say. Why not?"

"Because."

"Why not? You would say it to somebody else."

Christine laughed. She couldn't escape her own personality. Zaffino knew her well. Christine was never one to take any back talk from anybody—especially cops.

"What kind of message did you leave me?" Zaffino asked. "Real descriptive, or what?"

"No."

Zaffino went on to tell Christine to calm down. "And tell Tony to do the same. Nothing is gonna happen." He wanted the second set of business cards left on her door by the CAPU and promised he would stop by her apartment in a few hours to pick them up.

Instead, Christine decided to meet Zaffino in the parking lot of a strip mall in Fairlawn, just east of

Akron, a few miles from the Tangier. When she hung up, Christine was frazzled. So she called Vince Felber. "He wants me to meet him, I'm scared."

"Relax," Felber told her. "Let me get back to you after I get some things together."

The CAPU took Zaffino seriously. Christine couldn't say enough about how dangerous a face-to-face meeting with Zaffino was now. So Whiddon got every available detective he could find, along with members of the SWAT team, and set up surveillance at the strip mall, where they were scheduled to meet. They decided Christine would meet them first at another location, where they would hide a listening device on the floor of her car. With any luck, this would be the first and last time she would have to lie to Zaffino and try to entice him into admitting his role in Jeff Zack's murder.

"Never, under any circumstances, get into his vehicle," Felber warned Christine as her car was fitted with the device.

"OK."

A while later, Zaffino pulled up to Christine as she sat in the mall parking lot. Then he got into her car and immediately went into a rant. She could tell he was screaming mad by the look on his face. "What the f- - - do you think you're doing? Don't ever say that on the phone again. Are you f- - - - - - crazy? You're going to send me to jail."

"Calm down, John."

"I didn't do anything. They really can't do anything to me. But still, don't *ever* say *anything* like that *ever* again on the phone. I mean it."

"What do you want me to do, John?"

"What if they're recording our conversations, for crissakes. Are you f- - - - - - crazy?"

What have I gotten myself into? Christine thought. *Oh, my God.*

Nothing of substance came out of the first meeting; however, the conversation proved to detectives—and Christine, for that matter—that Zaffino was now more paranoid than he had perhaps ever been. The fact that Christine was mentioning him in reference to Zack's murder only heightened his fear that she was beginning to protect herself. In fact, Zaffino was so concerned the cops were listening to his cell phone calls that he used two cell phones, Christine explained: one to roll his calls over to the other, thinking that forwarding his calls to the second number would block the CAPU's recording and tracing abilities. Christine laughed to herself at the prospect. She had worked in telecommunications for the better part of her adult life and knew it didn't matter. "It showed me, really," she said later, "how stupid he actually was."

"I'll be in touch," Zaffino said as he got out of her car. "Remember what the f- - - I said."

"Bye, John."

67

After Russ McFarland and Mike Shaeffer finished interviewing Nancy Bonadio and Russell Forrest, McFarland grabbed the cell phone from his waist, snapped it open and dialed his boss, Dave Whiddon. McFarland had some great news to share. They had all been waiting for this for quite some time. Shaeffer and McFarland had seemingly cracked the case, not only locating the bike, but what Bonadio and Forrest had to say regarding how Zaffino had dropped it off was significant.

Dave Whiddon wasn't at the office. He was with his wife and son at a Little League game. Whiddon was a dedicated cop, but family, some of his colleagues suggested later, came first. It was one of the reasons why he had taken the lieutenant's job in the first place; he could delegate the work instead of going out there and doing it himself. It would keep him closer to home and, as much as he could bear it, off the street.

Near 6:30, or perhaps it was closer to 6:45 P.M., he couldn't remember exactly what time, Dave Whiddon was standing in the third base coach's box out on the field in the middle of a game, cheering on his son's

Little League team—when his cell phone rang. Although Whiddon is not one of those fathers who argues with the umpires and lets the game get the best of him, he does, he said, "get pretty intense when [he's] coaching." So the call, although expected, startled him.

At the time, the game had taken the case temporarily off Whiddon's mind. He knew McFarland was going to call; he just didn't know when. Standing, coaching third base, with his back to the bench of his son's team, Whiddon could almost feel the parents sitting in the gallery just beyond the dugout breathing down his back. So when his cell phone rang, the entire bench and bleachers of parents could hear it. It was right in the middle of an inning; there were two kids on base.

Looking back toward his wife, shrugging, Whiddon picked up the phone.

McFarland was barely able to contain his excitement. "Lieutenant, we got the bike. The Pennsylvania State Troopers were wonderful," he said.

"Great, Russ. That's great." Whiddon punched the air. One of his players was up at bat.

Pitch.

Hit.

The ball went into the outfield.

Whiddon, trying to watch the game and talk to McFarland, kept his eye on the ball.

"Hold on," McFarland said over Whiddon's excitement, "I've got even better news." McFarland could tell there was a commotion going on in the background.

"What is it?" Whiddon had zoned out of the game and lost track of what was happening on the field.

"Me and Mike interviewed Nancy Bonadio and Russell Forrest. Zaffino brought the bike over to Pennsylvania in the middle of the night. . . . [He put] *duct tape* over the paint to cover the colors." Whiddon was stunned. The play in the field was still going on. He didn't know it, but the parents and players in back of him were staring at him. "They gave us their word," McFarland added, "that they would not say anything to Zaffino."

As McFarland continued talking, one of Whiddon's base runners had made it past second base and was heading toward third—coming right at Whiddon, and looking for direction. Still on the phone talking to McFarland, Whiddon waved the kid home. "Go, run . . . run."

"What?" McFarland asked. He thought Whiddon was talking to him.

"Nothing."

Later, Whiddon said, "Needless to say, I was overjoyed, so much so that I was now screaming very loudly into the phone. I was very relieved that we finally had a great stroke of luck in this case and everything turned out better than I could have imagined."

When the conversation was over, Whiddon turned around to see all of the parents and kids on the bench staring directly at him. He didn't realize how loud he had been talking and how much the excitement of the moment had inspired him. Whiddon's wife knew he was expecting to hear from McFarland, and she was now focused on him—half embarrassed, half thrilled that the case, obviously, was moving in the right direction.

Whiddon was overjoyed. After the inning, he called Captain Daugherty and told her the good news. After all, it was Daugherty who broke the motorcycle lead to begin with. "That's great, Dave," she said. "That's wonderful."

68

The interviews of Nancy Bonadio and Russell Forrest that Russ McFarland and Mike Shaeffer recorded cleared up some loose ends in the case, as much as they interjected several new questions into the mix. The CAPU had always wondered how and where the motorcycle had fit into the murder of Jeff Zack. Now they felt they knew. According to Bonadio, it was back on June 17, 2001, the day after Zack's murder, when she first heard about the bike. Bonadio was generally in bed by nine o'clock on most nights, and considered any telephone call to her house after that hour "late." While she was nestling herself in bed next to her fiancé, the telephone startled her at about 10:00 P.M., she said. Her heart pounded. Any call at that hour generally meant bad news. "Hello?" she said, groggy, worried.

"It's John."

He sounded "very upset," Bonadio told McFarland. She could hear it in his voice.

Bonadio hesitated briefly. *Great, it's John.* The guy was a damn nuisance. She couldn't get rid of him. "What do you want? It's late. What's the matter?"

"I know. I know. I gotta get rid of this bike. I'm going to get into trouble with it someday."

"A bike?"

"I need to get rid of it. I want to trade it for a vehicle Russell has on the lot."

"Why do you need to get rid of a bike, John?"

Zaffino sounded hurried. Frantic. Even manic. "I was chased by the cops . . . a few times for speeding. I need to get rid of it or I'll lose my CDL license, or worse, kill myself." Zaffino claimed he had never ridden a high-performance motorcycle with such road supremacy, Bonadio explained. It wasn't what he was used to. She had no idea why he bought the bike to begin with if it wasn't what he was used to or wanted.

"OK," Bonadio said, "sure, you can bring the bike to me. I don't know if Russ will work with you on it, but we can ask him. We can talk to Russ and see what he thinks."

Bonadio assumed that the conversation would end there. Her ex-husband had gotten what he wanted. Maybe he could cut a deal with Forrest and dump the bike. But then, "I'm coming tonight," Zaffino said.

This startled Bonadio. *Why now? Why the urgency?*

"Maybe two in the morning or something," Zaffino said next. "I want to leave when no one is out on the road."

On Monday morning, June 18, 2001, two days after Jeff Zack's murder, John Zaffino called his ex-wife again. They had spoken during the morning on Sunday as Zaffino traveled into Pennsylvania. But later that morning, he called to say he was at a local Super 8 Motel, right up the road from Russell Forrest's used-car lot. He wanted to stop by with the bike as soon as possible and get rid of it.

Bonadio said she was too busy.

The next day, Tuesday, Zaffino called back. It was 7:00 A.M. "What time can I come out? I need directions." Zaffino hadn't been to Bonadio and Forrest's house before. Whenever they exchanged their child, they met halfway between Ohio and Pennsylvania. He wanted to drop the bike off at her house, not the used-car lot.

At about 10:00 A.M., Zaffino showed up with the bike. Bonadio later described the bike as being "gray with green neon striping on it . . . a high-performance motorcycle." But when Zaffino first arrived, she couldn't see any green on the bike. "John had covered the green stripes up with gray duct tape."

Standing, looking at the bike, Bonadio asked, "Why'd you cover up the stripes?" It seemed strange, over the top, even for Zaffino.

"Because I didn't want the green stripes to catch anybody's attention."

But he had traveled in the middle of the night. All this for a speeding ticket?

After Zaffino peeled the duct tape off the bike—"He didn't want me to scratch the paint," Bonadio said—he asked his ex-wife for a ride back to Ohio, or the keys to a Jeep in Forrest's lot. Bonadio called her fiancé and told him what was going on. "He wants to exchange the bike for a Jeep. Would you be interested in doing that?"

"No." Bonadio discussed the situation with Forrest and hung up shortly.

"John," she said, "we can't help you out. We can't take the bike in on a trade. We can't trust you to take on a car payment when you haven't been able to pay me child support for years." Bonadio expected Zaffino, knowing his temperament and history of anger, to snap. Go off on some tangent, screaming that the deal was over. *Forget it. I'm keeping my bike.* But, "Actually," Bonadio said later, "he was OK with it. He didn't give me a hard time."

"I just need to get rid of that bike," Zaffino said. "Now I need a ride home."

"I'll take the bike for the back child support, since it's worth what you owe me," Bonadio said. "I'll call Domestic Relations in Warren County and clear up your account and tell them you paid me and we can start all over again."

To her utter amazement, Zaffino agreed. ("He was OK with it.") Suddenly, Mr. Disagreeable, someone who, in the past, hardly ever wanted to work with Bonadio on anything that didn't benefit him directly, was willing to go along with whatever she said.

I need to get rid of the bike.

Bonadio agreed to drive Zaffino halfway. Maybe somebody could meet him. Zaffino pulled out his cell phone and dialed up a number while Bonadio stood by, waiting. "I'm calling Cindy, my girlfriend," Zaffino made a point of saying.

As they drove, Bonadio questioned her ex-husband about how he could have possibly come up with the five thousand to buy the bike to begin with. "Where'd you get *that* kind of money, John?"

Zaffino smiled. "Cindy bought it for me."

69

John Zaffino grew up in Warren, Pennsylvania. According to a few of his former friends, as soon as Zaffino got a couple of drinks in him, he became vicious and violent. Quite stocky—his weight was proportioned well—he had brown eyes and brown hair. Zaffino generally kept to himself, but wasn't afraid to step into a situation and voice his rather stern opinions. One of the things that made Zaffino angry was when people didn't conform to his wishes. It might be at a fast-food restaurant. Something simple, as when the restaurant failed to make his meal to his liking. He'd go off on a rip. There was one time, an acquaintance later said, when Zaffino didn't like a hamburger Burger King had given him and he screamed at the clerk for *fifteen* minutes before leaving the restaurant and ranting about the hamburger during the entire thirty-minute drive home. It was those little things that flipped a switch in Zaffino and turned him from a quiet guy into a loaded gun. His son, when he was two years old, squirted him in the face with some water one night. Zaffino snapped, put the boy in his room and screamed at his wife, throwing her against the refrigerator before striking her in the face with an open hand. All because the kid, having a little fun, splashed some water in his face.

Nancy Bonadio met Zaffino at a bar in the Kinzua Dam area of Pennsylvania in 1987; they married two years later. She was twenty-eight; Zaffino, born on September 22, 1966, twenty-two. Later, she would tell police, "Well, he was rather angry all the time. Anything would set him off. Sometimes he was the nicest guy in the world and then he would just turn around and just be the meanest guy." According to both of his ex-wives, Zaffino liked to verbally abuse women: he loved to shoot obscenities and nasty remarks at not only them, but anyone who pissed him off. Bonadio, from the early months of the marriage, lived in fear of what type of guy she would come home to at night.

A week after Bonadio was interviewed by McFarland and Shaeffer, she picked her son up from Zaffino after a scheduled visitation. There was no mention of her talking to police. He never asked about the bike or the helmets. That night, she called the CAPU to fill them in. "I saw him," she explained. "He told me he had hired an attorney, but had not talked to police yet. He said he wasn't going to talk to you guys without an attorney. He denied being involved in the murder. I told him he had nothing to worry about then."

Bonadio feared that if she failed to allow Zaffino to see his son, he would "become suspicious"—it was the only reason she agreed to let him take the boy after she learned about the bike and his possible involvement in Zack's murder. She told McFarland she was going to continue to allow Zaffino to visit the boy. She was convinced, she said, that he would never harm the child and promised to call the CAPU every time she dropped her son off in Ohio. Yet, she was worried about something: "What if he asks me about the motorcycle?" Bonadio wondered.

"Have Russell generate a pseudoreceipt of sale on the bike and keep a copy of it," Detective McFarland suggested. "If John ever brings up the bike, say you guys sold it. If he challenges you guys on it, show him the receipt."

Bonadio sounded scared of the prospect, but agreed.

"One more thing," McFarland warned. "Show him the receipt *only* if he expresses doubts about you guys selling the bike."

"OK."

"Never," McFarland concluded, "volunteer the receipt."

70

Vince Felber and Dave Whiddon were certain the mysterious blonde in the Suburban who showed up at Zaffino's apartment at various intervals was, in fact, Cynthia George. By Zaffino putting Cynthia down on his rental agreement as a "friend" to call in case of an emergency, it convinced the two detectives that Cynthia and John had an ongoing relationship. Were they friends, however, or lovers?

McFarland got a bead on a woman who lived one house away from Zaffino when he resided at the upscale complex. Two CAPU detectives had already spoken to her, but McFarland wanted to follow up and lock down a statement.

Meanwhile, several other detectives scoped out Zaffino's Rittman, Ohio, apartment, where he now lived, but saw no sign of him. He was obviously onto what the CAPU detectives were up to and stayed away from the apartment as much as he could. While the CAPU had never conducted twenty-four-hour surveillance, they were about to begin watching the place more than they had in the past. There was no chance the CAPU was going to approach Zaffino at this point. It was still too early. They needed more evidence against him. If he had killed Jeff Zack, someone had sold him a gun. They needed to find that source.

Zaffino's former neighbor was certain the woman who had been over to his apartment on occasion was Cynthia George. The time frame was between May and June 2001. McFarland pulled out a photograph of Cynthia. "That woman in the photo has the last name George and her family owns the Tangier," the woman said. "She was often out there to see John Zaffino. I know it was her. She had Medina plates on her Suburban."

"How do you know for certain who she was?" McFarland asked.

"Well, John told me during a conversation I had with him one day. He called her Cindy, and he said she was a model. I remember because my daughter used to be into modeling."

In late June, Christine Todaro called Zaffino one night to try to get him to talk about the murder. Christine didn't want to record any more of her calls, though. As each day passed, she grew more scared that Zaffino would find out what she was doing. "It was that simple for me," Christine said later. "I thought he would kill me."

After some small talk, Christine and Zaffino got into a bit of minutia about the case the CAPU was building against him. Zaffino knew they had something and were working on it. He could sense the net closing. Christine was desperate to get him to say anything substantial. Zaffino carried on about what she should say and do when the cops questioned her, adding, "Don't say anything. Tell them to f- - - off."

Christine repeatedly said she couldn't do that.

Zaffino was worried she would say the wrong thing without realizing it. "I don't want them to know about Nancy [Bonadio]," he said. "She'd turn me inside out, whether she knew anything or not."

Unbeknownst to Zaffino, however, it was too late for that. The CAPU had the bike, which Zaffino was undoubtedly referring to when he mentioned Nancy Bonadio to Christine.

"All right," she said.

"If she could, she would."

After a laugh, Christine said, "You haven't heard anything from her yet? Did you call?"

"No, not yet. I was supposed to go in and see my lawyer yesterday, but I couldn't make it."

A while later, Christine brought up the CAPU and asked Zaffino if he was going to call them. "That's why you wanted their cards, right?"

"No. I'm not calling them."

They talked a little more regarding how Christine was going to pay her bills. She was out of money. Wasn't working. And was having a tough time making ends meet. She blamed it all on Zaffino, saying that she had gotten herself mixed up in his life and it was destroying hers. But Zaffino didn't seem to care much about what Christine said. "Whatever you do, if you get panicked, don't say nothing on the phone. I mean, if you sound panicked and they are listening to you, they'll . . . there's a reason for all of this. . . ."

"All right," Christine agreed.

As June ended and the scorching heat of July began, Zaffino kicked up his communication with Christine. Whenever he brought up the idea that she might be turning on him, Christine smartly mentioned Cynthia

George. Christine had admitted to Zaffino that CAPU officers were still showing up at her house and asking questions about him. But she insisted she was playing it cool and not telling them anything. "You need to be concerned about trusting *her*," Christine said once. "Not me. You don't even know Cindy. You don't even know what she's like. Who is she, John? Do you even know?"

Whenever Christine brought up Cynthia's name, it rattled Zaffino and pushed him into changing the subject. But on this particular call, Zaffino broke into a rage centered on Christine and her "friends" talking to the police. He had heard the cops were moving in on her friends and interviewing them. He felt they would crack sooner or later and say something to hurt him.

Christine said, "Why don't you just go in and talk to them yourself?"

"No f- - -ing way."

"Well, if you didn't do anything, as you say, then go talk to them. I'm sick and tired of them coming to my house talking to me about you."

"F- - - them. I'm not saying nothing to them. I'll get my lawyers."

"Fine, then, John. I'm going to get me a lawyer, too."

Once she said that, it was important Christine follow through, she said, because she knew Zaffino would check it out.

"That's good," Zaffino said. "Them cops will have to go through your attorney, not you."

71

Dave Whiddon and Vince Felber took a ride out to Christine's house one day and asked her if she had a minute to listen to a tape. It was that threatening message somebody had left on Jeff Zack's answering machine a few days before the murder. Whiddon and Felber believed it was Zaffino, but had a feeling it could be Seth, the guy in Florida Jeff Zack had quarreled with over that aluminum-siding project. Seth had passed a polygraph, but if the case against Zaffino ever made it to court, the CAPU had better be prepared to show it had investigated every potential suspect thoroughly. Zaffino had hired Larry Whitney, an attorney the CAPU had a long relationship with. Whitney was meticulous. He would attack the CAPU's case on all sides.

Standing inside Christine's kitchen, Whiddon put the tape into a recorder and pressed play: "All right, buddy, you've got one more out. You need to start carrying your cell phone, OK? I'll be talking to you."

Whiddon then looked at Christine for her immediate reaction. "So what do you think?"

Whiddon later wrote in his report, Christine stood and "immediately" said, "That's definitely John. I cannot believe he was that stupid enough to leave a message on Jeff Zack's machine before he killed him." (Later, Whiddon told me, "There was no doubt in Christine's mind that the voice was Zaffino's. And, after we started recording his conversations with Christine, I, too, was convinced by listening to his voice on those tapes.")

At about the same time, Russ McFarland drove over to the apartment complex and played the message for one of Zaffino's neighbors. "It sounds like him," she said, "but I cannot be sure."

"Thanks," McFarland said.

By the Fourth of July holiday, Whiddon had contacted Herbert Joe, a voice analysis expert. Out of his Texas laboratory, Joe's firm did comparative examinations. Whiddon felt that since he had a few conversations recorded between Zaffino and Christine, Joe could take those samples, along with the voice mail message, and make a comparison.

Joe said it would take some time. He told Whiddon to send the tapes, along with the actual answering machine. Whiddon packaged everything up—including a sample of Seth's voice—and sent it to Texas. ("I was told it was going take a long time for Herbert Joe to come up with an opinion.")

72

CAPU officers were looking for a connection between Ed George and John Zaffino. The idea that Ed could have hired Zaffino couldn't be ruled out. They believed the common denominator was Cynthia; however, there was, at this juncture, no proof that Cynthia George was anything more than Zaffino's friend. To the CAPU, Cynthia was a bona fide—albeit, promiscuous—wife of a well-respected Akron businessman. They had to be careful. On paper, however, Cynthia looked more like the conduit through which a connection could be made between Ed George and Jeff Zack's murder.

Captain Daugherty wanted more than speculation and theories, though. She knew there was something out there. During her career, Daugherty said later, she had always been attracted to the document side of investigating. She loved the tedious repetition of rummaging through scores of documents looking for a needle. For most investigators, the process of combing through thousands of pages of mind-numbing text is a part of the job they loathe. Yet Daugherty was from the school that believed documents, providing they hadn't been tampered with, told a fairly truthful story. They could reveal parts of a case no other piece of evidence could. That being said, the best documents, Daugherty asserted, are bank and telephone records taken directly from the source. If you subpoena a bank or phone company and get those documents directly from them, no one has had a chance to manipulate them.

With that, Daugherty took out hundreds of pages of bank and telephone records connected to the Zack case that were stacked in several large boxes, sitting near her desk, and started to go through them, looking for, of course, any connection between Zaffino and Cynthia, or Zaffino and Ed George. "Generally speaking," Daugherty explained to me later, "when you get bank records straight from a bank, the bank could care less about them, so we know they're not altered."

The CAPU had subpoenaed Cynthia George's bank. The was no real plan as Daugherty sat down and started sifting through the records. She wasn't looking for anything in particular, more like she was searching for something that stood out. But while looking at the day Zaffino had purchased the motorcycle, Daugherty noticed Cynthia had withdrawn $5,300 in cash. When she matched up the withdrawal with the price Zaffino paid for the bike, the amounts matched almost identically. More than that, within a five-hour window, Daugherty noticed as she checked the times, Cynthia had withdrawn the money and Zaffino had purchased the bike.

It could be a coincidence, sure. But if nothing else, it was enough to look deeper. In fact, the one glitch in the paperwork, Daugherty soon realized, at first seemed like a major hurdle to get around. When Daugherty noticed the close proximity in which the time of the withdrawal matched the sale of the bike, she called the bank to find out which branch, exactly, Cynthia had withdrawn the money from. She was trying to time the purchase against the sale of the bike: the location where Cynthia had taken out the cash as compared to the location where Zaffino had purchased the bike.

The bank representative told Daugherty the withdrawal was made in Michigan.

Michigan? Daugherty wondered. It didn't make sense. Why in the heck would Cynthia drive to Michigan to withdraw money when she could do it right in town?

Then again, Daugherty thought, maybe the trip was part of the plan? But after further analyzing it, *There's no way,* Daugherty thought, *Cindy could have withdrawn the money in Michigan and made it to the bike shop in five hours.*

Maybe she wired Zaffino the money?

After going through it over and over, Daugherty learned that she had given the bank rep the wrong set of routing numbers. The actual physical withdrawal, she found out after calling back and giving the woman the right numbers, was in Montrose, Ohio, a town that, centrally speaking, is in between Akron and Medina, where Cynthia lived with Ed and the kids. This, of course, made more sense. Yet, what further piqued Daugherty's interest was that the bike shop was a twenty-minute drive from the bank. "I ended up," Daugherty said later, laughing at her own mistake, "making several unnecessary phone calls and talking to a bunch of unnecessary people for unnecessary reasons because of a couple numbers I transposed."

"It certainly started to look like Ed [George] was involved, once we found that connection between John Zaffino and Cindy George," said one of the detectives. "We just had to prove it."

PART THREE

73

On July 14, 2002, Christine Todaro decided to tighten the noose around John Zaffino's neck with the hope of stirring a reaction. Her days of undercover work and sleuthing for the CAPU needed to end. It was excruciatingly nerve-racking, not to mention danger-ous. Thus far, all those telephone calls and meetings be-tween her and Zaffino hadn't yielded what the CAPU could classify as a smoking-gun admission. Zaffino had been smart in one way, not giving Christine too much in the form of relative information regarding Jeff Zack's murder and his possible connection to it.

"Hey," Christine said when Zaffino picked up his tele-phone that night, "you really actually may be a suspect, you know that?" During their few previous conversa-tions, they had talked about how much of a suspect the CAPU considered Zaffino. He would ask Christine what they had spoken to her about and, through her answer, try to gauge where the CAPU's focus was heading.

"How the *f*--- could I even be a suspect?" Zaffino said in a fit of aggression. "They just threaten."

"Yeah, well . . . gotta check it out, I guess. There's a lot of ins and outs—"

"Like what?"

"What you gave me."

"Do *what?*" Zaffino misunderstood her.

"*Something* that you gave me."

"What'd I give you?"

"You gave me those [bullets]."

"No," Zaffino yelled. He was screaming mad that Christine had mentioned such a thing over the telephone.

"I mean, I don't know what for."

"Yeah, yeah, yeah, yeah, yeah. That's, uh, why would you even talk like that, talk about stuff like that." He started mumbling under his breath. Huffing and puffing. *Why would you talk about guns over the telephone?*

"Because I want to make sure I don't go to jail for any reason."

"Well . . ."

"You have to tell me everything."

"Well . . . ," Zaffino said. Christine could almost hear him laughing.

"Cause if I go there, then I don't look like an idiot. That's going to make me look bad in front of them, you know?" She was trying to convince him to give her something to feed to the CAPU. If he did that, they might get off her back.

"Well, who knows that other than you?" Zaffino asked.

"Nobody," Christine responded.

"All right, then."

Christine started talking about Cynthia, referring to her as "that chick." How much did *she* know? Was Zaffino being careful?

"No, no, no," he said smartly. "You know me better

than that. That s---'s pissing me off." Zaffino then broke into a tirade about the CAPU recording all of his telephone calls. He said he knew they were. And it didn't matter what she told them in person, because now she was spouting off at the mouth over the telephone and perhaps giving them all they needed. He told Christine she needed to stop. "I told you they listen. They're recording all my conversations right now."

"You know that for a fact?" Christine asked. "He [Chris's attorney] said he doubted that very much. They don't even have that kind of technology over there."

"He said that?" Zaffino seemed to calm down. It gave him a sense comfort to hear that Christine's lawyer had disagreed.

"Yeah, he deals with them all the time."

"He said they wouldn't be listening to my calls?" He paused, then added, "Well, before you dig yourself a hole you can't get out of, I would assume that they can."

They decided to meet the following day. "But remember," Zaffino warned, "you don't talk to *anybody* . . . not even the pope." He managed to sneak out a quick laugh. "*Anything* you say can and will be used against you in a court of law."

The following morning, Christine called Zaffino and, being guided by Whiddon and Felber, tried the angry ex-wife approach, to see if she could get a rise out of him. "Hey, it's me."

"What?"

"I talked to my attorney. Now I *know* that you have been f------ lying to me for a long-ass time."

There was a pause. Christine sounded angry.

"What are you talking about?" Zaffino wondered.

"Oh, how 'bout Cindy George?"

"What about her?"

"That you and her f------ ass were dating and I asked you about that specifically and you denied it."

"Why would you say that?" he fumed.

"Because I asked you that when it started."

"No, why would your attorney say that?"

Christine realized she had better think of something fast. She didn't expect such a comment. "Because they're . . . they're checking things out. They know that you lived on [his former address]. They know that you, that she's been over there and she knows and they know a lot more than that too, which I'll get into later on today. But that's one thing that I wanted to say to you over the phone. That's f---ed up and—"

Zaffino cut her off. "Shut up . . ."

"And let me tell you something else while I'm talking to you and you're going to listen to me." Christine knew how to turn the tables. "That chick has f---ed around on him (Ed George) for years . . ."

"You gonna come meet me?"

". . . and years and years and—"

"Did you hear what I said?"

"Yeah, I heard you."

"Uh, meet me over where we meet up at—"

"What time?"

"Now." Zaffino was livid. Christine could feel his negative, furious energy channeling through the telephone. But after he calmed down a bit, Christine explained that she had just gotten out of the shower and it would take her some time to get ready and drive to Fairlawn.

"An hour?" Zaffino wondered. He wanted a time. He was upset that it was going to take so long.

"Yes," she said. "I'm pissed at you for that. I don't appreciate it. That's f---ed up and I'm telling you right now that she's a whore and I hope you didn't waste your whole life on that bitch, OK?"

It was the perfect statement. Get Zaffino to feel like he was taking the fall for someone else. Still, covering himself, he said, "I don't know what you're talking about. Cause I don't, if you believe everything you hear, then you're f- - -ed up."

They both started yelling back and forth. Christine, to her credit, held tough. She said she didn't appreciate being lied to. They had built their relationship since the cops started coming around on trust and she was put off that Zaffino had broken that agreement in some way. But it was all, of course, nonsense—a well-scripted, intelligent argument on Christine's part.

"Well," continued Christine, "I don't appreciate being lied to."

"Well, you can't believe what you hear, I don't want—"

"I do believe that. . . . Why else would she be at your house?"

"Well, who said that, first of all?"

"Huh?"

"Who in the hell said that?"

"I don't know. There were people talking over there where you used to live. They know what you used to drive. They know everything about you, John. . . . That pisses me off. I sure hope it was worth it."

"I don't know what you're talking about."

Christine needed some time before they met, she said.

"Hurry up," Zaffino urged.

A while later, Christine called him back to let him know she was on her way, further playing up her role, saying, "I'm so pissed at you. You have no idea how pissed off I am."

"You have no idea how pissed off I am at *you*."

"I don't care how pissed you are at me. I really don't care at this moment. I'm leaving here in fifteen minutes."

"OK."

74

In some respects, John Zaffino was a smart criminal. During a meeting on July 14 with Christine Todaro, Zaffino kept fairly quiet about his role—if any—in the death of Jeff Zack. While sitting next to Christine in her car, Zaffino screamed at her for ten minutes, hooting and hollering about why he was right and why she was wrong regarding the argument they'd had about Cynthia George on the telephone earlier that day. When he was finished with his earsplitting diatribe, Zaffino told Christine to call him the following day. "OK," she said. *Jesus. What an animal.*

The next morning, they spoke and agreed to meet at the same strip mall in Fairlawn, which had become, by now, a place they could refer to over the telephone without naming it. This satisfied Zaffino. He liked the idea. But what he didn't know was that before Christine met him on any occasion, she would first meet Whiddon, Felber and other members of the CAPU at a housing development a few miles away from the mall to get set up with a wire. The equipment the CAPU had was outdated and shopworn, several detectives later told me. It wasn't the best recording gear an undercover officer or informant would hope to have at his or her disposal. On this day, Whiddon strapped a fake pager to Christine's side and sent her on her way. Felber reminded her, "Whatever you do, don't get in his vehicle."

About five minutes later, Christine was sitting inside her car calling Zaffino. When she arrived at the mall parking lot, she didn't see Zaffino's black Ford Explorer. "Where are you?" she asked when he answered his cell phone. "I don't see you."

Zaffino was just pulling in. He was likely parked across the street in the Wal-Mart parking lot, scoping Christine out as she arrived. "I'm here," he said.

"Oh, all right," she said, turning, looking toward the entrance, watching Zaffino pull in, "there you are."

Zaffino pulled up next to Christine, took a hard look around the parking lot—Whiddon, Felber and the rest of the CAPU surveillance team were in unmarked vans scattered throughout the parking lot and across the street.

Christine sat in her car, expecting her ex-husband to jump out of his vehicle and sit down next to her in her car.

But not today.

"Get in," Zaffino said from the driver's side window of his truck.

"What?" Christine yelled back.

They had always met inside Christine's car. She had never gotten into Zaffino's vehicle. It was way too dangerous. Inside her own vehicle, Christine had a slight advantage. At least that's how she felt: in control. With Zaffino at the wheel, she believed she had no chance. On this day, something was up, she could sense it.

"Get in my truck," Zaffino said again.

Son of a gun, he knows something, Christine told herself. Looking around the lot, Christine realized that if she didn't get into his truck, he would think something was going on. She couldn't chance it. All the work she'd put into helping the CAPU—in a way, it all came down to this one decision.

So she opened the door to Zaffino's truck and sat down. Christine was dressed rather provocatively, according to Dave Whiddon, and seemed to do that, he suggested, for Zaffino's sake, knowing it was what Zaffino would have expected. The listening device—the pager—the CAPU had given her was attached to her waist. Inside the pager was a small microphone. As Christine sat down, Zaffino started the conversation: "I found out today."

"So why'd you lie?"

"I didn't. . . . My lawyer said that before they got to you or one of your friends—" but Christine wouldn't let him finish.

"No way. None of my friends know anything, John. That's f- - -ing bull- - - -. You lied to me about that s - - -." Christine was still using the Cynthia George ruse as her core argument, knowing it would keep Zaffino focused on the one thing she could defend.

Zaffino looked around the inside of the vehicle. "They're saying all kinds of s- - -," he screamed.

"Well, they said she's been to *your* house."

"You're the one that lied . . . ," Zaffino said, losing his train of thought for a moment. Then, "In the snake's belly in the ground."

Christine ignored the comment, saying, "Tell the truth."

"What?"

"Before I get f- - -ing ticked off."

"I never had anything to do with her."

"Why was she at your house?"

"She was *never* at my house." Zaffino was getting louder, more animated.

"Why would they say her name? That doesn't make any sense."

"Why would they say *everything* they've said?"

"Why would they say her *name*, John?" Christine was getting heated herself. She knew she was pushing the conversation in a direction she shouldn't, but with the questions Zaffino was asking, she had to keep him focused on Cynthia George.

"I have no idea."

"You're lying to me. You always said I was the liar. *You're* the liar."

Zaffino started to say something. "The only thing I know about that, uh, anything is—"

But again, Christine wouldn't allow him to finish. "That's why you told me to stay out of the Tangier."

"No, it's not."

"Yes, it is. Yes, it is. Don't lie to me."

"We're not married."

"We *were* married."

"Not then."

Christine continued to call Zaffino a liar, keeping the focus of the conversation on Cynthia. She could tell Zaffino was feeding into it. In this manner, she had control over the situation, which was what she had always tried to maintain whenever they got together.

"You better not have screwed up your life for that thing. I'm telling you that right now."

"I have done nothing to screw up my life." He pounded on the steering wheel. "You're the only one I see digging my grave here."

Christine talked about Cynthia's vehicle being spotted at the apartment complex. Zaffino said it was a lie.

Then he said he might have worked on Cynthia's vehicle once—that was maybe why the cops and neighbors thought he was seeing her, because he had done some work for the George family.

Then, "Where's the money?" Christine asked. She wanted five hundred dollars from Zaffino to pay off several of her mounting bills. It was the least he could do.

Zaffino didn't answer. He began to look around his vehicle, searching for something. She sensed he was on edge, ready to snap. He had a look about him. Something was on his mind.

Zaffino said he had to use the restroom. Looking toward McDonald's, two blocks away, he started to drive. "I'm goin' to McDonald's."

"You need to quit lying, John," Christine said as he exited the mall parking lot, drove a block south, but missed the turn into McDonald's.

After turning around and pulling into McDonald's, Zaffino reached into the backseat and pulled out a small black box with an LCD display on its front face. It had a small antenna on the top of it.

"What's that?" Christine asked. She was alarmed. He was up to something.

Zaffino shut off the truck. Christine could see the van Whiddon and Felber were in pull into the parking lot of McDonald's. She felt a mild sense of comfort with that, but still knew Zaffino had something on his mind.

"It's an RF [bug] detector," Zaffino finally said. He smiled, looking at it. Holding it.

"What's an RF detector?" Christine asked.

"*This*," Zaffino said piercingly, pointing to the LCD light display, holding the detector in his hand, "is what's going to tell me if you're wearing a wire or not."

Christine froze. *Holy s- - - -.*

75

If John Zaffino managed to turn on the radio frequency (RF) detector, Christine Todaro was in big trouble. "He would have snapped my neck right there in that truck," she told me later. "For a moment, I didn't know what to do."

In the scope of the situation, what *could* she do?

But in a split-second decision, Christine grabbed the RF detector out of Zaffino's hand as he flipped the on switch and the bars of the LCD screen began to go from right to left (red to green). The unit was on and beginning to figure out that Christine was wearing some sort of listening device—the reason why Zaffino had brought the unit to begin with.

As the LCD lights started to hit the color green, Christine managed to shut it off and throw it into the backseat of the truck—all in one swift, smart motion, while screaming at the top of her lungs, "You bastard."

"Quit it now," Zaffino said as Christine tossed it, "you'll wear my battery down."

"Remember what I told you. I'm the *only* one you can trust."

Listening to what was going on, from inside a van nearby Zaffino's truck, Felber and Whiddon looked at each other.

Zaffino motioned toward the back of his truck, then addressed Christine. He was stunned. All he had to do was reach into the backseat and grab the unit, turn it on and confirm what he obviously knew.

But he didn't. Instead, Zaffino said, "If that's what you have to do to make you feel lucky. Make you feel like you're not talking to the cops."

Christine said later she believed Zaffino realized at that moment that she was wired. That's why he brought the unit to begin with—to prove what he already knew. "In some strange way," she recalled, "I think he wanted to get caught."

"I'm not talking to anybody," Christine said immediately, not breaking character. "But I'm going to protect myself, too."

"Well, that's like a catch-22, then," Zaffino murmured.

"No, it's not . . . that means I'm going to talk to my lawyer and see what I can get in trouble for and what I can't."

"Well, you don't know anything."

Zaffino asked Christine if she was going into McDonald's with him. She said no. When he came back, Christine asked him why he shaved off his mustache. Zaffino was a goatee guy, rarely without one. It was odd for him to shave his face clean.

But then, the conversation shifted back to the cops knowing that Cynthia was at his onetime residence. Zaffino talked about how the cops work—how they like to trick people into believing what they wanted. Christine questioned him on that theory.

Then Christine told him to "quit lying" so much. She

knew he was seeing Cynthia. Just 'fess up and be done with it. It was no big deal. Christine didn't care.

"Listen to me," Zaffino said, ignoring the comment about Cynthia, "the way you talk on the phone, you're feeding me to the wolves."

"Well, I get pissed at you."

"So it's OK to feed me to the wolves?"

"I'm not feeding you to the wolves, John. Somebody else is talking and it's *not* one of my friends."

"I know somebody is talking, but I don't know who it is."

For about ten more minutes, they went back and forth. Christine would call Cynthia a "cheater," and Zaffino would claim he knew nothing about her. Then Zaffino, in a patronizing fashion, repeated what Christine had been saying for the past few days—that she wasn't about to go to jail for him.

"That's correct," she kept saying.

"And," he added, "what you're going on is what somebody else told you. So, if someone calls me and says, 'Hey, your old lady, your ex old lady, she's a whore, she's got HIV, she's got f- - -ing AIDS, uh, she killed some guy.' Would I believe them?"

"No."

"OK. Now you're going to believe that stuff about *me?*"

"Well, it's an awfully big, *big* coincidence that she's at your house," Christine said, staying on the Cynthia George theme.

Sometime later, "You're so superficial, you don't realize it."

"Huh?" Christine replied.

"Look at, look at, look at . . . if they pin this on me, I'm gone for life," Zaffino said.

"I understand that."

"And maybe the electric chair. But the only thing between me and there is *you*."

"No, *her*."

"No, you."

"No, her."

"No—"

"Bulls- - -. Don't pin that on me. It's bulls- - -," Christine challenged.

"The only thing that would ever put me in prison and to death is you."

"I'm getting out. I don't buy that. No. You better check her out and find out what her lips are saying. OK?"

"I know she's—"

Christine wouldn't let him finish, saying, "You . . . don't even know that snob. You don't even know she's a whore. That's how stupid you are. What, are you stupid? I don't understand you, John."

Zaffino yelled, and then explained that if Christine could only keep her mouth shut, none of what was going on would continue. She told him again to go in and talk to the cops. He had nothing to worry about if he didn't do anything. But Zaffino said his lawyer advised him not to do that. Christine, finally realizing she was getting nowhere as far as an admission, said, "I'm getting those bullets back from my dad and I'm giving them back to you and you can do whatever you want with them."

"They're .32s, dear," Zaffino said in a jarring, sarcastic tone.

"Well, I don't care."

"If I were you, I'd leave them there and I'll come and get them."

"No."

Zaffino kept warning her, saying that if she went and picked up the guns, she was getting herself even more deeply involved, adding, "It's like a plague, man," regarding his troubles with the law.

"Yeah, you *are* the plague."

"I guess I can't stay out of trouble, no matter where I go."

As the conversation wound down, Zaffino reminisced about the days when they were married, saying it was all right for him to "f---" his ex-wife, they didn't need to be married.

"You wish," Christine said.

"What if I knocked on your door tonight? In about five hours?"

"Well, you think so? Like I said, you're the plague. You're staying away from me, dude."

"Pull the skirt down, put in a CD," Zaffino said softly.

"Do not get me worked up now."

"I better calm down before you kick me out the door."

Christine laughed.

"Then why are you encouraging me to do it?" Zaffino said.

"Oh, I'm *so* sorry. . . ."

"You know how that voice gets [to] you."

"Uh-huh. Now you gotta calm down." Christine paused.

Zaffino pulled out of McDonald's and drove back to the mall parking lot. As Christine stepped out of his truck, she promised she'd call later.

"Talk to you then," Zaffino said as he pulled away.

Christine composed herself before she left. Close call. She was overwhelmed. *That's it,* she told herself, *I'm not meeting him anymore. Too dangerous.*

"Christine Todaro," Dave Whiddon told me later, "was the most courageous witness I had ever seen. She showed a tremendous amount of tenacity and fearlessness. She was incredible. But we knew then, once John Zaffino pulled out that bug detector, that she could never meet him again."

With no admission from Zaffino, where did it leave the case the CAPU was building against him?

76

The CAPU knew its days of using Christine Todaro as an informant were finished. They agreed she should never meet Zaffino again; but she shouldn't necessarily cut off all ties with him. It would look too suspicious. "Just keep making excuses not to meet him until we can figure out what to do next," Whiddon explained to her.

Christine wanted more than ever for the CAPU to arrest her ex-husband. Why couldn't they drag Zaffino in now and get him behind bars so she could stop looking over her shoulder? Didn't they have enough?

The short answer was no. They needed more—much more.

With that, the investigation into Zaffino's whereabouts during the time period of the murder became a priority. Also, where was the murder weapon? It had to be somewhere—yet, in theory, it could be anywhere. Felber and Whiddon held out hope they'd eventually find it, but knew it was a long shot.

The next telephone call between Zaffino and Christine failed to yield much in the form of any evidence the CAPU could use. Christine had moved again.

Zaffino had no idea where she lived. But on July 24, Zaffino called, saying he wanted to stop by. "I bought a new Ford Expedition. It's green with a mocha bottom panel." He seemed to be bragging, like a new truck would impress her.

"John, what are you going to do?" Christine asked. Then she said something about the cops showing up at her door, pressuring her to talk. *You can't just ignore the situation and call and talk about a truck like your life is going fine.*

"I'm going in to talk to them next week," Zaffino promised.

She didn't believe him. When they hung up, she called Felber right away to tell him what was going on. "Thanks," Felber said. "Keep us informed."

Later that same day, a reporter from the *Akron Beacon Journal* called the CAPU. Whiddon took the call. "I heard that the hit man's ex-wife was working with you guys?" the reporter asked.

Son of a gun. "No comment," Whiddon said. "I have to go."

With this new development, the CAPU needed to keep the pressure on Zaffino by interviewing everyone it could to find out how deeply involved he actually was. Cynthia, too, had become a suspect. The more Whiddon and Felber looked into the relationship Cynthia had with Zaffino, they more they realized that they needed to talk to her. But arresting Zaffino was the CAPU's main focus—and on August 8, 2002, things finally began to move in that direction. Whiddon and Felber, who had basically taken over the investigation as a team, spoke to *Albert Stevens,* an inmate at the North Coast Correctional Treatment Facility in Grafton, Ohio. Stevens said he knew a woman, Mary Ann Brewer, who had worked for the George family as a nanny for the

better part of thirteen years. Mary Ann had essentially
lived in the George mansion, or spent enough time
there—from 8:00 A.M. to generally 10:00 P.M.—to claim
she had.

A convicted thief, Stevens lived next door to Brewer,
and, through that relationship, had been hired by Ed
George as a handyman and carpenter to do some work
around the house. "I remember," Stevens said after
Whiddon read him his rights, "being there the day of
the murder and Ed speaking to Mary Ann."

"What'd Ed say?" Whiddon asked.

"He told her that if the police approached her, she was
not to say anything and tell them to speak to his attorney."

"What about [Ruby]?"

"I knew she was Jeff Zack's daughter."

"How?"

"Just by watching the way she was treated. . . . I also
knew Cindy and Zack were lovers. One of the girls, I
heard, had caught them kissing in an upstairs bedroom. I also saw them myself holding hands and acting
as if they were more than just friends."

"Why did Mary Ann stop working for them?"

"She told me it was too much work."

"You know anything about Jeff Zack?"

"Mary Ann told me Zack came and went at will and
she asked Ed why he allowed it." But Stevens said Mary
Ann never told him what Ed had said about it.

When Whiddon and Felber left the prison, it was
rather obvious where they needed to go next. "Let's
put in a call to Mary Ann Brewer," Whiddon suggested.

Mary Ann Brewer was a hardworking sixty-seven-year-
old woman, who probably knew more about Cynthia

and Ed George than they knew about themselves. She had, for the most part, raised all of the George children. Cynthia was rarely ever home, Mary Ann later said in court. She was always out and about, working out at the gym, bike riding, or just gallivanting around town, doing God knows what. Ed, on the other hand, was a dedicated father, she testified. He dropped the kids off at school every day, took the kids to dance classes and sporting events, and did all he could as their father.

When Whiddon and Felber caught up with Mary Ann a few days after speaking to Stevens, she seemed at first a bit apprehensive about talking, but soon warmed up to them. She had felt slighted by then, Whiddon told me later. She had raised the children and Cynthia had not only turned her back on her, but, in her opinion, she also believed Cynthia was beginning to turn the children against her, too.

Mary Ann told detectives one of the kids had just been over to visit her. Cynthia's daughter told Mary Ann that her father, Ed George, had been "kicked out of the bedroom and was sleeping on the couch." Cynthia and Ed were having serious problems. Cynthia had retreated inward. Closed up. She wasn't talking to many of her friends. Once a woman who would go out on the town to clubs and frequent bars in Cleveland, Cynthia hadn't been hanging around with anyone lately.

"Did Cindy ever talk to you about Jeff Zack?" Whiddon asked.

She hesitated. "Yeah, well, she said she was afraid of him, that's why she wouldn't break up with him. . . . Cindy had a black eye once and told me that Zack had hit her and that's how she got it." In the coming days, two more of Cynthia's friends, on separate occasions, would tell detectives the same thing about the black eye Cynthia once had.

Mary Ann talked about the children, who were, Whiddon and Felber could easily tell, an important part of her life. She missed them dearly. It pained Mary Ann to speak of them in the past tense. Taking care of them had been more than a job; she loved them.

Whiddon took out a photograph of John Zaffino and asked Mary Ann if she had ever seen him.

She thought about it. "He definitely looks familiar. I'm sure I've seen him, but I just don't know where."

After giving Whiddon and Felber the address and telephone number of a family who had lived on the George property in a farmhouse for about ten years, Whiddon promised they'd be back. He asked Mary Ann to call them if she thought of anything else, no matter how insignificant.

Mary Ann said she understood.

Over the next several weeks, Whiddon and Felber spoke to several of Cynthia George's close friends, all of whom were, according to the reports filed by Whiddon, "sneaky" in some aspect of their responses to questions. One woman hired an attorney, saying she wanted to "protect her friend." Throughout it all, they got nowhere. Time and again, they heard that Cynthia was an upstanding citizen who had a "great marriage."

Meanwhile, John Zaffino found out where Christine had moved and began to harass her in his own self-indulgent way. One night, while he was drunk, Zaffino called to say he was coming over. It was close to 2:30 A.M.

"You know what time it is?" Christine lashed out. "No, you're not coming over here."

"Go buy some beer," he said, "I'm bringing a friend."

"Go get your beer somewhere else—you're *not* coming over here."

Christine hung up.

Zaffino called back.

"Go get some beer. I'm coming over to have sex with you." Zaffino sounded belligerent and crude, laughing.

"Where's your *girlfriend*, John? Call *her*."

"What girlfriend?"

Christine hung up.

Zaffino kept calling. So Christine, after several more calls, stopped answering the telephone. Zaffino left a threatening message, saying he was on his way over.

Christine left and went over to a friend's house for the night with her son.

A few days later, Zaffino called and asked her to meet him behind the Tangier. "I need to talk to you," he said.

"No way."

Christine was terrified by this point. She wanted nothing to do with Zaffino and felt she needed protection. The CAPU had cops from the town Christine lived in keep an eye on her apartment best they could—just in case Zaffino decided to show up. When she spoke to Zaffino again a day later, he said he was going to "kill" her and Fred Abers "with a handgun."

"I need you to arrest him," Christine told Felber after receiving the message from Zaffino.

"We're working on it," Felber told her.

With that, Christine told Whiddon and Felber that she remembered something. "John told me [a while back] that he got Cindy pregnant once and she ended up getting an abortion." Later, Christine told me, "He

[also] said that she had a miscarriage. He told me that for two reasons. I would not have a child by him—he thought it would hurt me, I guess—and just to try to hurt my feelings."

Neither of which worked, Christine added.

As the end of August approached, Christine went out to her car one morning to find it had been keyed. She knew it was Zaffino trying to send her a message. Things were escalating quickly. Something needed to be done— quickly—about John Zaffino.

77

On September 20, Detective Mike Shaeffer was sitting at his desk, studying an unrelated case, when his telephone rang. "Persons unit," Shaeffer said in his soft, comforting voice.

"Detective, this is Russell Forrest."

"How have you been, Russell?"

Forrest explained that Zaffino's son had just celebrated a birthday and his father had given him some money, with which the boy went out and purchased a BB gun. While they were eating dinner one night a few days ago, Forrest explained, the subject of guns came up as table talk. "He told us," Forrest said, "that his dad previously had a gun. He described it to us as a .45 pistol revolver with a large wooden handgrip, a large barrel, and chrome-plated. He said his dad kept it in a plastic case."

"No kidding. Did he mention anything else about that?"

"He told us that someone named 'Cindy' had bought the gun for his dad," Forrest continued.

"Anything else?"

"No. But I thought that was important."

"It is. Thanks. If the boy says anything else, let us know."

Forrest's information was helpful, but it didn't prove anything. The break the CAPU needed to arrest John Zaffino finally came on September 24, at 11:03 A.M., when Whiddon and Felber took a chance and drove over to North Canton Transfer, the company Zaffino had worked for. They spoke to a guy who had worked with Zaffino and knew him fairly well. He said he had talked to Zaffino just two weeks ago. Zaffino had stopped by looking for work. "I don't like him much," the guy added. "We didn't get along well. But I know Mike Frasher and Bob and Randy Cole do like him."

When Felber and Whiddon left, they had a feeling the guy was leaving something out. He seemed to be hiding information, like he didn't want to get involved. Sure enough, later that day, the head of security for North Canton Transfer called Felber and told him that the guy they had spoken to earlier had come up to him after they left.

"What did he say?" Felber wondered.

"He said Bob Cole told him that he was sure Zaffino was going to do something like a homicide and that he had tried to talk him out of it."

Whiddon and Felber had spoken to Bob Cole the previous day, but he hadn't mentioned this. So Felber called his connection at North Canton Transfer after receiving the information from the security guard. "Look," he said, "Bob told me that he knew John was going to do something to his girlfriend's ex-boyfriend and Bob Cole had tried to talk him out of it."

For Felber and Whiddon, it all seemed to lead back to Mike Frasher.

78

Whiddon and Felber pulled into Mike Frasher's Canal Fulton, Ohio, residence at 8:32 P.M. on September 24. Frasher, they believed, was the key to getting an arrest warrant signed for John Zaffino. What would become an important part of the investigation later on, Frasher's Leaver Road address in Canal Fulton was a 19.5-mile, twenty-minute ride from Home Avenue in Akron, where Jeff Zack had been shot in the head—even a shorter ride on a Ninja-style motorcycle.

"Bob Cole called me earlier today," Frasher said. "He told me you guys were around, asking questions about John Zaffino and a murder." Then Frasher explained that Zaffino used to live up the street from him, adding, "John used to come up to my house last winter a lot for dinner. We became close. He doesn't have many friends, you know. I was probably closer to him than anyone." Continuing, as Whiddon and Felber listened, Frasher said he knew Zaffino was "dating a woman who owned the Tangier. I met her at John's on more than one occasion."

For Whiddon and Felber, Zaffino's relationship with

Cynthia George, as they talked to Frasher, took on an entirely new arrangement. It appeared that Zaffino, at least from what Frasher believed, was a kept man. It wasn't a simple work-related relationship, as Zaffino had said. "She would stop at John's daily. She drove a Jeep Wrangler and a Ford Expedition. She pursued John. She even convinced him to quit his job so they could get together anytime she wanted." As Frasher spoke, he shifted his language: from using the pronouns "her" and "she" to "Cindy," without being told by the detectives that they knew he was talking about Cynthia George. "Cindy was paying his bills. He told me that the motorcycle he had, Cindy bought it." (Mike Frasher would later testify in court to this same allegation.)

It was important to Felber and Whiddon that Frasher referred to the woman as "Cindy," because they had never mentioned her name.

Suddenly, Frasher explained, Cynthia ran out of money for Zaffino. So he had to get a job anodizing machine parts.

"Did John ever mention any problems *she* was having with an ex-boyfriend?"

"No."

They asked Frasher when he last spoke to Zaffino. Frasher said it was the previous day—and the telephone call scared him. "He told me to keep my mouth shut. He said, 'I'm being set up and now you're involved.'"

This comment was quite alarming to Frasher. He thought he was good friends with Zaffino. For crying out loud, Frasher's wife used to cook the guy dinner and invite him to the house to eat over because she knew he was broke and had little money for food.

Is this the way you treat a friend?

Above all else, when Frasher spoke to Zaffino the last time, Zaffino made a point to talk about "the day" of the murder. He reminded Frasher—*listen carefully*—that he was "sitting" on his "porch" on the day of the murder.

"Was he at your house that day?" Whiddon wanted to know.

"Yeah. It was the day of the Massillon Car Show. We did talk on my porch. My wife and I had to go to a wedding that day, that's how I remember it so well. John came over and asked me to go to the car show with him."

"What time was the wedding?"

"Around five o'clock." Whiddon looked at Felber. "I spoke to John on the porch until my wife was ready and then I got ready."

"Did he leave?"

"Yes. He said he was going to hook up with the Cole brothers and go to the [car] show."

The wedding was at 3:00 P.M., Whiddon later found out. But either way, it didn't matter. The timing worked. It was vital information. Frasher was certain it was well after noon, which gave Zaffino enough time to commit the murder and head over to Canal Fulton, meet with Frasher, develop a timeline and then possibly meet the Cole brothers and head out to the car show.

"My nephew got married that day," Frasher later recalled in court, "and that's the only reason I really remember that day, that car show. . . . I had originally told them (Whiddon and Felber) the wedding was at five o'clock and come to find out the wedding was at three. The *reception* was at five. . . ."

A crucial point Frasher later made was that Zaffino was likely at his house on June 16, 2001, between 12:40

and 12:45 P.M. He was wearing, Frasher later explained, jeans and a T-shirt. He was acting "normal." Even more important, Zaffino wasn't driving his green-and-black motorcycle; he was driving a Ford Contour.

What did this mean? Well, Zaffino lived six houses away from Frasher—which allowed him plenty of time to stop at home, change, park the bike and make it to Frasher's by 12:40 P.M.

Leaving Frasher's, Whiddon was convinced that they had enough to present an arrest warrant to the Summit County Prosecutor's Office.

John Zaffino called Christine Todaro early the next morning. She was getting ready for the day, drying her hair, putting on makeup. As soon as the telephone rang, she knew who it was.

Damn it all. "What do you want? I'm busy."

"Hold on, hold on," Zaffino said. He sounded different. Worried. In a rush. "Have the cops been to see you? Have you *talked* to them this morning?"

What else could she say? "No." This time it was an honest answer. ("I could hear the panic in his voice," Christine later recalled. "I tried to question him, but he wasn't going to answer me. So we hung up.")

Christine immediately telephoned Felber. He wasn't around. Then she tried Whiddon. He, too, was gone.

79

At about 2:30 P.M., Dave Whiddon met with Summit County prosecutors Sherri Bevan Walsh and Mary Ann Kovach, as legal advisor Tom Dicaudo sat in on the meeting, listening to the conversation. Whiddon explained the case in full, detailing how thirty-six-year-old John Zaffino had become the CAPU's prime suspect in the murder of Jeff Zack. The prosecutor's office had been briefed about the case as the investigation continued over the course of the past year, but Whiddon was conducting a formal briefing that morning to assure everyone that he believed they finally had enough to bring Zaffino in.

Walsh, Dicaudo and Kovach, after several pertinent questions, unanimously agreed. And so an arrest warrant for John Zaffino was put into action.

At 3:30 P.M., detectives from the APD's narcotics unit drove over to Zaffino's Rittman, Ohio, residence and knocked on the door.

Zaffino, it appeared, had been expecting them. He put up no fight and calmly agreed to be handcuffed and brought into the CAPU.

Inside interview room number three on the sixth

floor of the APD, where the investigation had started so long ago, Whiddon and Felber waited, discussing how they were going to question Zaffino. Would he admit his role in Jeff Zack's murder, or prove defiant and say he had nothing to do with it?

Felber read Zaffino his Miranda rights as the alleged murderer sat down. He looked tired, stressed, a bit beaten down, as if he'd been on the run, which, in a way, he had. "You can stop this interview," Felber said a few times, just to make sure Zaffino understood, "anytime you want, and ask for your attorney. You understand that?"

"I spoke to Larry Whitney earlier today," Zaffino said. "I told him I wanted to come down and talk to you guys. He told me not to come down. You guys would come to me."

"Are you saying that you *want* to talk to your attorney?" Felber asked.

"I'll answer your questions. . . . I have no idea what you're going to ask."

"You can stop this anytime you want and call Mr. Whitney, you know that, don't you?"

"Yeah. Let's go. I'll answer your questions."

Zaffino was playing it off as if he had nothing to hide. Still, he had been arrested on charges of aggravated murder. At the least, he had to offer some explanation.

Whiddon asked about the day of June 16, 2001. It was important to lock Zaffino down to an alibi. Get him to put a story on the table immediately.

"I was at Mike Frasher's house that day . . . I don't know, about ten A.M. And then I spent the rest of the day at the car show. Mike, Randy and Bob [Cole] all went to the car show with me. We spent the entire day there."

Whiddon and Felber knew he was lying. They had

several witnesses by then committed to a far different timeline.

"Do you know what time the murder of Jeff Zack occurred?" Felber asked.

"No. I didn't even know about the Zack murder until . . . I read about it."

"Two months ago, you mean?" Felber was referring to the anniversary article in the *Akron Beacon Journal.*

Zaffino nodded his head. "Yeah."

After a while of back-and-forth chitchat, with Zaffino unwilling to answer questions in any detail, Felber threw Cynthia George's name on the table and asked Zaffino about his relationship with her.

"She's an acquaintance . . . someone I ride bikes with."

"When did you last see Cindy?"

"Last week at Staples in Montrose. She asked me about going for a bike ride." At some point after this, Zaffino said, he had spoken to Cynthia about the murder only because the police were asking several people he knew about his possible involvement.

Whiddon stepped up and asked Zaffino when he first heard about the murder. Repetition. Ask the same questions two, three, even four times—see how he reacted.

"My ex-wife told me about it when you guys came around asking her about it."

And there it was: the first discrepancy. Two different stories regarding how he had heard about Jeff Zack's murder.

"Did you know Jeff Zack?"

"I never met him. Never talked to him. I know nothing about him."

"Did you know he had a relationship with Cindy?"

"No."

Then the subject of motorcycles came up. Zaffino said "hell yeah" he had owned motorcycles. "All you have to do is check the motorcycle endorsement I have on my driver's license."

"What kind?"

"Honda," he answered smartly. "What other kind is there? You should know, I still have it in my garage."

As Whiddon started to ask another question, Zaffino hesitated and said, "I'd like to talk to Larry. I feel like you guys have one up on me."

They concluded the interview and put him in a holding cell.

When Felber returned to his desk after interviewing Zaffino, he put in a telephone call to Christine Todaro. She deserved to hear, Felber knew, that they had finally arrested her ex-husband; her days of sneaking around, lying to the guy, looking over her shoulder, were over— at least for the time being. She could breathe a sigh of relief. On top of that, Felber had become close to Todaro. He genuinely cared for her and her children and worried about them.

"I was happy to finally have him off the streets," Christine recalled later, "because I didn't want him to find me and hurt my son or my dad like he claimed he would. But at the same time, I was sad for him, because he decided to throw his life down the toilet. . . . He was too stupid to realize that he was totally used by [a woman] for one purpose and one purpose only—to get rid of a problem that looked like it would never go away and that problem was Jeff Zack and his claim to his daughter. I cried for him. Then my next thought was, 'Is he going to get out on bail? He knows for sure that I am working with the detectives now.' I was frantic."

80

The day before John Zaffino was arrested, Whiddon and Felber interviewed Robert "Bob" Cole, one of the three men the CAPU knew John Zaffino was using as an alibi for the day of Jeff Zack's murder. What neither detective mentioned to Zaffino when they interviewed him was that Bob Cole had sold Zaffino out—in a big way.

Bob Cole was forty-eight years old. He still worked for North Canton Transfer, just coming up on his eighth year. He had known Zaffino for about two years. At times, Zaffino and Cole had spent ten, even twelve hours together in a truck, driving loads of goods all over the Ohio region. Bob Cole said Zaffino had told him that Cynthia had bought him the motorcycle, but beyond that, he said he really didn't know much about her. Zaffino had kept his personal life "pretty vague," Bob Cole added.

Whiddon wondered if there was anything else.

Bob Cole thought about it. He said Zaffino told him that Cynthia was having problems with an "old boyfriend who was bothering her, calling and going over to her place, harassing her, basically."

"So this guy was going over to [Cindy's] place?" Whiddon asked, pushing him to be more specific.

"Yeah . . . and, uh, apparently she must have said something to John and, and, ah, John took it upon himself to, you know, do something, or whatever."

Bob Cole explained that he had spoken to Zaffino over the telephone about Jeff Zack. Zaffino told him he was "tired" of Zack bothering Cynthia and said he was going to do something about it.

"Did John ever talk to you about firearms, any weapons, anything like that?" Whiddon queried. It was worth a shot to ask. Felber and Whiddon had already heard Bob Cole sold Zaffino some guns, but they obviously wanted to hear it from him.

The witness said, "Yes. He bought, uh, two, two . . . handguns off me."

Whiddon asked for a description of each.

"The first one I sold him was a Davis .32 caliber, chrome-plated with wooden handles. It was semi-automatic. . . . The second was a, uh, Smith and Wesson revolver. It was chrome-plated, model 66, with a four-inch barrel. It had wooden grips on it, too."

Whiddon was intrigued by the statement.

After a pause, Bob Cole said, "It was a .357."

Jeff Zack was murdered with a .357-caliber, copper-jacketed bullet. That much was known.

To the best of his recollection, Bob Cole said he had sold the .357 to Zaffino in March 2001.

Interestingly enough, at no time during the conversation did Bob Cole say Zaffino admitted that Cynthia George had specifically asked him to murder Jeff

Zack. To the contrary, based on Bob Cole's recollection, it would seem that Zaffino had come up with the plan himself and acted on his own behalf, perhaps with the thought that he was protecting his "girlfriend."

81

On October 2, Vince Felber received a call from the Summit County Jail, where John Zaffino was being held. The sergeant on the other end of the line said that an inmate had walked up to him and claimed to have information about the Jeff Zack homicide. Felber made arrangements with the jail to have the inmate transported to the APD.

A few hours later, the guy was brought into an interview room. Whiddon asked him what he wanted to say. It wasn't all that uncommon for prisoners to have sudden epiphanies regarding other inmates. Convicts wanted deals. Good investigators know this and even expect it. Whiddon and Felber weren't inclined to cut anyone a deal; they had done well for themselves thus far and were building a strong circumstantial case against John Zaffino on their own.

This new source claimed he met Zaffino a few days before. They had both been to court and were put in the same holding cell. Zaffino's court appearance was formal: he was officially charged and held on a whopping ten-million-dollar bond.

"He seemed lost," the guy told Whiddon and Felber, "so I walked up to him and started talking. I asked him what he was in for." According to the inmate, Zaffino said, "I'm being accused of shooting a guy at a gas station." Further explaining the conversation, the informant added, "I could see he was uncomfortable with his surroundings, so I said, 'Don't worry. It'll be OK. I've been in jail before. It's no big deal.'"

This seemed to relax Zaffino, so he started talking more openly. "It has something to do with this girl I was f---ing all the time," Zaffino explained to the guy. "[Her ex-boyfriend] owed me some money for some drugs and the girl wanted to get some insurance money."

Was it a confession?

Hardly.

Was it from a reliable source?

Probably not.

Nonetheless, it told Whiddon and Felber something about John Zaffino—when put under enough stress, he might crack.

Heading into the first week of October, Dave Whiddon took a call from a detective in the narcotics unit who had spoken to Cuyahoga Valley National Park ranger Beverly Haywood. Apparently, Haywood had some information regarding a run in with John Zaffino. With Zaffino's name now on the front page of the newspapers, Haywood recognized it.

The Cuyahoga Valley National Park is located in an isolated part of Cuyahoga Falls, between Stow and Akron. It spans several miles of woods, with glistening streams and nature trails coexisting against the backdrop of spectacular views of Ohio's brilliant natural game and wildlife. A drive by the park during certain times of the year yields stunning views of herds—hundreds—of deer grazing in open fields. Coyote have been spotted in recent years, and sightings of bald eagles are not uncommon. According to the National Park Service, Cuyahoga Valley National is "a short distance from the urban environments of Cleveland and Akron. . . . [The] winding Cuyahoga—the 'crooked river,' as named by American Indians—gives way to deep forests, rolling hills, and open farmlands. The park is a refuge for flora and fauna, gives a sense of times past, and provides recreation and solitude for Ohio's residents and visitors."

More important to Whiddon, he knew that the bike trail running through the park was a popular meeting place for Cynthia George and Jeff Zack, when they used to ride bikes together. Speaking to Whiddon over the telephone, the ranger explained that her office, located in a whitewashed building no larger than a utility shed, situated right on the bike trail by a marvelous wooden bridge, had "contact" with John Zaffino on May 8, 2001.

After receiving the tip, Whiddon and Felber headed out to the ranger's headquarters on Riverview Road. Just down the way from the office, maybe a mile or so, was one of several parking lots, this one angled perfectly adjacent to the beautiful red covered Everett Bridge, projected over the Crooked River on one side, and a very thickly settled wooded area going uphill across the street from the parking lot. Standing on the foothill, going up the beaten path, one had a clear view of the parking lot.

As Felber and Whiddon were about to learn, this was important.

When they arrived, Whiddon and Felber learned that Ranger Lois Neff was the first cop to have made contact with John Zaffino on the night of May 8. It was about 9:25 P.M., according to Neff's report. She had pulled into the Everett Bridge parking lot after noticing a green Ford Contour parked by itself. It was unusual to see a car at that time of the night.

With a feeling that something was wrong, Neff approached the car. She parked her cruiser in front of it so she could shine her headlights on it. Then she got out and started looking inside with a flashlight. Walking around the car slowly, Neff saw a "triangular-shaped gun case on the passenger floorboard" inside the vehicle.

It was empty.

Right away, Neff called for assistance. Then she got hold of the APD to run a check on the license plate. It was cool outside and quiet, just the chirp of crickets passing the night away. A foggy mist hung in the air just above the fields as Neff waited for a return call and wondered where the driver of the car was.

One of the things Neff had asked the APD to do was a "welfare check" regarding the owner of the car, whom she now knew to be John Zaffino. She was worried, albeit seeing a gun case without a gun, that the driver of the car had parked, taken his or her gun, then walked out into the woods to commit suicide.

Very soon, backup arrived. As the two rangers sat together and waited, Zaffino came out of the woods across the street—the foothill—and walked slowly into the parking lot. Both rangers approached Zaffino, shining a flashlight in his face. "What are you doing out here?"

Zaffino seemed spooked. He didn't speak at first.

"What's going on with the empty gun case?" one of the rangers asked.

"Oh, shit, my gun is at home," Zaffino said.

"We're going to have to pat you down, sir."

"I'm a truck driver, you know, I have to carry a gun sometimes."

"What are you doing out here?"

"Well," Zaffino started to say with a look of embarrassment on his face, "I've been out here about three hours waiting for my . . . my girlfriend. She's married. She just called me and told me she's not coming."

"Look, before you leave, put that gun case in your trunk. OK?"

"Sure," Zaffino said.

With nothing to hold him on, the rangers let him go.

Whiddon and Felber were amazed by the story; however, what did it mean in the scope of the investigation? The date was close to the day Jeff Zack was murdered. Why was Zaffino in the woods that night? Who was he meeting? Was it Cynthia George?

Ranger Beverly Haywood then explained what happened on her shift eight days later. It was May 16. A quiet night. Not much going on. After receiving a call to go check something out in the park, Haywood ran into a man named David Amstutz. "Hey, Ranger," he said as she approached, "I found a loaded handgun out in the woods."

"Can you show me where?"

They walked from the Everett Bridge parking lot, across the street from the woods—the same parking lot where the rangers had questioned Zaffino—and up Furnace Run Trail, where Zaffino had come walking out on the night of May 8. Amstutz explained that he had been out in the woods, about five feet off the main trail, sixty paces from the trail entrance, looking for wild mushrooms, when he came upon the gun just lying there on the ground underneath some brush. It appeared to be placed there and covered over, not so much dropped. The gun was fully loaded—six rounds. It was a semiautomatic, chrome-plated Davis Industries .32 caliber, with a 2½-inch barrel—the exact type of weapon, in fact, Robert Cole had claimed he sold Zaffino.

"The parking lot where Zaffino's car was parked," Whiddon said later, "and the trail where the man found the gun were directly adjacent to each other. Vince [Felber] and I walked up the trail at night and stood where the gun was found and we could clearly see the parking lot. We believe John Zaffino was going to kill Jeff Zack in the woods that night after Cynthia George called Zack and asked him to meet her there. But something happened and they ended up calling it off."

The park rangers gave Whiddon and Felber a Polaroid of the gun and told them they had sent the gun itself to the Bureau of Criminal Investigations (BCI) for fingerprinting and ballistics, as well as a sample of Zaffino's prints.

82

Inside the Summit County grand jury room on Monday, October 7, John Zaffino was indicted for the murder of forty-four-year-old Jeff Zack. Zaffino was formally charged with aggravated murder "for allegedly causing Jeff Zack's death by prior calculation and design." If convicted, Zaffino faced a possible twenty years to life in prison. On top of that charge, Zaffino faced a separate charge of "murder for allegedly causing the death while committing a felonious assault," a charge that carried an additional maximum sentence of fifteen years to life.

If John Zaffino was ever going to serve up Cynthia George—who the CAPU detectives were now focused on pursuing—to secure a lighter sentence for himself, time was running out.

What some found rather ridiculous was that Zaffino, who had pleaded not guilty, was being held in the Summit County Jail on a $10 million *cash* bond. Why so much money?

For one, several involved with the prosecution later agreed, the CAPU was afraid for Christine Todaro's life, not to mention her son and father. The large bond would insure Zaffino sat in jail until he had his day in court, which looked like it was going to take place during the spring of 2003.

Bonnie and Ashton Zack had moved. They couldn't bear to be in the Stow house any longer. Bonnie needed to start over. Through her lawyer, Frank Pignatelli, Bonnie released a statement to the *Akron Beacon Journal*: "[She] is very relieved that there has been an arrest and law enforcement has done an excellent job in an extremely difficult and complex case."

In December, Dave Whiddon, rather anxious to hear from Herbert Joe's Texas laboratory he had sent the ominous voice mail message to, along with the voice samples from Zaffino and Seth, got his answer. It had been months and, he said later, he had almost forgotten about it. Still, that one telephone message could help seal the APD's case against Zaffino.

In his detailed twenty-page report, Herbert Joe believed that the voice on the tape was indeed John Zaffino's.

As the CAPU began interviewing people connected to John Zaffino, some had rather bizarre stories to tell. One woman, whom Zaffino was buying his anodizing products from, said he would often tell "inappropriate" stories about his life that were, at times, appalling. In one instance, she said, Zaffino told her he had tied a string around the genitals of his cat and was waiting for "them to fall off." He thought it was funny, she claimed, that the cat had suffered so horribly. This same woman also said Zaffino loved to "brag" about being with Cynthia George. "Married women are the best," he'd say jarringly.

Through Christmas and the New Year holiday season, the CAPU kept building its case, while Zaffino consulted with his lawyer, Larry Whitney, trying the best he could to come up with a plausible defense. Whitney knew, of course, the CAPU's main witness, Christine Todaro, was going to be devastating to his case; yet, as Zaffino began telling it, Christine had some skeletons herself. And when the time came, Whitney was going to pull those old bones out of the closet and expose them to the jury, discrediting Christine's integrity.

At what first looked like a trial slated for the spring of 2003, by February, the *State of Ohio* v. *John Zaffino* was under way. As preliminary hearings and voir dire concluded by February 24, with a jury of twelve, plus two alternates already chosen, the Honorable James Murphy, the judge, slapped his gavel and adjourned until opening statements, which were set to begin on February 26.

The only setback thus far, at least from Dave Whiddon's point of view, was that Judge Murphy ruled the results of the voice mail message test Herbert Joe had conducted, in which he believed that the voice threatening Jeff Zack was John Zaffino's, would not be permissible. According to Whiddon, that decision sent him into a rage. He had worked hard at putting together the evidence. To have it thrown out—even though Chief Assistant Prosecutor Mike Carroll, who had taken over the case, insisted it wouldn't matter—was devastating. Whiddon couldn't believe it.

Larry Whitney filed a motion to suppress the testimony of Herbert Joe, writing that Joe's forensic testing on the tapes was considered "junk science"—a tired, overused term if there ever was one in today's courtrooms. Joe was a nationally recognized expert. He had testified in dozens of cases and was willing to back up his findings with documented evidence, not just an opinion. "I'm happy to fly in and explain it all to the judge," Joe had told Whiddon.

A suppression hearing was called. Whiddon wanted to set up Herbert Joe and have him ready to testify. But others involved in the prosecution didn't think they'd need Joe for the suppression hearing.

"In fairness to [those who didn't think Herbert Joe needed to be there]," Whiddon recalled, "no one thought Judge Murphy would react the way he did."

But still, Whiddon insisted that it wouldn't hurt to fly Joe in and at least have him ready in case Judge Murphy wanted to hear from him.

The problem was that no one had made plans with Joe. So when the time came and Murphy, sure enough, wanted him in court to explain the science behind his findings, Joe was off in Australia studying Aboriginal language and couldn't make it back in time.

Prosecutor Mike Carroll did his best to explain to the judge that Joe would be available for trial, but Murphy wasn't hearing any of it.

Whiddon was upset, but Carroll insisted that it wasn't the end of the case. They could get the voice mail message in another way and make a connection to Zaffino through his ex-wife Nancy Bonadio, Russell Forrest and Christine Todaro, who had spoken to Zaffino over the telephone and could clearly identify his voice. Then jurors could take the message themselves, play it and make up their own minds.

"What else could I do?" Whiddon explained later. "In the end, I knew it would all work out and I was upset with myself for making such a big deal out of it."

83

Standing a thin six feet four inches, Mike Carroll has an unassuming way about him—a Clark Kent type of demeanor that boded well for his job. He was an evidence man all the way and didn't come across as some sort of overbearing prosecutor who knew more than anyone else, as some do. Carroll wanted to see a case on paper before he went after it with a vengeance in court. The Zaffino case was going to be a challenge. Carroll had no forensic evidence and no eyewitness testimony. What he had, however, was a plethora of circumstances that pointed to John Zaffino as the murderer. A major part of Carroll's case was set to hinge upon telephone records, inch upon inch of stacked records sitting in Carroll's corner office, located in the same building as the APD. At one point, Carroll and Whiddon spent days going through the records to see if they could put together a paper trail explaining how and when Zaffino and Cynthia George spoke. Carroll knew that if he was going to eventually bring a case of conspiracy against Cynthia George—although, Zaffino so far hadn't mentioned that she was the least bit involved—he was going to have to expose part of that alleged culpability during Zaffino's trial.

On top of that, Carroll admitted to me that he didn't have the most sympathetic victim to present to the jury. "It was going to be hard in respect to Jeff Zack."

Even so, on the morning of Wednesday, February 26, 2003, after Judge Murphy read the jury its instructions, Carroll, with his rosy red complexion, salt-and-pepper hair, stood up from his seat and began his opening statement as the most high-profile trial to hit Akron in some twenty years commenced under the umbra of a throng of media and courtroom watchers.

For Mike Carroll, the case against John Zaffino came down to one main point—and he wasted little time getting it across to the jury. "You're going to find out from the evidence in this case," he said in his soft, comforting tenor, "that Cindy George had a problem—and that problem was Jeff Zack." After briefly pausing, he added, "The solution to that problem"—he pointed now at Zaffino, who was dressed in slacks and a sweater obviously too small for his protruding belly—"was John Zaffino."

It was an eye-opening line, one that clearly spelled out for the jury how, in Mike Carroll's opinion, this incredible murder case, which took the CAPU over a year to solve, boiled down to a triangle of deceit, adultery and, of course, cold-blooded murder.

Finally, "The reason we're here," Carroll said sternly, without reserve, "the reason Jeff Zack was murdered, surrounds Cindy George and the affair she was having with these two men."

84

The one thing, Mike Carroll told me later, you never want to do, is make your opening statement too long so it lulls the jury into a deep, comforting coma, where they begin to hear everything in one blur, thus forgetting the main position of your argument. For Mike Carroll, it was simple: Cynthia George wanted to get rid of Jeff Zack because he wouldn't leave her alone. Jeff Zack, Whiddon and Carroll speculated, might have even threatened to take Ruby—their daughter—away from Cynthia; so Cynthia, who had already found herself a good, solid brute of a man, asked him to take care of her problem.

But John Zaffino, on the other hand, had never played into the prosecution's hand: he, in fact, was saying that he'd had nothing whatsoever to do with Zack's murder, or that it was Cynthia George who had asked him to do it. And this was the only part of the state's argument Carroll did not address during his opening: Why hadn't Zaffino turned on his lover and fingered Cynthia for the mastermind behind the crime, if she had been involved? Why not give up the architect and cut a deal? What did Zaffino have to lose at this point?

Carroll spent an ample amount of time laying out his case, step by step, then concluded by saying, "You will be firmly convinced that based on this evidence and it will prove beyond a reasonable doubt that John Zaffino . . . is the man who rode that motorcycle to BJ's . . . [and] shoots Jeff Zack before he even has a chance to get out of that Explorer to pump any gas. Based on the evidence, John Zaffino is guilty of aggravated murder beyond a reasonable doubt."

The jury didn't flinch. It was a quick opening statement, devoid of the rigorous detail some attorneys like to get caught up in.

But now, it was Larry Whitney's turn, the one man who could save Zaffino from a life behind bars. Whitney, a middle-aged man with stringy gray hair like a mad professor's, could be as caustic as a political strategist when the situation warranted it. Here, he was defending a man who had steadfastly denied his guilt. Whitney was determined to prove to the jury that the prosecution was going to have to come up with more than circumstantial evidence to convict his client. After all, no one had identified Zaffino. Not one person could walk into the courtroom and call him the shooter. Nor was there any forensic evidence linking him to the scene or any part of the crime. Sleeping with Cynthia George wasn't a crime. Neither was hating Jeff Zack or getting into bar fights. "All of us have done our homework here," Whitney said after an opening few lines introducing himself. He spoke fluidly, clearly, nonthreateningly. He moved like a candidate running for office, using his hands when the moment struck him. "We anticipate what a witness will say because we've talked to those witnesses. We know what the evidence is in this case. Everything you've been told, I've known. Everything

that Mr. Carroll has told you, we know. And everything
probably that I tell you right now, he knows."

For the next several minutes, Whitney told the story
of Jeff Zack's life and how it ended on June 16, 2001.
Then he went into Zaffino's alibi, before ripping apart
Christine Todaro's undercover work, saying she tried
to get Zaffino to admit to killing Zack, but the problem
with her testimony and countless hours of tape recordings the jury was about to hear will be that Zaffino
never did. And that was the bottom line: Zaffino never
admitted killing Jeff Zack. "We're not going to argue
with the state that [Zaffino] knows Cindy George. What
we argue about is whether or not his knowing Cindy
George, his buying a motorcycle, amounts to his being
a murderer. Because we think the evidence will not
convince you beyond a reasonable doubt that these
things add up to murder."

When he finished, Whitney sat down. He didn't look
so good. He moved slowly near the end of his opening.
Several courtroom watchers later said he appeared
sickly, pasty, white. He seemed nervous, anxious and, at
the same time, withdrawn.

Something was wrong.

During the first day of testimony, through a multitude of witnesses, Mike Carroll proved several things to
the jury. For one, Carroll showed how, in early June
2001, John Zaffino purchased a .357 Magnum Smith &
Wesson revolver, and that the bullet used to kill Jeff
Zack was from a .357. On June 13, Zaffino called the
Zack home and left that now-infamous threatening
message, Carroll suggested, as several witnesses identified Zaffino as the man behind the voice.

Powerful evidence—that is, if jurors bought it.

Through another round of witnesses, Carroll then ex-

plained that three days after John Zaffino left that
threatening telephone message, a Ninja-style motorcycle
was seen circling the parking lot near BJ's minutes
before noon. Carroll insinuated, with each witness, that
the person on the motorcycle was in fact John Zaffino.
How? He and Dave Whiddon had gone through scores
of telephone records. According to them, that nauseat-
ing work had paid off: the records showed how John
Zaffino spoke to Cynthia George from 11:49 to 11:57
A.M. on the day Jeff Zack was murdered—but didn't
speak to her again until 12:29 P.M., which would have
given him just enough time to kill Jeff Zack, speed away
and allegedly let Cynthia know the deed was done. Carroll put up poster boards with the cell phone records
blown up and highlighted all the telephone calls between the two lovers.

It was powerful evidence—but all of it circumstantial.
There was nothing to prove what Zaffino and Cynthia
had talked about, only that they had called each other.

Larry Whitney answered Carroll's attack by saying that
during the normal course of a day, Zaffino and Cynthia
talked on the telephone like teenagers, generally during
those same times. He provided records to show that
Zaffino and Cynthia had spoken on the telephone for
days and days before the murder during those same time
frames. Just because they spoke on *that* particular day,
at *those* particular times, it didn't mean they were planning or discussing Jeff Zack's murder, Whitney implied
through his questioning of witnesses. They could have,
after all, been planning a wild night together.

How does one make the leap, Whitney wondered,
from a telephone call to murder—without knowing
what was discussed?

85

During the first day of testimony, the *State of Ohio* v. *John Zaffino* was full of sordid details alleging an adulterous triangle between Jeff Zack, Cynthia George and John Zaffino—one that ended, so claimed the prosecution, in murder. Many expected the second day of trial to be even more tawdry, with additional witnesses coming forward to paint a picture of Cynthia George's love life as if it were a subplot in a steamy romance novel. But the second day of testimony would not commence for another week, as even more drama was injected into the case.

After the first day of testimony concluded, Larry Whitney went home and lay down on his couch. He still hadn't felt quite right. As the night wore on, Whitney became extremely disoriented, and after being rushed to the hospital, he was told he had suffered a mild heart attack.

With that, Summit County judge James Murphy halted the trial and sent jurors home on Thursday morning. Fifty-four-year-old Whitney, still being treated at Akron General Medical Center, was expected to remain in the hospital for several more days.

Late in the morning, it was reported that Whitney had called Judge Murphy's office from his hospital room. "I'll be ready to return [next week]," Whitney promised. "I don't want a mistrial declared."

When the trial resumed the following week, Mike Carroll put Nancy Bonadio on the stand, her fiancé Russell Forrest and a long list of supplementary witnesses. Bonadio and Forrest explained how Zaffino drove the bike to Pennsylvania in the middle of the night less than a week after the murder, and its fluorescent green colors had been covered up with duct tape. It was riveting testimony, and spoke to Zaffino's character and mind-set near the time of the Zack murder. He was scared. He was doing things a guilty man would do. He wanted to get rid of a motorcycle. He had avoided paying child support in the past. He had never given Nancy Bonadio a damn red cent without getting something for himself, she claimed. But on that night, John Zaffino didn't care; he wanted to be rid of an alleged connection to the crime and handed his ex-wife the keys to a five-thousand-dollar motorcycle without asking for anything in return.

Two witnesses later, the star of the trial walked into the room. Forty-eight-year-old mother of seven, wife of sixty-three-year-old Tangier owner Ed George, Cynthia George, sauntered into the room like a celebrity. Cynthia wasn't the Mrs. Ohio America third runner-up she had once been; the past year had taken its toll on her. She appeared thin and frail, as if she had spent many a night agonizing over what had become of her existence. Cynthia could have had the life of a queen— castle and all—but she had given it all up to bed down with two men—and now she was being asked to expose that secret life in public.

Zaffino stared Cynthia down, cracking a devilish smirk, perhaps knowing what was to happen when she spoke. It was March 6, 2003, almost two years since they'd first met.

Carroll went through a series of nondescript, pertinent questions regarding where Cynthia lived and whom she was married to. Cynthia answered tersely: "Yes" and "no," without adding any detail.

When Carroll asked Cynthia how many children she had, not a minute into his questioning, Cynthia asked through her attorney that the jury be removed from the courtroom.

With the jury gone, Cynthia's attorney stood. "Your Honor," he said, "my client contends to assert her Fifth Amendment rights at this time to any further questions with regard to this matter."

"Mrs. George," Judge Murphy asked, "you've consulted with your counsel or counsels, have you not?"

"Yes, I have." She seemed content. Unbreakable.

The judge then excused Cynthia and asked Mike Carroll to call his next witness.

Elayne Zack, Jeff's mother, Bonnie Zack, his wife, Detective Bertina King and Cynthia and Ed's housekeeper, Mary Ann Brewer, filed in next. Each gave the jury a well-rounded view of the case from their perspective. Nothing groundbreaking came out of the testimony, but Mary Ann Brewer set the stage for Carroll's next witness, Ed George.

Ed answered several of Carroll's questions regarding his restaurant and how he had called Paul Callahan a few weeks before Jeff Zack's murder to say he was being harassed. But other than that, Ed had nothing of substance to add. Carroll knew he wasn't going to be much help, but the fact that Ed was on the witness stand answering questions was important in and of itself. His presence alone, Carroll told me later, showed the jury how serious the case against Zaffino was—that a man of Ed's status and wealth had been dragged into court to sit and face his wife's alleged lover.

Uncomfortable couldn't come close to describing the look on Ed's face as he sat in front of John Zaffino.

When Whitney had his opportunity to question Ed, he asked him if he had hired Zaffino to murder Jeff Zack.

"I don't even know John Zaffino," Ed said firmly.

86

On Friday morning, March 7, Mike Carroll called perhaps his most important witness, Christine Todaro. Christine was terrified to sit in front of her ex-husband and talk about how she'd recorded her conversations with him, but she was determined to see the case through. Zaffino had put the fear of bodily injury into Christine for years; he wasn't going to do it anymore. On this day, she was taking back her life.

After having her describe how she met Zaffino and when they married, Carroll began a series of questions that would bring the trial its most powerful testimony thus far. "All right, then, let me ask you a few specific things," Carroll said, looking down at his notes. "Did he (Zaffino) talk to you about some incidents that had occurred with another man . . . ?"

"Yes." Christine shifted a bit in her chair, but appeared calm, cool and ready to tell the jury what she knew.

"Tell me about that."

"He came over [to] my house . . . and told me that he had gotten into a fight with a guy, and he never said his name or whatever . . . and he basically said he, you know, beat the shit out of him in front of his posse, or people. . . . And he wanted to warn me about the guy to make sure that this guy wasn't around. He described him to me and, you know, wanted me to make sure that I made sure that he was not after me or, you know, around me."

"And is there an explanation of why that warning was necessary—why he would be around you?"

"I think he said the guy had made a threat about me. . . ."

Carroll paused and shook his head. He knew, of course, where the conversation was headed. Then, "And you said he described this fellow?"

Christine didn't hesitate. "Yes!" How could she forget? It was such a bizarre description.

"How did he describe him?"

"White-haired Israeli."

Christine went on to explain how the conversation came up and how she figured out, after seeing Jeff Zack's photograph in the newspaper, that Zaffino was talking about the guy killed at BJ's by someone on a motorcycle.

From there, she went on to explain how she began to wear a wire for the CAPU and recorded her conversations with Zaffino. Carroll played several of the tapes for the jury. Then Christine told the jury about Zaffino's gun collection and how she had seen a semiautomatic pistol in his car one day.

Near the end of what amounted to an hour of questions and answers, Carroll asked Christine about State's Exhibit #58, the microcassette tape of that threatening voice mail message left on Jeff Zack's answering machine.

"Do you remember any of the words that were on [the tape]?" Carroll wanted to know.

"Um . . . pretty much."

"Just give me an idea of what you recall."

"I think he says, 'OK, buddy, you have one more out.'"

"And when the [CAPU] played that tape for you . . . explain to the jurors your reaction as you begin to hear that tape. What do you *say* when you listen to that?"

"I said that it was definitely his voice. I mean, it was just—it was just his voice to me."

"No doubt in your mind?"

"No."

"Miss Todaro, the man we have been talking about, John Zaffino, is he present in the courtroom today?"

"Yes, he is."

"Where is he sitting and what's he wearing?"

"A brown-green sweater. Right there."

"Man in the second chair there?" Carroll pointed as Zaffino sat with a look of disgust on his face.

"Yes."

For the next hour, Whitney tried to take the wind out of Carroll's sail by questioning Christine on every minor detail regarding her statements to police and the tape recordings she had made, but she held firm and never backed down.

After Christine left the stand, Carroll called Vince Felber, his final witness, who explained how the case against John Zaffino was managed by the CAPU.

87

Larry Whitney had a job in front of him. He needed to counter each piece of damaging testimony against his client. If all went well, he also needed to put his client on the stand and have him explain to the jury, in his own words, that he was in no way involved in the murder of Jeff Zack. Juries want to hear from defendants. They want to look into their eyes and watch them as they speak. They want to feel the emotions and develop a sense of a defendant's moral compass.

Everyone was going to have to wait. Whitney wasn't saying one way or the other whether his client would sit in the witness chair.

The first witness Whitney called was Mike Frasher, who explained the day—June 16, 2001—he and John Zaffino had sat on his porch and talked.

By the time Frasher finished, Zaffino looked more guilty than he ever had. Frasher's words gave the jury an understanding that John Zaffino had the *time* to murder Jeff Zack and also make it to that car show.

Next up was Odell Lyde, who was a recording studio producer. He and his wife were inside the BJ's parking lot when they heard the whip crack of a gun go off. When he heard it, Lyde said he turned quickly and got a good bead on the motorcyclist. Larry Whitney read parts of Odell Lyde's statement to police. Lyde had described the motorcycle. Whitney thought he was giving the jury an alternative theory—that it could have been someone else besides Zaffino on an entirely different bike.

But Whitney's plan didn't go quite as well as he might have planned. "And it says," Whitney said to Lyde, reading from the statement Lyde gave to police, "'I thought there was a backfire of a car, saw bike speed away, and then it says, bike, white and black.'"

Odell Lyde answered right away. "Right."

"So—so this would—does this refresh your recollection as to what you saw?" Whitney sounded cocky and somewhat arrogant.

"I'm not going to say," Lyde answered, "the bike was white and black, per se, the whole bike." Whitney's jaw dropped. "Those were the colors on the bike that I remember."

Whitney couldn't get the words out of his mouth fast enough: "OK."

"I wasn't trying to describe the bike as a whole."

"I got you," Whitney said, his voice rising. "I got you. So what you saw as the bike sped away, the colors you saw, was white and black?" He was trying to get Lyde to disagree, in other words, with ten other witnesses.

"Colors that stuck in my mind was white and black," Lyde said.

"I got you," Whitney said, trying to stop Lyde from expanding on what he was saying. "OK."

On cross-examination, the prosecution pointed out the obvious: Odell Lyde saw a man on a bike speed away from BJ's after shooting someone. The bike was white and black, Lyde said, but could have also been painted other colors, too. All he saw was white and black.

Whitney called a landscaper next, Mike Bruce. He had hung around with Jeff Zack and went bike riding with him "every week or every other week" right up until the day of his death. In total, Bruce was on the stand for about five minutes. He answered approximately fifteen questions. The one Whitney no doubt wanted to float in front of the jury most was an exchange between Bruce and Whitney regarding Jeff Zack's demeanor during the last weeks of his life. "And did you ever at any time notice that—that Mr. Zack," Whitney asked, "had been beaten up or appear to you to be beaten up?"

"No."

"OK. Did he continue to ride bikes with you?"

"Yes."

Apparently, Whitney wanted to establish that Jeff Zack didn't appear to have sustained a beating by anyone, especially John Zaffino, as some had speculated. But the fact—at least according to Mike Bruce—that Jeff Zack didn't show signs of being beaten up didn't answer the question of whether he had tussled with anyone. With his second witness, Whitney seemed to be dancing around certain factors without coming out and talking about them specifically.

Whitney next put on another witness who was in the parking lot of BJ's, someone who spent a total of six minutes on the stand explaining nothing that proved John Zaffino was or wasn't the person on that motorcycle on June 16, 2001.

Whiddon and Mike Carroll, sitting, listening to each of Whitney's witnesses, couldn't help but think, *Is this all he's got?* "We couldn't believe that Larry Whitney," Whiddon explained later, "who we knew was a competent, good defense lawyer, wasn't putting on a case."

And then, Whitney called Cheryl Johnston—shockingly—his final witness. John Zaffino wasn't going to testify.

Johnston was also at BJ's on the day in question. She said at about noon, she was sitting at a stoplight on Home Avenue.

"And what do you see?" Whitney asked.

"Something catches my eye."

"What is it that catches your eye?"

"It turned out to be a motorcycle," Johnston said, "with a rider on it. And it was kind of an odd thing. It just"—she stopped, hesitated, then—"there was something about the color or the way he was dressed or something just caught my eye. And I watched him pull out of the gas pump area and come down the driveway . . . and tried to figure out the color of the bike, which I know the colors of the bike was—to me, they were sour apple green and cream."

Whiddon and Carroll looked at each other and smiled.

"OK."

"And—"

"Let's stop right here," Whitney said. "So the bike you saw leave the pumps and come down the driveway was sour apple and cream?"

"Yes."

Mike Carroll had convinced the judge to allow him to place the motorcycle the CAPU had taken under a warrant from Nancy Bonadio and Russell Forrest in the courtroom. This way, witnesses could take a look at it up close. It was a brilliant move on Carroll's part, more drama than actual legal strategy. Just having the bike sitting there for the jury and anyone else to look at made the impact of it that much more powerful.

Whitney asked, "Did you go in and look at that motorcycle sitting in that courtroom next door?"

Johnston said, "Yes, I did."

"Was that the motorcycle you saw that afternoon?"

"Absolutely not."

"Thanks."

After a few more inconsequential questions, Whitney asked Johnston to describe the driver she saw on the motorcycle. She had noticed what he was wearing because he was dressed "really odd," she said.

"Tell us about how he was dressed."

"Well, he had brown shoes on, brown socks on, brown dress pants like you wear for a suit, and he had a silk brown zip-up jacket on, long, you know."

A few questions later, Whitney asked, "How much of his face could you see?"

"All of it actually. I could see his lips. He didn't have a mustache. I could see his eyes, his forehead. I didn't see any hair."

"OK. I want you to look at this man," Whitney said, pointing to Zaffino, "sitting right here, John Zaffino."

"Uh-huh."

"Is this the man that was riding that motorcycle?"

"No."

"OK."

"Definitely not."

Later in her testimony, Johnston said she thought the guy driving the motorcycle was "Iranian."

On cross-examination, the prosecution got Johnston to admit that when she realized—after reading the newspaper—that she had perhaps seen the shooter leaving BJ's, she didn't call the police. Instead, she called Larry Whitney. Not one or two days after the murder, however, but almost eighteen months after the crime had occurred.

With Johnston's testimony concluded, Larry Whitney, apparently feeling confident he had explained the prosecution's case away, rested.

88

Four days after Christine Todaro lit up the court-room with her story, perhaps sinking Zaffino's ship in the process, after a total of twenty-seven witnesses—five of whom were called by Larry Whitney on Zaffino's behalf—the jury heard closing arguments.

Whitney argued that the evidence against his client was strictly circumstantial, that Zaffino had maintained his innocence since the day the CAPU had him on its radar, and there was nothing the state provided that should convince them he had murdered Jeff Zack. A white-haired Israeli and some tape-recorded conversations, an ID of a voice mail and a roll of duct tape, weren't enough to convict a man of murder and condemn him to a life behind bars.

The jury had obviously been sold on the notion that there could be no other person responsible for Jeff Zack's murder than John Zaffino. Because after fewer than four hours of deliberations—one of which they spent breaking for lunch—John Zaffino was found guilty of aggravated murder.

While Zaffino was being led out of the courtroom

in utter amazement that he had been convicted on such shoddy, circumstantial evidence, security later reported that he cried his way to jail.

One of Zaffino's relatives, who was in attendance every day of the trial, bolted from the courtroom after hearing the verdict, running into the street in tears.

During Zaffino's sentencing on March 17, 2003, Bonnie Zack finally got her chance to address the man who had killed the father of her son. Here was another victim of this tragedy, a woman who had sat through rigorous questioning by the CAPU, a polygraph test, and heard detectives describe a husband who had cheated on her time and again. Yet Bonnie was an empathetic human being if there ever was one; she had accepted Jeff Zack's flaws, raised their child and, by middle age, been through more emotional pain than most see in a lifetime. Now it was Bonnie's turn to express *her* feelings. To speak out. To tell the man who had killed her husband *exactly* what she felt. She had seen and heard enough.

Through the first few words of her impact statement, Bonnie Zack pointed to the white elephant that had been sitting in the courtroom during the entire trial. "If it wasn't for Cindy George," Bonnie said in open court, "my husband wouldn't have been shot, my son wouldn't have lost his father and you (John Zaffino) wouldn't be looking forward to spending the rest of your life in jail. You are just the fall guy. Do you think [Cindy] cares about you now? Are you willing to take all the heat for this and let her continue to live her extravagant lifestyle?"

Bonnie held Ashton's hand as she spoke. But she had gotten it out of her system. There, she had said it: *Cynthia George*. Where was her head? People wanted

Cynthia to be next in line. Even jurors later said they wondered throughout the trial why Cynthia hadn't been sitting next to Zaffino as a codefendant? Why wasn't she being charged?

When it came time for Ashton Zack to speak, he explained how sorry he was that he had argued with his dad on the morning of the murder. He was upset, he said, that he never got a chance to say good-bye. The child felt guilty. What a boy Bonnie had raised. Incredible. He sounded like the man he was destined to become.

Then, looking at Zaffino, who sat totally stiff and unemotional, with some sort of "I can't believe this is happening" look on his face, Ashton asked him, "Was it worth not seeing *your* own son again?"

What an astute observation for a young boy to make. If there was any consolation, Ashton knew Zaffino would never spend a day with his son again; they would have to see each other now amid the confines of barbed wire and steel bars.

"Was it worth killing my dad for Cindy?" Ashton asked next. "I know my dad did not always do the right thing, but he did not *deserve* to be killed."

Another incredible encounter.

Christine Todaro was unnerved by the entire process of the trial and Zaffino's subsequent sentencing. In a way, she still felt guilty about helping the CAPU nail him. As his sentencing went forward, Christine stood in the back of the courtroom (on the victim's side) next to her best friend, Sharon George (no relation to Ed George). As the judge read Zaffino's sentence, Christine, thinking about what Ashton had said, cried. Sharon, who had been there for Christine throughout the entire ordeal, consoled her. "It's OK, Christine. You'll be all right."

The judge gave Zaffino life in prison. He would spend at least twenty-three years behind bars before he could consider sitting in front of the parole board to plead his case for early release. When the judge finished, Christine ran out of the courtroom toward the back stairs, Sharon right behind her. Before they entered the stairway, reporters rushed Christine for a comment. "Are those tears of joy, or tears of sadness?"

What a cliché, she thought. *Could they not think of anything more original?*

"Both," Christine mumbled. "I cannot believe John didn't think of his own son." As Christine spoke, she started fumbling with her words. The tears were too much. The emotion of the day. So Sharon grabbed her by the hand and dragged her down the stairs.

When they reached the bottom of the stairs and turned the corner to walk out of the building, Ashton Zack was standing in front of them. Christine was startled. The boy was crying. She didn't know what to say.

Ashton looked at her. "Did you know my dad?" he confusingly whispered through tears. "Why did John kill my dad? Do you know why John killed my dad?"

Christine felt terrible. She was at a loss for words. So she instead hugged him. "No," she finally said, "I didn't know your dad. I don't know why John killed your dad."

After that, Christine and Sharon ran out the door and made it to Christine's car without being accosted by another reporter.

As the media, family members, detectives, interlopers and townspeople gathered outside the courtroom, shaking their heads in disbelief, the question loomed: would Zaffino open up and sell Cynthia George out now that, one could argue, he had nothing left to lose?

After the proceedings ended, reporters tracked down

Mike Carroll: "What are you going to do about Cynthia George? Is she going to be arrested? What's next?"

Cynthia and Ed were still married and living together. Cynthia's affairs had done little to destroy the marriage, at least from an outsider's perspective. In fact, there was word that the Georges had retained two of Akron's most high-powered attorneys to protect Cynthia. By this time, the CAPU and Mike Carroll were convinced that Ed George had had nothing to do with Jeff Zack's murder. The focus was specifically on one person—Cynthia. "We suspected Ed George for the first year on the investigation," one detective later told me, "but by the time of Zaffino's trial, we were confident Ed had had nothing whatsoever to do with the conspiracy to kill Jeff Zack."

Mike Carroll took a long pause while standing in front of a throng of reporters after Zaffino's sentencing. After all, Carroll and his team had done one hell of a job in getting a conviction. Couldn't he just let that verdict and sentence sit for a while before thinking about whether to go after Cynthia?

"So, Mike," one reporter asked, "what are you doing about Cindy George?"

Whiddon was standing beside him.

"The case is still open," Mike Carroll said softly before walking away.

Kimberly Cefalu, one of the jurors the *Akron Beacon Journal* tracked down after the Zaffino case was over, told a reporter, "There was an overwhelming amount of evidence, a lot of it circumstantial, but a mountain of evidence against John Zaffino." The article went on to explain that the juror "cited the importance of the cell phone records, which showed calls between Zaffino and [Cynthia] George before and after Zack was murdered."

Moreover, during the trial Mike Carroll proved that on the night when the two park rangers at Cuyahoga Falls came upon Zaffino as he emerged from the woods, there could have been a more sinister plot in play. Telephone records from Cynthia and John's cell phones proved that they had spoken on that night for hours. Mike Carroll and Dave Whiddon later told me that they theorized Cynthia was trying to lure Jeff Zack down to the park so Zaffino could kill him in the woods. But the plan was botched, they claimed, when those park rangers showed up. And that was when John Zaffino, in a panic, tossed the gun into the woods and covered it up with leaves, believing no one would ever find it.

"After we convicted Zaffino," Mike Carroll told me later, "we took a deep breath—and began to zero in on Cindy George."

89

In July, Dave Whiddon, Vince Felber and Russ McFarland took off on a trip to the East Coast. They had been listening to John Zaffino's telephone calls from prison. Through those calls, some rather shocking developments emerged. "[Someone close to Zaffino] had fabricated some of our police reports, sent letters to some of our witnesses," Whiddon explained to me later, "and we ended up serving a search warrant partly because of that."

During that search, Whiddon said, the CAPU found a number of e-mails between this person and Larry Whitney. In one, Whitney wrote back, **Your letters created quite a stir.** Those letters he was referring to had been sent to witnesses by a Zaffino relative. In some of the letters, Whiddon claimed, police reports were misquoted and even, he insisted, fabricated to some extent, thus turning two of the state's witnesses against the CAPU. It became a huge problem for the CAPU to gain back the credibility it had spent months shaping.

The conversations the CAPU recorded between Zaffino and family members painted a pretty clear picture for Mike Carroll. It was obvious to him, he said, that money had changed hands between Cynthia George and John Zaffino's attorney, which offered an explanation as to why Zaffino had never fingered Cynthia in the murder of Jeff Zack. In theory, the prosecution believed that Cynthia was helping Zaffino pay for his attorney— or, as Carroll put it, "financing his defense."

How did Mike Carroll and the CAPU know this? During one conversation, Zaffino was recorded telling a family member to get "a message to the George family." He said the Georges needed to hire him a "big-time lawyer like Johnnie Cochran" to represent him on his appeal. "[The Georges] are either going to help me," Zaffino said jarringly, "or *else.*"

That "else," Carroll maintained, was Zaffino dropping a dime on Cynthia.

Later on during the call, Zaffino upped the ante, saying sharply, "Because if I start making calls, shit's going to happen."

About nine weeks after that, Mike Carroll confirmed to me, he believed Cynthia George "funneled" a check for ten thousand dollars to Mike Bowler, her attorney, for the sole purpose of financing Zaffino's appeal. Bowler, Carroll claimed, then gave that money to Larry Whitney. Even more disturbing was that the CAPU uncovered a deposit of five hundred dollars into Zaffino's commissary fund at the prison where he was serving his sentence. They wondered where he got the money and traced it back to a relative, who had gotten it from Larry Whitney, who had gotten it from Mike Bowler, who had gotten it from Cynthia George.

Their heads were spinning after exposing the trail of "hush money," the prosecution later told me and several reporters.

90

Any hope John Zaffino had that the appeals court would find a reason to force another trial diminished by the first of the year 2004, when the court ruled Zaffino had lost his appeal. Larry Whitney had argued that because Cynthia had invoked her Fifth Amendment right against self-incrimination, she somehow prejudiced the jury against Zaffino. Hindsight doesn't work, however, with the appeals judges: since Larry Whitney didn't object to it during Zaffino's trial, the appeals court ruled, it made little difference now.

In a way, the court's decision cleared the path for Mike Carroll to focus exclusively on Cynthia George—and for the next year, that's what he and the CAPU did. Piece by painstaking piece, they built a case against the former Mrs. Ohio America runner-up. By Monday, January 10, 2005, a little over a year after Zaffino lost his bid for a new trial, Carroll thought he had enough. After stealthily watching the Akron socialite for a better part of the day, the Northern Ohio Violent Fugitive Task Force cornered Cynthia at the Bath & Body Works inside the West Market Plaza not far from her mansion in Medina. Cynthia knew why they were there. She put up little resistance when cops slapped the cuffs on her at 7:59 P.M. and walked her to an APD patrol car.

Once they got Cynthia down to the APD, she refused to answer any questions—big surprise—and asked for Mike Bowler and Bob Meeker, her attorneys.

On the day she was arrested, Cynthia was fifty years old. Her oldest child was nineteen; her youngest was ten. At the APD, she was charged formally with complicity to commit aggravated murder before being processed into Summit County Jail.

Cynthia George was now part of the judicial system, just another female inmate wearing the scrubs the state of Ohio provided. Appearing in Akron Municipal Court via a video satellite hookup the next morning, dressed in an orange jumpsuit, a sad, defeated look about her face, Cynthia said nothing while sitting stoically in a chair staring into the camera. It was hard for some to believe she was facing her demons for the first time. It had been almost four years since her lover was murdered. For the CAPU detectives working the case all along, it was comforting to see that Cynthia was finally going to have to answer to her involvement (if any).

Mike Bowler asked Judge Carla Moore to lower Cynthia's enormous bond, insisting that she wasn't a flight risk. After all, Bowler argued, she knew the CAPU had been after her since the day Zack was murdered. She had never left the state. Never hid from them. Why should she be forced to sit in jail until her trial under a bond that was, in truth, extreme?

Ultimately, Judge Moore sided with Mike Carroll, who had urged the court to slap Cynthia with a $10 million cash bond, the same amount John Zaffino had when he was arrested two years earlier. Why should the two be any different?

Bowler was upset with the decision and said there was no good reason why his client's bond should be so "unnecessarily high."

During a hearing before Summit County judge Mary Spicer a day later, Bowler, standing alongside longtime George family attorney Bob Meeker, once again argued that Cynthia was being treated unfairly with a bond that was ridiculously high.

On the other hand, Mike Carroll's office was saying it had "new information" regarding Cynthia's guilt. He believed a $2.5 million bond, if not $10 million, was appropriate for the situation, still insisting Cynthia was a "risk" to flee.

Judge Spicer, however, didn't agree. She said George had known of her "pending arrest for three years and has made no effort" to leave town. The fact of the matter was, Meeker and Bowler were right: compared to other murder suspects, Cynthia's ten-million-dollar bond was exceptionally outrageous.

So Spicer set Cynthia's bond at ten percent of two million dollars. She could walk out of jail with a cash payment of $200,000, an amount Ed George could certainly afford. The question was, would he do it? Was he still supporting a wife who had cheated on him repeatedly and was now suspected of participating in the murder of one of her ex-lovers?

Ed was in the courtroom with his and Cynthia's nineteen-year-old daughter. In his late 60s, Ed was showing his age. His once curly black hair had turned gray and wiry. He appeared tired, sullen, withdrawn. He wanted this over with. Still, to the shock of many, he was determined to support his wife. No matter what.

Within an hour, Ed arranged for the $200,000 cash payment. That night, he left the jail at five-thirty. with Cynthia on his arm. She had been in custody a total of four days. One could say Cynthia was a free woman, but the court permitted her to travel only in Summit, Stark or Medina Counties. She was told to report once a week to the county probation office.

Mike Carroll was disappointed, but respected Spicer's judgment. "In order to be a flight risk," Carroll commented later, "Cynthia would have to have been streetwise in order to survive, and I somewhat doubted then that she was. She had the means, obviously, and the money, which, if you want to flee, can be helpful. So although we lost that battle, if you will, we knew it was a long shot and accepted the judge's order. I kept my focus on the trial."

Cynthia's case was then formally assigned to Judge Patricia Cosgrove and scheduled to get under way immediately.

91

Several issues needed to be resolved before Cynthia's trial could begin. Number one on Mike Carroll's list was the notion that Cynthia had funneled what Carroll now publicly called "hush money" into John Zaffino's defense team. If that were true, Cynthia's attorneys, Carroll argued before the court, were going to be called as witnesses during the trial, thus relinquishing their right to represent her. Conflict of interest didn't begin to explain what Carroll thought of the behavior. Aiding Carroll was Summit County chief assistant prosecutor Mary Ann Kovach. She was competent and experienced, not to mention well-versed in both the Zaffino and George cases. The two together, many said, were unbeatable.

Mike Bowler told the judge during a hearing on the matter that the payments were part of a "common legal strategy used when two people are suspected of the same crime."

To the dismay of many, the court agreed. On March 5, Judge Cosgrove ruled that Bowler and Meeker could, in fact, remain on board Cynthia's defense train, which was growing into a Buckeye State version of the dream

team. More than that, Cosgrove's decision made it clear
that the prosecution couldn't call the lawyers as witnesses. If Mike Carroll and his office wanted to look
into charging the lawyers with misconduct, they could
always pursue those charges later. "[Courts have to ex-
amine] where an adverse party may try to call an opposing lawyer as a witness simply to disqualify that lawyer,"
Judge Cosgrove said in her ruling, "thus creating an
unfair tactical advantage, or to harass opposing counsel."

It was a blow to the state's case, for sure. Still, Carroll
and Kovach were confident. By the middle of March, as
both sides began preparing motions and arguments,
Bonnie Zack, on behalf of herself and Ashton, filed a
wrongful death suit against the George estate. In the
suit, Bonnie's lawyers claimed that "four months after
John Zaffino was convicted, the Georges moved $2 mil-
lion in property located in Medina County into a privately held trust in order to avoid paying any damages
that might arise from a lawsuit."

It seemed money was changing hands as though
people were playing a game of Monopoly. Bonnie was
overwhelmed that the Georges would go to such lengths.
It showed where their mind-set was heading into Cynthia's trial—or perhaps had been all along.

By November 11, 2005, both teams of attorneys had
fought it out in court over moving the trial because of
pretrial publicity, allowing the telephone calls Zaffino
made from prison and just about every minor matter
one could think of pertaining to making the trial a fair
balance for both sides. After a few days had been spent
questioning a long list of potential jurors, at the last
minute, in a move that would surprise many, Cynthia

waived her right to a jury trial and opted instead to have her case tried in front of the judge.

The news stunned the community. "We just didn't feel we could get a fair and impartial jury in this county," Bob Meeker told the *Akron Beacon Journal* after the agreement was reached. "Despite people seeming to be promising that they would make every effort, we just felt they were tainted so severely by this extensive publicity, so many news articles and so many news reports, that it was just asking more than a jury could fairly do."

It was a risky, albeit unorthodox move, to say the least. One person—a judge, mind you—was going to decide Cynthia's fate. For a trial with such a high-profile status surrounding it to be decided by a judge was rare. Defendants seldom chose this route. More than any of that, however, appeals courts hardly ever challenged a verdict made by a judge, simply because a judge is thought to have a better understanding of the due process and weigh the balance of justice on a much more impartial scale. In theory, Cynthia George was better off with a twelve-man/woman panel, even if one or two held on to a bias. The idea that her lawyers could convince a judge far more easily than a jury, however, won out. Cynthia's life was in the hands of another woman—a judge with a strong track record for running her courtroom with the respect, honor and integrity the scales deserved.

92

On November 14, 2005, Cynthia sat and listened to opening arguments in the *State of Ohio* v. *Cynthia George*. Mike Bowler wasn't going to try to paint Cynthia as some sort of golden girl, a sitcom mom, free from any problems in life. He wanted to explain to the judge exactly how he saw it. Talking about the month after Cynthia and Jeff Zack split up, Bowler said, "At this point, she didn't have a problem with Zack anymore. The relationship was over because Cindy George took steps in her life to end the relationship. She was gaining strength. The plan was working and she could feel good about it."

Those who knew the case sat in utter disbelief of the statement. Many saw the split between Zack and Cynthia as anything but amicable.

Bowler said nothing of Ed George's calls to the APD, insisting that his wife was being harassed. If the breakup had gone so well, so fluid and problem-free, why was Jeff Zack having a hard time letting go? Why was Cynthia stressing over not being able to get rid of him? And why, for crying out loud, had she changed her telephone number and canceled all of her e-mail accounts?

None of it made any sense.

Bowler blamed Cynthia's adulterous behavior on Ed George's seemingly workaholic nature, claiming the restaurateur was rarely around and, in effect, not there for his wife when she needed him. The bottom line for Bowler was, what would Cynthia's motive be if, by chance, she'd had something to do with the crime?

There was none, he insisted. "She had no need to. She had no want to," Bowler said near the conclusion of what amounted to about fifty minutes.

Mike Carroll had a different view of Cynthia George. For the past four years, he believed that she'd had a major hand in Jeff Zack's demise—that is, she had masterminded the plot to kill him. "My goal," Carroll told me later, "was to present the same exact case I had put on for Zaffino. There was no difference to me. . . . Murder's a dirty business. I was determined to prove that."

Mimicking his opening statement during the Zaffino trial, almost word for word, Carroll said, "Cindy George had a problem in her life. That problem was Jeff Zack, and she solved that problem through John Zaffino."

Whereas Carroll spent an ample amount of time telling the judge that the telephone records between Cynthia and Zaffino detailed a concerted murder plot, Bowler disagreed vehemently, claiming, "The phone records don't come close to saying what the prosecutor said they say. There is *no* evidence of what was said."

It was a valid point. Records of telephone calls and their length certainly couldn't explain what was said during each of those calls. It was pure speculation on the state's part. Don't assume they discussed murder—prove it with *evidence*.

During the opening testimony, Mike Carroll put

Mary Ann Brewer on the stand and had her explain to
the judge what went on inside the George household
on a normal—if it could be called such—day, especially
after Cynthia's affair with Jeff Zack supposedly ended.
Through that testimony, it was clear Cynthia was scared
of ending the relationship with Zack. "She told me she
has to put up with him," Brewer said. "'I have to see
him,' [Cindy] said. 'You don't understand. He said he
would take my child with him to Israel.'"

It was Cynthia's main motive for murder, according
to the prosecution: Cynthia's secret love child would be
exposed to the world if Jeff Zack decided he wanted
custody—or worse, kidnapped the child and took off to
Israel with her.

Like she had during the Zaffino trial, Brewer said she
was "unclear" whether Ed knew of the affair or that one
of his children had been fathered by another man.

"Ed didn't understand why there were so many hang-
up calls to the house," Brewer told the judge.

Next up were Bonnie and Elayne Zack.

When Mike Carroll asked Bonnie if she knew of the
love child, Bonnie retorted, "I went into complete
shock. I just felt like I was hit."

Elayne discussed the secretly recorded telephone call
she made to Cynthia in the days after her son was murdered. And for the next several witnesses, the case
moved along at breakneck speed, Carroll calling a list
of witnesses nearly identical to those he called during
Zaffino's trial, painting a picture of Cynthia's affair with
Zack, showing the judge how Cynthia wanted to end
the affair but was being, basically, harassed by Jeff Zack.

All of it, Carroll insisted, added up to murder.

During the next few days, Nancy Forrest sat and told
the judge how her ex-husband showed up at her house

with the bike in the middle of the night, and then a bank official testified to the trail of money allegedly tying Cynthia and Zaffino to the purchase of the bike.

Bowler and Meeker did their best to poke holes in each witness's testimony. Although Cynthia had left what the prosecution was calling a paper trail of her relationship with Zaffino that juxtaposed with the murder of Jeff Zack, it was mere speculation and theory. None of it proved Cynthia conspired with Zaffino. All it proved was that Zaffino and Cynthia had contact.

Many of the state's witnesses had already been through one trial and were sharp and direct with their words. Christine Todaro walked in and seemed to be stronger than she had ever been, undoubtedly a bit more confident due to the fact that her ex-husband was sitting in prison. The two park rangers further tightened the noose by telling their stories of finding Zaffino roaming through the woods, waiting for his girlfriend, and the mushroom hunter finding a gun in the same general region where Zaffino had been seen. Both rangers' testimony was further lifted by the fact that Mike Carroll presented blowups of the telephone records proving how many times—and for how long—Cynthia and Zaffino spoke on that day and night.

But again, all Carroll could prove was that Zaffino and Cynthia—or, more to the point, their cell phones—had communicated.

On Monday, November 21, Mike Carroll played a tape of a telephone call between Zaffino and a relative, which had been recorded on April 5, 2003. Zaffino must have known the conversations were being recorded. During the call, he told this person to let his "friends" know that he needed to get out of jail on bond. If they don't understand what he means, Zaffino said, they will "lose their freedom. . . . They've just put two-and-a-half million dollars in[to] their restaurant," he said rather frankly, with a cold, threatening chill in his voice, "while *I've* been in *jail.*"

People in the courtroom gallery were taken aback by the calls. Without coming out and saying as much, it certainly seemed as if there had been a conspiracy between Cynthia and Zaffino that he was ready to talk about anytime he felt Cynthia wasn't keeping up her end of a bargain they had possibly made.

For the most part, Cynthia seemed relaxed during the trial. She had even managed to laugh during portions of testimony and smile as witnesses identified her after being asked to point her out by Mike Carroll. She came across as cocky, though, which didn't sit well with some. She was above the law, at least it seemed that way as she grimaced and smirked and walked with her head high as she came to and from the courtroom. Ed George was there in the courtroom to support his wife, sitting once again next to his and Cynthia's oldest daughter. Ed and Cynthia made eye contact on occasion and embraced for everyone to see, appearing as a happily married couple.

Nothing seemed to bother Cynthia as she watched and listened to her adulterous life unfold in public. Yet, what was coming next would be cause for Cynthia to want to curl up in a ball and hide underneath the oak table where she was sitting. Because Mike Carroll had some rather squalid, shocking evidence to present to the judge—which had not been part of Zaffino's trial.

93

There's a saying: never put in writing what you don't want the world to read. Cynthia George had obviously not heard of this age-old proverb. Because every letter she had written to John Zaffino after his arrest became public record as Mike Carroll began introducing the letters as evidence. According to the letters, Cynthia was still in love with John Zaffino and couldn't bear to live without him. She wrote "how sorrowful" she had felt for her lover. The letter was dated a few weeks after Zaffino's conviction. She said her "heart aches for" him "every day."

The laughing, smiling, walking in and out of the courtroom as if she didn't have a care in the world, were temporarily over for Cynthia George. As excerpts from letters she wrote to her lover were read into the record, Cynthia bowed her head and cried into a tissue.

The letters were obtained in 2004, when the CAPU served a search warrant to a Zaffino relative. This person had collected all of the letters for Zaffino. A match and some gasoline would have probably saved Cynthia a lot of embarrassment, but something told investigators and the prosecution that Zaffino had held on to the letters as some sort of insurance policy. In one, Cynthia wrote how her "days" after Zaffino's conviction started with visits to her local church "every morning." In church, she sat and prayed during "a mass . . . offered" in Zaffino's name. She said she began her morning by lighting one candle for him and a second for his son. "They burn throughout the day. . . ." At night, Cynthia wrote, if she couldn't sleep, she would think about the candles "burning" as she quietly read excerpts from her Bible, drifting piously to sleep.

In his telephone calls during the same time period the letters were written, Zaffino seemed to give the impression that he was getting impatient with the Georges. Had Cynthia ladled on the charm in order to keep Zaffino quiet? Her letters seemed to say as much, as well as a look into the mind of a woman torn between reality, a perpetual counterfeit bond and devotion to Christianity, along with a touch of pure narcissism. She claimed she wanted to meet and speak with Zaffino, adding, "if only a few words," but insisted that they both must "listen to counsel."

God, Cynthia wrote in one, *was working through them.* She wanted Zaffino to "pray for wisdom." Then, perhaps giving the state its most damaging piece of evidence, Cynthia wrote Zaffino, *We cannot make one mistake.*

When Dave Whiddon first got hold of the letters and sat down to read them, he was amazed by the candor Cynthia displayed. He believed much of what she wrote was her way of keeping Zaffino in order, dangling on puppet strings. If she could have, Whiddon said, Cynthia George would have immediately written John Zaffino off when he was arrested. "But she had to make sure he didn't say anything."

The gallery sat in stunned silence as Cynthia's words,

which she had to have believed would stay private, echoed throughout the day as the letters became part of the record. *We will never loose* [sic] *contact,* she wrote. *We are still steadfast.* Then she talked about building "strength in each other." In what could be classified as an example of purple prose, she wrote, *[The] storm is quite great and devastating, but plant your feet and dig.*

The second letter was weighed down by several Bible passages and references to Jesus Christ. It was rather strange for some to hear a woman quote Scripture to a guy who was perhaps as far removed from God as an atheist. Cynthia spoke of how "difficult" it was for her to make it through a day knowing that Zaffino was locked up. She thanked him for making a "difference" in her life, before writing she missed him and *all your stuborn* [sic], *bullheaded, pigheaded ways.*

According to Cynthia, Zaffino had written to her saying he cried himself to sleep most nights with the thought of never "seeing" her again. She referred to herself in her letters as the most *gentle, levelheaded, patient, funloving, wonderful* and *humble* person *in the whole wide world.* But she wrote about Zaffino as the most *obstinent* [sic], *cantancerous* [sic], *stubborn, strongest person* she had *ever met.*

Johnie, Johnie, Johnie, Johnie, I worry so about you. . . .

Here was a side of Cynthia George no one had seen. She came across as a love-swept teenager, begging for the love of a man she claimed to be—without coming out and saying—her soul mate.

Many had to wonder what Ed George thought as he sat and listened to the letters his wife had written to her lover as they were presented in court for the entire community to hear. But Ed wasn't talking. Instead, he continued to stand by his bride and support her.

* * *

After the letters were read, Detective Vince Felber took the stand to tell his version of investigating the case. Felber's perspective was a good representation of the case. He and Whiddon had basically taken over a majority of the investigation as it shifted from Zaffino to Cynthia. Some later said Felber had become "obsessed" with the case and couldn't get his mind around anything else.

But none of this changed Felber's expert investigating skills and how much he had contributed to the case. Without Felber, many agreed, the cases against Zaffino and Cynthia George would have never materialized.

After Felber, the testimony moved the case back to how Jeff Zack called Cynthia obsessively in the weeks after she told him the relationship was over. Zack and Cynthia had talked a lot on the telephone, but nothing compared to how much Zaffino and Cynthia had. In total, Mike Carroll presented evidence that suggested Zaffino and Cynthia talked between 1,000 and 5,300 minutes per month. Keeping score, averaging it out, they spoke on the phone for approximately fifty hours per month.

In the end, the state had presented a carbon copy of the Zaffino case and felt it was enough to convict Cynthia.

Shortly before lunch on Tuesday, November 22, Mike Carroll rested the state's case, confident the judge was going to see how intimately Cynthia George was involved in the planning and plotting of Jeff Zack's murder. After all, Cynthia's defense presented little evidence to suggest otherwise—that perhaps Zaffino acted on his own behalf because he was a jealous lover, which was, legal experts agreed, Cynthia's best chance at freedom. John Zaffino had been brought from prison to the court in case he wanted to testify at the last minute. But he refused. Without Zaffino backing Cynthia up, or testifying against her, some thought she was going to walk.

As the day ended, Bob Meeker and Mike Bowler addressed the press outside the courtroom. They said they were "unsure" whether to put their client on the stand, but promised to make a decision within the next twenty-four hours.

94

The following morning, Bob Meeker and Mike Bowler didn't waltz into court saying anything about Cynthia testifying. Many knew it likely wasn't going to happen, seeing how devastating it could be for Cynthia if she happened to say the wrong thing and open a vein of her life that had yet to be explored. Maybe it was safe if she kept quiet and hedged her bets, knowing full well that a judge might view her silence as a weakness.

Cynthia's defense called two witnesses. Cynthia had been seeing a therapist, Alan Kurzweil, during the period shortly before she and Jeff Zack had split. At first, Kurzweil talked about how Cynthia had been referred to him by her psychiatrist in January 2001. Kurzweil called himself a counselor, someone who sat, listened to problems and then offered solutions.

Ed George's wife was "depressed and stressed," Kurzweil stated, when he began evaluating her condition. Cynthia's demeanor mimicked that of a child's, the doctor seemed to say. She was caught between a Cinderella world of wealth, which she had dreamt of as a young teen, and a lonely life inside that castle, once she realized she had gotten what she wanted. For years, it was a melancholic state of emotional pain and retreat that she fed by having affairs with strangely tarnished men she related to in a way that was representative of her childhood. The woman had been lonely. With a husband working all hours of the night and day, she became bored. She filled that void with affairs.

Kurzweil said Cynthia spoke of a "friend" who was rather "abusive" toward her and that she wanted to end the relationship, but couldn't find a way to do it.

In a sense, Kurzweil's testimony boosted the prosecution's case, ostensibly laying a foundation for the theory that Cynthia could not get rid of Zack in a traditional way, so she resulted to one of the oldest tricks in the book.

Jeff Zack, the doctor admitted, referring to him as Cynthia's "friend," had been calling her, at one time, every two hours, acting quite "bizarre" and irrational. Cynthia had even told Kurzweil that he had threatened to put a contract on her life, saying something to the effect of, "If I can't have you, no one can."

Kurzweil suggested to her as part of his treatment that she should tell her husband about the affair. Admit her shortcomings, plead for forgiveness, and have Ed help her deal with a man who had become a major problem in her life.

In response to that, Cynthia cried. She said she was living with what was then an older man who was "severely depressed" himself. She had always viewed their relationship, she admitted, as a "father-daughter" type of love, and felt she couldn't confide in him the way she could with her various lovers.

Three months after she started the counseling sessions, Cynthia stopped going. Three months later, her problem was gone; Zack was dead.

Next, in what would be Meeker and Bowler's final witness, Ed George walked slowly up to the stand and took a seat. One had to admire a man who stood by a wife who had cheated on him repeatedly throughout their marriage. Ed was a pillar in the community. He and his family had been in the restaurant business for over five decades. Many people didn't like Ed George, but most respected him and viewed his success as a symbol of what hard work could accomplish.

Ed initially talked about how he and Cynthia met. He seemed confident and sure in his words. Even sincere. Then he discussed how he and Jeff Zack, along with Cynthia and Bonnie, became "acquaintances" in 1991 after meeting inside his bar. For a while, things went well. Christmases. Halloween parties with the kids. Thanksgivings. Birthday parties. They were all friends. He didn't think anything more of it.

Much of Ed's testimony seemed to center around how much he worked. "It's the business I chose," he said at one point.

Ed's work had had an impact not only on his life, but on his marriage. He knew that. It was during Christmas Eve, 2000, he explained, while he and Cynthia and the kids were attending holiday services at St. Vincent Church, when he understood that the problems between Jeff Zack and Cynthia were beginning to affect the marriage. He wasn't aware of the affair then, he insisted, or that Ruby had been fathered by Zack, but the story he told the judge seemed to echo with reverberations of a man beginning to acknowledge that his wife was stepping out on him. "I heard a loud voice," Ed testified, talking about that incident inside the church, "but I couldn't decipher what was being said." Cynthia was talking on her cell phone. It was Christmas Eve.

They were in God's house. *What in the heck is going on?* "Cindy became very upset in church. She said it was Jeff Zack and she asked him to please just leave her alone. She just wanted to be with Jesus on that night."

She just wanted to be with Jesus. . . . It sounded so strange. So unlike something Cynthia would say. She was talking to a man she had been sleeping with then for nearly nine years. Not to mention, she was already involved with John Zaffino. But on that night, she had just wanted to be with her husband, children and, of course, Jesus.

Jeff Zack wouldn't accept that from Cynthia and lashed back with what Ed described as a litany of offensive remarks. It wasn't until one month later, Ed testified, that he contacted Paul Callahan at the APD and began talking to him about what he could do in regard to "a man harassing" his wife.

Meeker asked Ed why he didn't file a police report after talking to Callahan.

"I didn't want to air all of our dirty laundry and have the media and other people find out."

Again, Ed's words seemed to benefit the prosecution, pointing to the fact that Cynthia was out of options when it came to getting rid of Jeff Zack.

Ed admitted that he didn't learn of the affair between Cynthia and Jeff Zack until after Zack was murdered— and didn't have any idea Ruby was Zack's child until the APD came calling with a court order to get a buccal swab of Ruby's cheek.

Slowly, with a trace of sorrow in his voice, Meeker then asked the question that perhaps anyone following the case from day one wanted answered. It had to be said. "Why remain married to Cindy after learning those things?"

"Well," Ed said resolutely, with the natural ease of a

man who had come to terms with his wife's transgressions and had obviously forgiven her, "the first reason is, I took a marriage vow. . . . I firmly believe in that. I'm a devout Christian. I think a mother is important in raising the children. I don't think you can raise a family without a mother."

It seemed that the letters Cynthia wrote to Zaffino didn't matter to Ed. He was standing behind his wife and nothing was going to change his mind. He may have looked like a fool, a pushover, but what mattered to Ed George was the love he could *give* his wife, not the other way around. Anyone who knew Ed said later that he was devoted to his children. One would have to imagine that his devotion to the children was one of the reasons why he had put up with so much for so long. "I look at my wife," Ed added calmly, staring at Cynthia, "and the things we have been through. I see this person I met at that time. I have always hoped that person would return." He paused. Then quietly, "And she has."

Over a calendar week of testimony, Judge Cosgrove heard a case that was fairly cut-and-dry: either you bought the prosecution's version of events or you didn't. Cynthia's lawyers, on the other hand, didn't have to explain or prove her innocence.

The prosecution's case was all circumstantial. No forensic or witness testimony had tied Cynthia to the murder of Jeff Zack. Cynthia's lawyers were certain that was enough to allow her to walk out of the courtroom a free woman.

On Wednesday, November 23, both sides presented closing arguments. When they were finished, Judge Cosgrove announced she would study the evidence and present her verdict by 11:00 A.M. on Monday.

95

Cynthia and Ed George's children had all attended Catholic schools. They were a family of Christians. No one could deny them that. Cynthia, too, fashioned herself as a devout follower of Jesus Christ—yet her behavior hardly fit with what Jesus would have perceived as a devoted disciple. She had sinned. No doubt about it. But she had also come to terms with those sins—or so she claimed—had asked for forgiveness and, in some respects, had been granted it. At least the one man who mattered most to her had done so.

Judge Cosgrove, who had promised an 11:00 A.M. verdict, emerged from her chambers by eleven-thirty, walked into the courtroom, cutting a silence throughout, and began to read the results of her assessment of the testimony and evidence.

Cynthia sat smiling at friends and family, over a dozen strong, there to support her. She was seemingly undeterred by what might become of her life. She had kissed three of her children and Ed before heading to the table where her attorneys waited.

Cynthia's youngest daughter sat in the gallery with

a crucifix in her hand and mouthed what many assumed was the Lord's Prayer.

Judge Cosgrove sat at the bench and read from her ten-page verdict. As soon as she got a few paragraphs into it, a flurry of applause and "yeses" rang out from Cynthia's side of the courtroom. The judge explained that prosecutors had "failed to prove" Cynthia conspired with John Zaffino in an attempt on Jeff Zack's life that night at the Cuyahoga Valley National Park when the park ranger caught up with Zaffino as he came walking out of the woods.

Quieting the crowd, however, Judge Cosgrove made a point to say next that her "first verdict applied only to the conspiracy count."

This comment by itself silenced the room. Jolly faces turned serious. Cynthia's posse must have known that bad news was forthcoming. Why else would the judge even mention it? In fact, it didn't take long for the George crowd to go from pure elation to utter shock as Judge Cosgrove's verdict reading began to suggest guilt: "'The defendant claims that if Mr. Zaffino was the killer of Jeff Zack, then it was a spur-of-the-moment decision. The evidence does not support this decision,'" Cosgrove inferred. "'The one constant in this case is that Cynthia George has not completely told the truth to anyone.'"

Utter silence.

"'This court is convinced, but for the conduct of Cindy George in financing and inducing John Zaffino to commit a crime, Jeff Zack would not have been murdered.'"

Jaws dropped. *What? No . . . it can't be.*

In the end, those letters Cynthia wrote to Zaffino were what ultimately sunk her. Cosgrove quoted from one, saying, "'We must . . . listen to counsel, God is also working through them, too. Pray for their wisdom, we cannot make one mistake.'"

There was a brief pause.

As Judge Cosgrove continued, the George crowd gasped. Cynthia trembled and fell into the arms of one of her attorneys. She could be heard wailing and crying hysterically as the inevitable was read into the record.

In the thick of it all, as whispers and jubilation were heard from one end of the courtroom, Ed George yelled, "We support you."

"'Without Mrs. George's encouragement and influence in procuring and convincing Mr. John Zaffino to commit this murder, it could not have been accomplished on June 16, 2001,'" Cosgrove said. "'In conclusion, there is no "smoking gun" in this case. What there is, is an abundance of direct and circumstantial evidence proving beyond a reasonable doubt that she procured and/or solicited John Zaffino to commit aggravated murder in the death of Jeff Zack.'"

The judge said she had deliberated the case over the three-day Thanksgiving weekend. She explained how she had traveled to the courthouse each day to review evidence.

With the verdict in, Cosgrove said she would sentence Cynthia after she had the opportunity to speak for herself.

The judge's guilty finding came in regard to the complicity to aggravated murder charge. It was the worst possible scenario for Cynthia.

"First of all," Cynthia said through tears, standing and facing the judge, "I just want to tell you I didn't do it. I know it points that way, but I *didn't* do it. I was just

seeking help. I know this has been a tough decision for
you and I know you are fair and I know how it looks. I
will appeal this verdict."

Cynthia's sentence seemed to be the most sobering
detail of the late morning: life in prison without a
chance of parole for twenty-three years. Barring any
positive judgment on appeal, Cynthia would be in her
mid-seventies by the time she could face a parole
board and plead for her freedom.

While being handcuffed before she was led away to
prison, Ed George spoke out to his wife, giving her the
thumbs-up sign, saying in haste, "Keep your chin up,
Cindy, we're here right behind you."

On Wednesday of that week, Cynthia was driven in a
white van with bars on the windows to the Ohio Reformatory for Women in Marysville, more than a two-
hour ride from Akron. Ed had told his wife to keep her
chin up. When Cynthia was booked after she was
found guilty, her photograph was taken. In that booking photograph, she did exactly what her husband had
suggested—but on top of standing erect with her chin
held high, as if she didn't have a care in the world,
Cynthia smiled for the photograph. It was an awkward
smile, more Hollywood than anything. It spoke to how
pompous and arrogant the woman could be. Here she
was heading off to prison for the rest of her life and all
she could do was smile. Odd behavior for a woman
who was so concerned about not being able to see one
of her daughters that she reverted to allegedly sanc-
tioning the murder of the man who had apparently
made the threat. She couldn't have been smiling at the
notion that she would now only see her children at
weekly intervals—if she was lucky—in the confines of

a women's prison. Was there anything, really, left to smile about?

Apparently, Cynthia knew what no one else did: because, in the coming months, she would have plenty to smile about.

96

On January 3, 2007, Cynthia George, then a fifty-two-year-old women beginning to show her age, was once again in court. There she sat, wearing a pink suit coat, staring expectantly at a three-judge panel in the Ninth District Court of Appeals. With a look of bewilderment on her ashen face, her hand was cradled up against her chin, as she watched her new lawyers go to work.

If anyone had wondered where Ed George stood in the face of having a wife tucked away in prison, he answered by showing up in court to support Cynthia once again. Ed had always claimed to be a devout Catholic, and perhaps he had forgiven Cynthia with every aching muscle of his pious heart. When asked by a local newspaper, Ed said he "continues to stand by his wife in her efforts to prove her innocence and is in total agreement with the arguments of her new lawyers."

The main cusp of Cynthia's argument centered on the notion that she was "denied her constitutional right" to a reputable defense during her 2005 trial.

How?

Cynthia's new lawyers, Max Kravitz and Bradley Barbin, claimed Bob Meeker and Mike Bowler, her former attorneys, should have never been allowed to represent her in the first place. In fact, Kravitz and Barbin argued, Cynthia would not have even been indicted if Meeker and Bowler hadn't arranged for the payments of fifteen thousand dollars and five hundred dollars to her lover, John Zaffino, and Larry Whitney, Zaffino's lawyer, as part of what they termed "a joint defense agreement." In theory, Cynthia's new lawyers were saying the state's most telling and damaging evidence against Cynthia was that so-called "hush money" she had supposedly paid Zaffino to keep quiet. Without that evidence, they said, the state had no case.

Attorney Barbin explained to the appeals judges that Patricia Cosgrove, the judge who oversaw Cynthia's trial, should have invoked a conflict of interest, as Mike Carroll and his office had originally argued when they filed a motion before trial. When that failed, Meeker and Bowler shouldn't have been allowed to continue representing Cynthia; they should have, Barbin said, "voluntarily" withdrawn from the case.

Addressing the judges, Barbin said quite portentously, "For the conduct of counsel in this case, Cynthia Rohr-George may not have been indicted, and most certainly would not have been convicted. . . . I think the court is aware that until January 2005, there was no indictment of Miss George. It was only *after* the investigation began, regarding the conversations between Mr. Zaffino and Mike Bowler (her former lawyer) . . . that this case became a complicity case. I would ask the court to look very carefully at the timing of the payments in this case. I would suggest that despite the prosecution's best efforts to remove Mike

Bowler and Bob Meeker . . . they didn't go far enough."

In that respect, it was the state's burden to get rid of a defendant's inadequate counsel?

Further along, Barbin added, "And the reason they didn't go far enough is, if you look at that motion that Mr. Bogdanoff (Mike Carroll's colleague) himself signed, you see fourteen instances of not just legal payment references, but actually conduct of counsel that goes *well* beyond legal payments. For instance, in the April 23, 2003, conversation, there is a clear suggestion in that both Mr. Bowler *and* Mr. [Larry] Whitney are going to be jointly representing both Zaffino and Cynthia George. That is *exactly* what [the cases I've referenced in my argument] are about. It is the type of problem that is discussed in [another case example] where lawyers get themselves thoroughly immersed in the case and almost become accessories after the fact. . . ."

Strong contentions made by competent lawyers now saying that Cynthia George deserved a second chance because she had been so thoroughly damaged by the conduct of what were incompetent counselors.

But wasn't it too late for all this?

According to the state, the problem with the argument was that in March 2005, during a hearing on the matter before Cynthia's trial began, Meeker and Bowler said they *should* be allowed to stay on the case because the transaction of exchanging money between defendants was in the due process of what was called a "joint defense fund."

Judge Cosgrove agreed. Nothing more was said of it.

Mike Carroll had moved on to other cases. In the state's rebuttal argument, Summit County assistant prosecutor Philip Bogdanoff took over and explained to the judges that "the issue of conflict of interest by defense lawyers" was never raised then and shouldn't matter now. "I can state on my experience that this defendant is not the first defendant to blame her attorneys for her conviction—and certainly won't be the last," Bogdanoff said in a somewhat subdued, comfortable and determined manner. He was sure of himself and the judgment, and wasn't about to allow Cynthia's new attorneys to walk all over Judge Cosgrove's ruling. "The attorneys in this case—and I will say to you there were *five* attorneys in this case [for the defendant]— were *not* ineffective. The defendant raises the actions of two attorneys, primarily one, Mike Bowler. . . . What I want this court to realize is, what occurred at the trial level. What the defendant's [claim] is, is that Mr. Bowler and Mr. Meeker had a conflict of interest in this case. That was *not* the issue at the trial level. The issue at the trial level was that when we were investigating this case, we saw payments between the defendant, through the law firm of Meeker and Bowler, to Larry Whitney, the attorney for John Zaffino, and then these funds were used to benefit John Zaffino. We also had statements—we were listening to Mr. Zaffino's phone calls while in prison—and he would call almost every day to [a family member]—and we would listen to these phone calls. And he was *told* that these phone calls were being recorded. He would indicate, 'I need money from my friends, and if they don't give me money, they are going to be in big trouble.'"

In other words, with or without trying, John Zaffino had cut Cynthia's throat by giving investigators information regarding that so-called "hush money." Larry Whitney and Mike Bowler had the opportunity to "testify about the joint defense agreement at the March

2005 hearing before [Judge] Cosgrove," the state prosecutor told the judges—an opportunity that had come and gone.

The three-judge panel said they would release their decision soon.

97

Primarily, appeals take months, if not years. Courts are continually hampered by convicted murderers and criminals alike pointing to the mistakes they believed were made during their trials. It hadn't worked for John Zaffino. His appeal was denied. Yet, on March 21, 2007, a little over two months after Cynthia George argued her case in front of the Ninth District Court of Appeals, two of the three judges agreed to reverse Cynthia's conviction on complicity to murder, writing that the prosecution had failed to prove Cynthia convinced John Zaffino to murder Jeff Zack.

In short, Cynthia George had won her appeal. She would be set free as soon as the paperwork was submitted by the court to the prison in Marysville, Ohio, where she had spent the past year and four months.

A collective gasp could be heard from Akron as the ruling—which meant Cynthia George was going to walk out of prison a free woman—was made public. It was what the prosecution, not to mention members of the CAPU who had worked so doggedly to build a case against Cynthia, feared most: a ruling that, in the way it was written, would not allow the state to pursue charges against Cynthia ever again.

"Money buys you freedom in this town," one person close to the case told me after the appeal decision was released.

This sentiment—that a rich woman was walking away from prison as a poor man lost his appeal and was forced to serve life behind bars—rang throughout the community like a church bell on Sunday morning. People in the community were upset. They felt slighted. They couldn't understand how it could have happened. The evidence seemed so clear-cut. So perfect.

According to two of the three judges, however, the evidence—or lack thereof—was the one component setting Cynthia free. "The evidence is insufficient to sustain a finding of guilt," Judge William Baird wrote, "and, as a result, the federal Constitution and the Ohio Constitution require the conviction to be reversed with prejudice to further prosecution.

"As will be explained . . . ," Baird continued, "there was very little evidence to connect Rohr-George to this murder in any way." The main crux of the court's decision hinged on the idea that circumstantial evidence alone was not enough to find Cynthia guilty. "Extramarital love affairs" were not a motivation or proof of a murder plot. Two of the three judges—Baird and Judge Beth Whitmore—agreed that "much of the state's evidence . . . focused on Rohr-George's possible motive," which the court decided wasn't enough to sustain a conviction. "Assuming, without deciding, that this evidence was sufficient to establish that Rohr-George may have had a motive to kill Zack, motive alone was not sufficient to prove that Rohr-George committed a crime." Baird cited a prior case, *State* v. *Nichols*, in which it was written into the record that "proof of motive does not establish guilt."

Quite shockingly, Baird made an assumption in his decision, writing that, "If Zaffino had been a stranger having no motive to kill Zack, it could be argued that an inference arises that Rohr-George must have solicited him to do it, because she was the only one of the two having a motive to kill Zack. As a lover newly coming upon the scene, however, Zaffino had a motive to want his competition out of that scene."

Thus, in effect, Baird was implying a motive on Zaffino's part; yet, in the same breath, he was saying that the state could not impart a motive on Cynthia's part. For many, this made little sense.

Further along, Baird suggested that a relationship between Zaffino and Cynthia was not enough to prove she was involved in the murder plan. Moreover, the telephone calls between them, which were a major part of the state's case (or, as Baird wrote, "The state placed a great emphasis on the many cellular telephone calls . . ."), did not imply that a murder plan was being hashed out during those said calls. "Even if it inferred from the gap in the phone calls," Baird wrote, "that Rohr-George knew about the murder beforehand, prior knowledge of a crime does not make one an accomplice."

As for the fact established during her trial that Cynthia financed the hit, supplying Zaffino with the money to buy the gun and the infamous Ninja-style motorcycle, Baird, writing on behalf of the court, wasn't buying that argument, either. "Although the state attempted to prove that Rohr-George gave Zaffino the money that he used to purchase the murder weapon, the record is devoid of any evidence to support such an inference."

It seemed, as the decision went on for twenty-four

pages, that the state's one great failure was that it hadn't produced Zaffino as a witness. It was as if Cynthia's entire conviction hung on Zaffino's lack of participation in the state's case.

Judge Lynn Slaby disagreed with her colleagues, writing separately that, "I would overrule the Defendant . . . because the State presented sufficient evidence to establish that Defendant procured Zack's murder. . . . The State presented evidence to prove that Defendant did several things that brought about Zack's murder or motivated Zaffino to commit it." Citing all the reasons why her colleagues decided to overturn the conviction, Slaby agreed with the state's version of events. "I would," she concluded, "affirm the judgment of the trial court."

Judge Patricia Cosgrove must have felt snubbed. Here were two of her counterparts saying that she should have found Cynthia George not guilty. It was an unprecedented decision, hardly ever written into Ohio judicial history.

All that the Summit County Prosecutor's Office could say was that it was a "shocking" turn of events. With that, they asked the appellate court to "reconsider" its decision, and vowed to fight Cynthia's release, at least until they could write an argument and take it to the supreme court.

Part of the prosecution's new argument claimed the appeals judges failed to take into account that in the text of the letters between Zaffino and Cynthia, there was evidence that he had not spoken to the CAPU because Cynthia had promised to take care of him. According to the Summit County Prosecutor's Office, Zaffino had indicated clearly during these correspondences that there was some sort of agreement between him and Cynthia to kill Jeff Zack and that his silence regarding her involvement would be compensated. "[Zaffino] is in prison for George and did exactly what he said he would do,'" the prosecutor's office said in a statement. "They had an agreement that George would use all of her financial resources, even selling her house [which she never did], to set him free if anything went wrong and he went to prison."

Meanwhile, Ohio could no longer hold fifty-two-year-old Cynthia George. During the evening of March 22, 2007, near seven o'clock, just a day after the decision was released, Cynthia walked out of the Ohio Reformatory for Women in Marysville, about 140 miles from her Medina home, stepped into a gray Ford SUV driven by her oldest daughter and headed for home. Later that night, at about nine-thirty, as all her children, Ed George—the irrefutably faithful husband—alongside about thirty family members and friends, stood outside the Georges' massive estate waiting for her. Inside the house was a WELCOME HOME banner above a celebratory cake.

Cynthia cried and smiled and held her hands over her mouth to the cheers and shouts of "Hi, Mom" as local news cameras captured her return. As Cynthia hugged her kids and said hello to friends and family, reported the *Cleveland Plain Dealer*, Ed George said, "Oh, God. Oh, this is great."

He was beside himself with joy.

Cynthia's brother handed her some sort of trinket, an angel pin. He told her to keep it forever. It was Helen Rohr's, Cynthia's mother, who had passed away in September 2006.

Cynthia looked thin in her blue sweat suit, her once porcelain skin hung in wrinkles off her tired face. For the first time in her life, perhaps, Cynthia was showing her age. Prison had sped up the process. It had been hard on her, certainly. She hadn't accepted the time, but instead sat in prison praying for her release. In total, she had spent a year and four months behind bars. But now, here she was: home. She couldn't believe it. A nightmare finally over.

Or was it?

EPILOGUE

Ed and Cynthia George, along with their attorneys, had several opportunities to speak with me; they chose not to. Cynthia George, I will say, spoke to NBC's *Dateline* and the *Cleveland Plain Dealer*. I didn't include the *Dealer*'s interview in this book because, to be honest, I felt Cynthia was not being totally honest. In that interview, she tells a story of Jeff Zack breaking into her home, raping her, beating her, truly making Jeff out to be a monster. This was the first time Cynthia had ever told this story. It seemed to come out of nowhere. She said she was terrified of Jeff Zack. The story ran during the middle of her appeal process. I believe she was speaking directly to the appeals court judges, looking to further bolster her case for freedom. During her *Dateline* appearance, Cynthia basically said the same things.

My point here is this: Cynthia George, her husband and family chose to speak to those people who would rally around them. If there was a chance that any sense of objectivity could be injected into an interview Cynthia gave, she wouldn't do it.

What does this mean?

In the grand scope of things: nothing. Cynthia George played her hand perfectly and, as of this writing, is sitting at home a free woman.

John Zaffino and his family wrote to me with their theories of police corruption, witness tampering and alleged perjury by witnesses, but when I asked for evidence to back up such outrageous claims, I never heard from them again.

I conducted over one hundred hours of interviews for this book, studied thousands of pages of documents— police reports, witness interviews and statements, transcripts of recorded interviews, transcripts of the meetings and telephone calls between Zaffino and Christine Todaro, over one thousand pages of trial transcripts from Zaffino and Cynthia's trials—and exchanged hundreds of e-mails with many of the players involved. I would also like to note that beyond the interviews I conducted with several of Cynthia George's former neighbors, on top of the family background research I did myself, articles published in the *Cleveland Plain Dealer* and *Akron Beacon Journal* helped me draw the brief biography of Cynthia's childhood and high-school days found in Chapter 36. In Chapter 43, where I describe Cynthia and Ed George's courtship and wedding ceremony, along with Ed George's history, several sources were helpful to me, including interviews I conducted with former George family friends, neighbors, people who wish to remain anonymous and former employees of Ed George, as well as Ed George's court testimony and articles published in the *Akron Beacon Journal* and *Cleveland Plain Dealer*. In addition, I think it's important to note that every phone call between Christine Todaro and John Zaffino I re-created in this book was recorded, and the dialogue during these sections of the book was taken verbatim from those recordings and the transcripts accompanying them. As an added authentication, the interviews I conducted with Miss Todaro helped me understand the context and nature of each call, along with re-creating what she was going through and feeling at the time. Furthermore, Lieutenant Dave Whiddon, who I also interviewed, listened to each phone call and provided me with his exclusive insight.

Why wouldn't John Zaffino, after his appeal was denied or before he was sentenced, come forward and talk about Cynthia's role—if any—in the murder of Jeff Zack? The first answer is, Cynthia was never involved (which the appeals court obviously believed); the second answer, some told me, is that Zaffino was bamboozled by Cynthia George and led to believe that he would be taken care of. One person close to Zaffino later told me, "He is nothing but a simple country boy from Pennsylvania. He should have never messed with the Georges, because they were never going to do anything for him. Cynthia, I told him, would toss him out with the rest of the day's trash—and she did." In reviewing the new twist in the case when Cynthia was set free, that same person added, "I think that John's anger will override his denial. I would imagine that he has tried to contact her [since her release] and that she has rejected him. Rejection fuels his madness."

Will John Zaffino now talk? That seems to be the question on everyone's mind. A source close to the case told me that several investigators went to see Zaffino in prison after it was announced that Cynthia won her appeal, yet Zaffino didn't have anything of importance, I was told, to say—and remains tight-lipped. Weeks later, the Court of Appeals refused to overturn its decision.

On August 29, 2007, the Ohio Supreme Court weighed in. It ruled 5–2 not to hear the Summit County prosecutor's case to overturn the appeal.

Thus, Cynthia George is, officially, a free woman.

This ruling closes the case.

She can never be tried for this crime again, and the Summit County prosecutor's office said she never will be.